THE INTELLECTUAL WORLD OF THE COUNTRY HOUSE
IN IRELAND AND BRITAIN

The Intellectual World of the Country House in Ireland and Britain

Terence Dooley & Christopher Ridgway

EDITORS

FOUR COURTS PRESS

Typeset in 10.5 pt on 12.5 pt Ehrhardt by
Carrigboy Typesetting Services for
FOUR COURTS PRESS LTD
7 Malpas Street, Dublin 8, Ireland
www.fourcourtspress.ie
and in North America for
FOUR COURTS PRESS
c/o IPG, 814 N. Franklin St, Chicago, IL 60610

© The various contributors and Four Courts Press 2024

A catalogue record for this title is available from the British Library.

ISBN 978-1-80151-136-0

All rights reserved. No part of this publication may be reproduced, stored in or introduced into a retrieval system, or transmitted, in any form or by any means (electronic, mechanical, photocopying, recording, or otherwise), without the prior written permission of both the copyright owner and publisher of this book.

Printed in England
by CPI Antony Rowe, Chippenham, Wilts.

Contents

ACKNOWLEDGMENTS		vii
INTRODUCTION *Vincent Comerford*		ix
1	Historic houses and their associations *Ben Cowell*	1
2	The painted decorations in the Long Gallery at Castletown House: new light on the intellectual lives of Thomas and Louisa Conolly *Deirdre Cullen*	13
3	'An effect rather than a reality'? The place of the country house in the Irish gentry's perception of their world *Ian d'Alton*	29
4	Mary Delany and the mental and creative world of Delville *Kristina Decker*	41
5	Frances Power Cobbe, daughter of the Irish country house *Cathal Dowd Smith*	52
6	Safe and unsafe houses: architecture, politics and the Irish cultural imagination *Roy Foster*	67
7	'A persevering proclamation of gospel truth': the 3rd earl of Roden and evangelical Christianity at Tollymore Park and Dundalk House, c.1820–70 *James Frazer*	78
8	Irish country house libraries and social change, 1650–1750 *Raymond Gillespie*	89
9	The Moore brothers and the library at Moore Hall: differing visions of its legacy in a new Ireland *Elizabeth Grubgeld*	99

10	An intergenerational chronicle: the library at Adare Manor, Co. Limerick *Anna-Maria Hajba*	108
11	Photographers and antiquarians in Paris: Goddard Orpen and Eugène Atget *Jeremy Hill*	122
12	From muniment room to online access: family and estate archives at Cowdray House, Knole and Ham House *Elizabeth Jamieson*	136
13	Reading the eighteenth-century print room *Kate Retford*	150
14	The house of ideas *Christopher Ridgway*	164
15	The library at Annes Grove *Aileen Spitere*	184

NOTES ON CONTRIBUTORS 195

INDEX 199

Acknowledgments

This volume marks a very significant milestone in the life of the Centre for the Study of Historic Irish Houses and Estates (CSHIHE) at Maynooth University, emanating as it does from the Twentieth Annual Historic Houses Conference. From humble beginnings in September 2003, when the first conference was held on the theme of 'The Irish country house: its past, present and future', the conference has grown exponentially to international status attracting speakers and delegates from across the world. Its growth reflects the sea change in political, cultural and public attitudes to the Irish country house, but also the much wider international expansion of research perspectives related to all its various dimensions.

We, the editors, are very grateful to all those who have supported us on this journey. This is the seventh volume of conference proceedings, all of which have been published by Four Courts Press. We would like to thank Martin Healy, Martin Fanning, Anthony Tierney and their colleagues for their unstinting support.

The conference title in 2022 was 'The mental world of the country house' and we are very grateful to Professor Sir David Cannadine for his stimulating opening address: 'How do we study country houses now?' For many years, David has been a steadfast supporter of the CSHIHE. It is fitting that Professor Vincent Comerford should write the foreword to the volume; as Head of Department when the first conference was organised, he was unsparing in his efforts to ensure the CSHIHE would prosper as an academic research unit. That it continues to thrive has much to do with the foundation he helped to build. We are also grateful to all the other speakers at the conference and contributors to this volume. Unfortunately, our esteemed colleague and wonderful friend, Professor Raymond Gillespie, passed away before he saw the end product. His brilliant mind and generous spirit is sorely missed by all who knew him.

As Vincent Comerford alludes to, the conference has over the years become a successful meeting place for scholars, professionals, and all Big House enthusiasts. Its ability to do so has been made possible by the ongoing support of the staff of the Office of Public Works, most especially Mary Heffernan over the life span of the Centre to date and, more latterly, Rosemary Collier and Katie Morris-Roe.

We extend a very special thanks to Carmel Naughton who, through the Stackallan benefaction, has made this volume and very many other important projects possible, all of which adhere to the original tenet of the Centre of reaching the widest possible audiences amongst those interested in the country house and, indeed, history more generally.

We are most grateful to colleagues in the Department of History at Maynooth University; and to our wider associates for their support, including the Attingham Trust, Historic Houses (UK), Historic Houses of Ireland, the Institute for the Study of Welsh Estates (Bangor University), and the Yorkshire Country House Partnership.

We owe a particular debt to Dr Ciaran Reilly, assistant director of the CSHIHE, and Veronica Barry whose dedication and professionalism made the running of the conference so enjoyable for all our patrons. As ever, Den Stubbs of Stubbs Design did a wonderful job in designing all the literature around the conference. We thank Dr Ciaran McCabe for his editorial expertise.

Finally, on a personal note, we thank our families – Annette, Áine, Conor and Rosie – for supporting us in doing what we love most to do.

TERENCE DOOLEY & CHRISTOPHER RIDGWAY

Introduction

VINCENT COMERFORD

The convening of the twentieth annual conference of the Centre for the Study of Historic Irish Houses and Estates was a significant landmark, far beyond the original time horizon of the initiative launched in 2003. The conference down the years has been remarkably successful as a meeting place of people from Ireland and abroad and from across a wide range of interests. Numerous contacts have been made and many discussions initiated and renewed, of enduring benefit to scholarship and public life.

The contribution of the Office of Public Works (OPW) and its staff has been particularly important. Following her recent promotion, Mary Heffernan has ended two decades of direct responsibility for the OPW's involvement with the CSHIHE. Over that time Mary's enthusiasm and tireless energy have been at the core of the centre's work and achievements, while she simultaneously managed the opening to the public of at least a dozen major houses and facilities in state ownership, including Dublin Castle.

The published conference papers capture the formal scholarly aspect of the annual gathering. For the leadership and the routine labour that go into organizing the conference and producing the volumes of essays everyone else is indebted to Professor Terence Dooley and Professor Christopher Ridgway.

This volume, presenting essays delivered at the May 2022 conference on the theme of mental worlds, is another collection of stimulating and valuable papers. Sincere thanks to each of the contributors.

In the opening essay Ben Cowell teases out the strands of English historic house activism in the twentieth century, implicitly providing scope for comparison and contrast with developments in Ireland, north and south. Good causes prosper most fruitfully when supported by astute promotional endeavour. In the case of England in the decades following 1945 political support for historic houses was enhanced by – among other things – association with the prosperity that is expected to accompany tourism, by an emotionally powerful exhibition at the Victoria and Albert Museum in 1974, and by a public petition that apparently garnered one million signatures.

Nowhere has been more closely associated with the work of the CSHIHE over the past two decades than Castletown. As it happens, this volume includes an innovative study by Deirdre Cullen of the decoration of Castletown's Long Gallery. That decorative work was achieved in the years 1775 and 1776 under the auspices of Louisa and Thomas Conolly, and it is recognized as a relatively rare example of a very specific 'antique' style that abounds with Classical references. Making connections such as these was what Thomas's classical education had prepared him for, as did especially his lengthy grand tour. At home there was a library of classics, in the original languages and in English translation, together with volumes of antiquarian engravings. Although her formal education was more limited, and she had not taken the Grand Tour, Louisa had the same library resources, and was part of a network in which classical visual culture mattered. Louisa had her own closely related project in the celebrated Castletown print room, in which classical subjects predominate. Modern scholars have identified the connections of most of the decorative items in the Long Gallery, but others have eluded recognition, most importantly a pair of matching oval paintings dominating the main entrance. Deirdre Cullen has solved the mystery through an interrogation not only of visual but also of literary sources.

Ian d'Alton weaves an evocative tapestry of the perceptions of Irish country houses as described by their imaginative residents and visitors. For this he draws on the imagery of twentieth-century novels and poetry. The reader is also reminded that the impermanence and loss invoked in the fiction were also a feature of life as lived, and not only in the early twentieth century. Long before the land war, and despite the intended objectives of the law of entail, country houses here and there together with their demesnes and estates were being abandoned and dissipated in response to the changing fortunes of life.

The survival of a rich seam of correspondence enables Kristina Decker to recreate the 'mental and creative world' of the celebrated Mrs Mary Delany during more than two decades that she spent at Delville, a villa in Glasnevin categorized by Jonathan Swift as 'too far from town for a winter visit and too near for staying a night in the country manner'. Decker draws an intriguing picture of Delany as an Enlightenment figure, combining international epistolary discourse with the creation of an interior domestic décor (it encompassed a private chapel, her husband being a clergyman) and with the cultivation, study and depiction of her garden and its plants.

Newbridge House is unusual in the completeness of its contents and surroundings when it passed from the Cobbe family into the ownership of Dublin County Council in the 1980s. A widely known figure connected with the house is Frances Power Cobbe (1822–1904). Here Cathal Dowd Smith draws on her papers and drawings in the Newbridge House archive, on her published works, and on a substantial secondary literature devoted to Cobbe, to outline the life of a significant nineteenth-century intellectual and activist.

Roy Foster's essay explores some of the themes that have problematized attitudes to the houses of the great (whether in town or countryside) in Britain and in Ireland. The commentators discussed include John Harris, David Watkin, David Cannadine, the Knight of Glin, Terence De Vere White, Terence Dooley,

Introduction xi

William Laffan, Erika Hanna, Ian d'Alton and Colm Tóibín. This essay also cites a range of novels allowing further exploration of the imaginative associations of Irish houses, with an interesting contrast between the imaginational impact of the great houses of the landed on the one hand, and the substantial dwellings of wealthy bourgeois Catholics on the other.

In the nineteenth century the successors of Louisa and Thomas Conolly had scriptural quotations inscribed on the kitchen walls at Castletown for the edification of the servants. However, the Conollys were not one of the minority of landed families to give themselves over to the evangelical mission. One that did have this conversion was the family of the earl of Roden, with land in counties Down and Louth. In his essay James Frazer summarizes the lifestyle, domestic discipline, devotional practices, and outreach to tenants and neighbours that characterized the evangelical career of the 3rd earl, Robert Jocelyn (1788–1870).

Raymond Gillespie's essay provides an analytical survey of what is known about book ownership by Irish families in the early modern period, much of this knowledge gleaned over a generation of scholarship by Raymond himself, Bernadette Cunningham, and Toby Barnard. Possession of manuscripts, old or newly commissioned, is also part of this story. Economic conditions in the later seventeenth century facilitated healthy development of the book market in Ireland and owners of country houses were prominent among the purchasers. Possession of a book is not evidence of having read it, and evidence is not always available to show whether a library was acquired primarily for use or display.

Elizabeth Grubgeld in her essay explores the complexities, ironies and inventions that abound in the life writings of George Moore. The context is that of a family history of privilege, travel, politics, writing, and indulgence in books. Even before it had exhausted financial and material resources a family might run out of determination to keep the show on the road. Grubgeld, drawing on Terence Dooley's evidence, muses on the possibility that locals may have secured some volumes from the great library when Moore Hall was ransacked in the hours before its destruction by fire in 1923.

Anna-Maria Hajba takes Adare Manor as an example of a great house library that reflected particularly well the personal interests of successive proprietors, in this case the 2nd, 3rd and 4th earls of Dunraven. While the house survives in style, the library has been scattered, but auction catalogues and related sources permit a reconstruction. Hajba's account of the acquisitions of the 2nd and 3rd earls amounts to a concise history of the Gothic and Tudor revivals in England and Ireland, and the intellectual backdrop to the building of the great house at Adare, including religion, politics and travel.

Jeremy Hill draws attention to the recent digitization of more than 2,000 photographic images created by the historian G.H. Orpen and preserved at Monksgrange, Co. Wexford. Orpen is best remembered for his four-volume

History of Ireland under the Normans (1911–20), but his use of photography was not directed exclusively to his study of the Irish past. He seems to have taken up the camera in the 1890s and he made extensive use of it in his study of medieval Paris.

Elizabeth Jamieson's chapter amounts to an intensive tutorial in the hazards and complexities of archival survival and preservation. Taking three historic English residences, Jamieson details the twists and turns that can lead from a medieval muniments room, or 'evidence room', to a place in the National Archives. But the pathway is seldom smooth, with fire, flood, war and especially proprietorial carelessness among the many hazards. Too much attention can also be a problem as when a reader inscribes his or her thoughts on a document. With so much source material now available online, the kind of knowledge and insight conveyed here will be ever more valuable in the education of researchers.

Kate Retford's contribution provides an intensive introduction to the rich complexity of the uses and circulation of prints in the eighteenth-century heyday of their culture. Bound prints might be scattered between the letterpress pages of the relevant book, or assembled at the front or the back or in whatever disposition pleased the owner. They might be glued to furniture or arrayed on complex principles along the walls of the print room. The subject matter was predominantly but not exclusively the sculpture and architecture of the Rome of the Grand Tour. This account is closely grounded in evidence from Clongowes Wood, Petworth, Wricklemarsh and Ston Easton Park. Carton House also enters the picture, as does the pioneering work of Mary Delany at Delville, the subject of attention elsewhere in the volume.

In the penultimate essay, 'The house of ideas', Christopher Ridgway takes an overview of the topic of the volume and invites reflection on various challenges that it poses, including that of relating tangible evidence to the things of the mind. Can visual portraiture convey mental states? Can scientific interest and endeavour such as that of the 3rd earl of Rosse or the 3rd earl of Salisbury be accorded appropriate weighting when in competition with dedication to the art and architecture that is foremost in the image of the residents of great houses? Is religion, agriculture and even history similarly disadvantaged in the prevailing view? Patriarchal prejudice is an obvious bias both in the sources and in the enshrined interpretations. And the mind is not only intellect but emotions. Christopher Ridgway explores several frontiers with a thoughtful reflection of the brittle mindset of Georgina Cavendish, wife of the 6th earl of Carlisle, based on a plentiful body of auto-writing and several professional portraits.

Aileen Spitere provides an introduction to the gardens of Annes Grove, County Cork. With an already long history behind it, the property in 1905 came under the management of Richard Annesley, aged 26. Weathering the upheavals of the following half-century, Richard cultivated the gardens until the 1960s, maintaining throughout a horticultural establishment of international standing.

Introduction

This was gifted to the nation by the Annesley family in 2015 and is now in the care of the OPW. Along with the garden itself, the glory of Annes Grove is the documentation of Richard Annesley's work in his happily surviving library and archive. Based on a thorough acquaintance with this material, Spitere provides a valuable guide to the mental and physical processes that sustained a remarkable achievement.

The published collections of conference papers provide a permanent record of the formal academic business of the annual gathering and register its scholarly function. At the same time the conference has a wider remit as a venue for personal interaction between academics and the far wider range of people with a professional or business or other interest in historic properties. The continued support of so many committed individuals and public bodies has made the annual CSHIHSE conference an important occasion for beneficial interactions and has enabled it to contribute to the defusing of once fraught discourse in an important area of public life.

Historic houses and their associations

BEN COWELL

Implicit in the dedication of Lord Montagu of Beaulieu's *The gilt and the gingerbread* (1967) was the stark metaphorical contrast between country houses as either historic homes or as roofless ruins.[1] In that book, Montagu drew attention to the importance of post-war tourism to country houses. Tourism had been key, in Montagu's view, to those houses' survival. Tourism had become the new intellectual framework within which the country house experience was to be understood, as Evelyn Waugh had articulated in the preface to his revised 1959 edition of *Brideshead revisited*, which was so withering of the effects of tourism in creating 'the present cult of the English country house'.[2] Lines were being drawn around the essential idea of the country house: as either a 'public' experience or as a private domain. Montagu made it clear where he stood, stating baldly that he would rather 'keep my home and surrender my privacy than have things the other way round.'

Montagu was a man of many talents, but he especially excelled at public relations. In many ways, he was responsible for developing a strong brand identity for UK country houses in the 1950s, 60s and 70s. Sensing the emergence of a new market for country house tourism, he opened his own house at Beaulieu in the southern English county of Hampshire to the public on Easter weekend 1952. Having inherited a single historic car from his father, a pioneer of motoring, he rebadged Beaulieu as the national motor museum. It gave an entirely new life to an otherwise largely disregarded house, that previously had been notable mainly for its adjoining monastic remains. Montagu made it his business to fill the national newspapers with images of himself hard at work at Beaulieu. In one image, widely used, he was seen scrubbing the floors in preparation for the arrival of visitors. 'It's enough to bring a peer to his knees' was the caption. Such images were deliberately staged, to generate newspaper coverage and media attention. (He later admitted that he was holding the cleaning brush the wrong way around in one of these shots.)[3] Montagu went on to contrive a 'stately home league table', in which the annual visitor figures at the major open houses were compared, as if those houses were rival football teams. Beaulieu, naturally, frequently came out on top.[4]

1 Lord Montagu of Beaulieu, *The gilt and the gingerbread* (London, 1967).   2 Evelyn Waugh, *Brideshead revisited: the sacred and profane memories of Captain Charles Ryder* (London, 2000 ed.), p. ix.   3 Lord Montagu of Beaulieu, *Wheels within wheels: an unconventional life* (London, 2000), pp 250–1.   4 For the heroic age of the post-war stately home, see Adrian

Applying the lessons of such boosterism more widely, Montagu's book served as a manifesto for how country houses needed to up their game to attract increasing numbers of visitors. His emphasis was firmly on the idea that the country house business needed to professionalize their activities. Montagu divided country houses into the Gentlemen and the Players: the Gentlemen being the old order of aristocratic houses such as Chatsworth and Blenheim, while the Players were those houses where a new, modern professionalism prevailed, among them Beaulieu, Burghley and Castle Howard, as well as Woburn and Longleat with their famous safari parks. Montagu was at pains to point out that the Players were not always 'easily distinguished from their rivals'. What set them apart, rather, was that they 'have an eye for the main chance' and that they 'are … willing to think of their properties as business ventures'.[5]

This was the optimistic spirit in which the Historic Houses Association (HHA) was founded in 1973: as an association dominated by the Players, with Montagu at its helm. The HHA was by no means the only such grouping of houses; nor would it be the last. The formation of the HHA was a political act, which projected country houses as a distinct political force in the UK, albeit one that faced specific threats and challenges. It helped to frame a certain public understanding of country houses: of untold significance and importance to national culture, albeit beleaguered by the threats of diminishing income from land and of new forms of taxation (fig. 1.1).

The idea of an association of house owners had already been some years in the making. The National Trust had experimented with instigating a 'country houses association' under its own auspices in the mid-1930s, as it commenced work on what would become its country house scheme. The idea had been for the Trust to forge alliances with private owners, which would have the effect of widening levels of public access as a condition for receiving support from government.[6] The idea drew on the example of La Demeure Historique, founded in France in 1924 to represent and support the owners of historic properties. But owners in Britain were reluctant to fall in with the National Trust in this way, and the idea of such an association was dropped. The Trust instead turned to the direct acquisition of country houses, amassing over a hundred of them during the 1940s and 1950s.

The idea of an association of private owners was revived after the war, when the perils facing country houses were considered by many to have deepened. The Labour government commissioned a report on what was to be done about the problem. The conclusion of the committee led by Sir Ernest Gowers was, famously, that the best solution for country houses was that they should be preserved as privately owned houses – preferably lived in by the families

---

Tinniswood, *Noble ambitions: the fall and rise of the post-war country house* (London, 2021). **5** Montagu, *Gilt*, p. 87.   **6** Merlin Waterson, *The National Trust: the first hundred years* (London, 1994), p. 108. Peter Mandler, *The fall and rise of the stately home* (New Haven and

1.1 Front cover of the first *Historic Houses Association Journal* (1976).

connected with them.[7] Such houses would be entitled to benefit from advantageous fiscal treatment, as well as from grants from the newly proposed historic buildings councils. The committee's report reaffirmed a rationale for this group of houses – perhaps no more than two thousand in number, although the Gowers' report could not be definitive on the matter[8] – being able to band together in solidarity.

In theory this was fine. But in practice, this group was still too diverse, and divided. A meeting of owners at the Dorchester Hotel in 1952 – convened by Sir

London, 1997), pp 299–304.   7 Ernest Gowers, *Report of the committee on houses of outstanding historic or architectural interest* (London, 1950).   8 'The information provided to us by the Ministry of Works and the National Trusts indicates a figure of about 2,000, but in

Harold Wernher of Luton Hoo – sought to gauge the appetite for a new association of private owners. But any enthusiasm for the idea at that time soon petered out. There was just too much separating the larger houses, which were already doing very well from tourism business, from the greater number of smaller owners, who were unprepared to make the financial commitment necessary for such a scheme to work.[9]

By the early 1960s, in the absence of their own dedicated association, many house owners had followed the example of Lord Montagu and had joined instead the British Travel Association (BTA). The BTA was an early travel industry body, effectively the principal tourism agency for the UK. The BTA was a private organization (albeit that it was supported by government) but it was possible for houses to join as members and thereby exert some influence on its activities. Over a hundred houses had done so by the early 1960s, which led to the BTA's chairman, Ross Geddes, to commission a working party to investigate how the needs of these houses might best be served. This led in turn to the establishment of the BTA's Historic Houses Committee in 1966, chaired by Hugh Wontner, managing director of the Savoy hotel group.

More informal associations were also being formed at this time. Brian Thompson, a former Irish paratrooper and farmer, bought Puttenden Manor in Surrey in 1966 and almost immediately opened it for public visiting. He soon realized that other smaller owners were in the same boat and so recruited forty-five houses in his area for the purpose of mutually supportive marketing as well as to act as a lobbying force to apply pressure on local councils for things like tourism-related road signage.[10] Thompson's initiative led eventually to his appointment to the BTA's Historic Houses Committee.

The Development of Tourism Act (1969) resulted in the British Travel Association being replaced wholesale by a new British Tourist Authority, the first UK government agency for the promotion of tourism. Len Lickorish, who had been general manager of the former BTA, was appointed the chief executive of the new agency, and had a significant influence in the subsequent creation of an owners' body. A consequence of the change in status of the BTA – from private trade association to public authority – was that it could no longer carry individual members, such as those historic houses owners that it had formerly recruited. But Lickorish was loathe to sever his ties with aristocrats such as Montagu, who were such well-known advocates for tourism – and who, through their positions in the House of Lords, had a ready-made platform for proselytizing the cause of the British tourist industry. Lickorish therefore initiated a conference of country house owners, held at the Mansion House in

---

fairness to our informants it should be said that this is highly speculative'. Gowers, *Report*, para 117, p. 29.   **9** Elena Porter, 'National heritage in private hands: the political and cultural status of country houses in Britain, 1950–2000' (D.Phil., University of Oxford, 2022), p. 89.   **10** See 'Union for owners of historic homes', *The Times*, 17 Nov. 1970, p. 4.

London in 1970. The success of the gathering led to the formation of a Standing Conference of historic houses, that would meet annually for the next three years.

The Historic Houses Association was an evolution of this Standing Conference. At its third annual meeting, on 8 November 1973, the Standing Conference determined that it should reconstitute itself as an independent association of historic houses owners, standing independently from the British Tourist Authority. The significance of the move lay in the freedom desired by the new association to speak its mind, untrammelled by the requirements of being a publicly funded organization. Nevertheless, the early HHA retained close ties to the British Tourism Authority. Its first executive secretary was a BTA staffer (David Coleman), and the association at first shared offices with the BTA on St James' Street. Such patronage and support was a conscious attempt by Len Lickorish to keep aristocratic owners onside and on board as advocates for the BTA's cause, which many of them would regularly demonstrate in their contributions to House of Lords' debates.

Soon, the value of having a public mouthpiece to articulate the country house cause would be made all-too evident. The UK was beset by historically high rates of inflation, a consequence of global energy crises and domestic industrial action. By early 1974, political and economic strife was the political context for the calling of a general election by the presiding Conservative prime minister, Edward Heath. Heath's call to the electorate was famously to ask, 'who runs Britain?' The answer was not conclusive, since the election returned no overall majority for either of the larger parties. Eventually, a Labour administration formed a minority government under prime minister Harold Wilson, whom Heath had beaten in the previous general election of 1970. Labour's manifesto committed the party to radical action to tackle social inequalities. The party promised to effect 'the redistribution of wealth by new taxation on the better-off', and announced plans to impose a new tax on those who held significant assets.[11] This wealth tax therefore promised to be a raid on the pockets of the 600 or so members of the early HHA.

The association wasted no time in building momentum behind the idea that a crisis faced country houses. In 1972, again with support from the BTA, it had commissioned John Cornforth to prepare a state of the nation report on the health of country houses in Britain. The report was intended as an update of the Gowers' Report on country houses from 1950. Cornforth worked on the study over the course of 1973 before it finally appeared in early October 1974.[12] Its gloomy front cover – a wild-looking monochromatic depiction of Rousham in Oxfordshire by John Piper – was a foretelling of the narrative contained inside (fig. 1.2). It was clear from the pages of the report that all was not well with

---

[11] *Britain will win with Labour* (October 1974 Labour Party Manifesto), retrieved from www.labour-party.org.uk/manifestos/1974/Oct/1974-oct-labour-manifesto.shtml. [12] John Cornforth, *Country houses in Britain: can they survive?* (BTA, 1974).

1.2 Front cover of John Cornforth, *Country houses in Britain: can they survive?* (British Tourist Authority, 1974).

country houses. The stark question that the report's title asked was 'Country houses in Britain: can they survive?' and the answer that it gave was a resounding 'no', in most instances. Cornforth pulled no punches. Country houses were in as sorry a condition as they had been just after the Second World War. Worse, new talk of capital taxation posed an existential threat to the future of these houses. Cornforth speculated that within fifty years, there might be no more than fifty of these houses left in Britain.[13] The rest would be sold off for development,

13 Ibid., p. 122.

Historic houses and their associations 7

robbed of their collections and their grounds, or converted to institutional use as offices, schools, or hospitals. Cornforth's report was part of the background evidence for peers when the House of Lords debated Labour's proposed wealth tax on 26 June 1974. Lord Montagu used his position there to underline the importance of historic houses and their essence:

> Britain cannot offer hot sun and beaches: what we have is living history, a panorama of which can best be seen in our historic houses and their contents. But unlike many European houses, which, though beautiful on the outside, inside resemble a mausoleum of a bygone age, Britain's historic houses are still homes. Their walls still breathe, and a 'lived in' atmosphere pervades the scene. It is just this that the overseas visitor finds so seductive – flowers in the hall, oak fires burning in the grate and perhaps children's steps on the back stairs.[14]

Because he was so involved in preparing his report, Cornforth was not able to join his colleagues Marcus Binney, John Harris and Roy Strong in preparing an exhibition that was, in parallel, being planned at the Victoria and Albert (V&A) Museum. This exhibition has also had a profound impact on the public and political understandings of the country house in the UK.[15] *The destruction of the country house* was the V&A's contribution to the European Year of Architectural Heritage that fell in 1975. The exhibition was the brainchild of Roy Strong, who had started as director at the V&A that January 1974, having previously been at the National Portrait Gallery. Strong intended the exhibition as a bold statement of his intent. This was about making the V&A an institution for the present and the future, as much as it was a hangover from the nineteenth century. The exhibition was a spectacle that projected a certain image of British country houses. Roy Strong's vision was to move visitors emotionally by presenting endless pictures of 'lost' houses. In so doing, he wanted them to think about the present-day situation, and what they could do to alleviate the pressures still facing country house heritage. It was a bold attempt to influence voting intentions by an institution that remained, formally, a part of the UK civil service.[16]

More than a thousand houses were identified as having been demolished in the preceding century, from 1875 to 1975. It didn't matter that the precise number was a matter of some conjecture. The more the exhibition's curators looked, the more they found. Strong conceived of the centre piece of the exhibition as being a series of newly commissioned pictures from Osbert Lancaster, who had collaborated with Strong in a show at the National Portrait

---

[14] HL Deb., 26 June 1974, vol. 352, col. 1536.   [15] See Ruth Adams, 'The V&A, the destruction of the country house and the creation of "English heritage"', *Museum & Society*, 11:1 (2013), pp 1–18.   [16] The V&A was at this time directly funded through the Education Department.

Gallery the previous year, 'The Littlehampton Bequest'. For *Destruction*, the idea was that new drawings by Lancaster would trace 'the trials and tribulations of a great estate', from late Victorian grandeur to the ignominy of their late-twentieth-century condition. Between these two points, the fortunes of an imaginary estate would be sketched through a chronological series of tableaux. In an early scene, the heir apparent would be shown to have been killed in action in the First World War. Soon after this 'the tax man cometh', waving his demand for estate duties. By the time of the next scene, it was apparent that the household servants had departed or died: the countess herself was sweeping in the Long Gallery. The East Wing would soon fall, while the West Wing would be blown up. The Van Dyck would be sold at auction. During the Second World War there would be a dual invasion of American troops and evacuees, with the gardens dug up as allotments for vegetables. After the war, everything was up for sale. The park would soon be bisected by a motorway and the rest of it built over by suburban housing. The house would become either a police college or local council office. By now, the full horror show had arrived: 'caravan rallies – motor museum – safari park – state robes on show – water skiing on the lake – mass catering etc. etc.'. The commissioning brief evoked where Strong felt the country house faced its greatest problems.[17]

In the end, the *Destruction* show depended ultimately on photography for the power of its impact. It was a spectacular event. Working with designers Robin Wade Associates, a schema was developed that saw visitors initially pass a small display about the history of the British country house. This was merely a prelude to the main event of the exhibition – the hall of lost houses. Visitors were presented with a panorama of tumbling masonry, with each block covered in a black and white photograph of one of the lost houses. Over the speakers could be heard the hiss and crackle of burning timbers. Against this, John Harris was recorded reciting the names of hundreds of lost houses, as if they were names on a war memorial. Strong claimed to have been successful in provoking an emotional response: 'Many was the time I stood in that exhibition watching the tears stream down the visitors' faces as they battled to come to terms with all that had gone'.[18] A book of the exhibition became a best-selling Thames & Hudson paperback, its black-and-white photography revealing even greater numbers of lost houses than were featured in the exhibition.[19]

It was all a highly political event, not least since, as it turned out, the exhibition opened just two days before the second general election of 1974. The subtext was clear: excessive taxation had been one of the factors that had led to the loss of so many country houses over the preceding century, and a fresh attempt to tax landed wealth would have similarly damaging consequences. Arts

---

[17] Roy Strong to Osbert Lancaster, 21 June 1974, V&A Archive, MA/28/243/1.   [18] Roy Strong, *Diaries, 1967–1987* (London, 1998), p. 140.   [19] Roy Strong, Marcus Binney, John Harris (eds), *The destruction of the country house* (London, 1974).

Historic houses and their associations

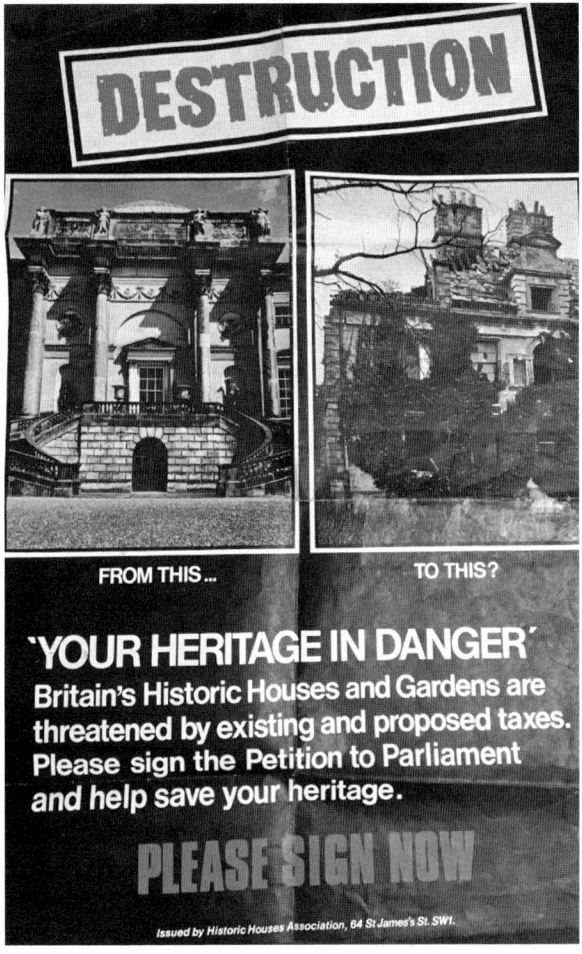

1.3 Poster seeking signatures for the petition against the wealth tax (1975).

minister Hugh Jenkin had no time for such emotive appeals, insisting that the fate of the built environment 'must take second place to the reduction of privilege and inequality'.[20] Such an insistence by a minister of the realm merely galvanized the early HHA into taking an even stronger stand. If something was not done, these houses faced imminent apocalypse.

It did not matter that the power of owners to demolish their houses had largely been removed in 1968, when explicit listed building consent was made a requirement for acts of demolition. In the five or six years after 1968, hardly any country houses had, in fact, been demolished. Nor did it seem to matter that,

20 Hugh Jenkins, *The culture gap: an experience of government and the arts* (London, 1979), p. 146.

something like ten per cent of the houses that featured in the exhibition had not been destroyed at all. They may have been partially demolished, but they may equally have been subsequently rebuilt. Few would describe Bowood, nowadays a very popular complex of gardens, a hotel, a golf course, as wholly 'lost' even though, admittedly, the major part of the eighteenth-century building had vanished. The core of the historic estate remained intact here, as it did in many other cases where the main house had been pulled down.

Nonetheless, country houses generally were presented as facing an existential threat, and an appeal was made for public support. In the summer of 1975, petitions were left in HHA member houses up and down the country, as well as in National Trust properties. The petitions called on the Labour government to reverse its planned wealth tax proposal in the interests of 'our heritage'. The HHA thereby successfully made the threats to country house owners a threat to the nation as a whole. Over a million people signed the petition, making it the single biggest such petition until the modern era of internet polling (fig. 1.3). The petition was presented to parliament in December 1975, accompanied again by stage managed photographs of Lord Montagu next to Labour MP Ted Graham.

The campaigning proved successful. In the same month, Denis Healey announced to the House of Commons that his wealth tax plans had been suspended for the time being. Healey had arguably made conditions a whole lot easier for country house owners, by giving them the option to exempt their buildings and land from capital tax charges in return for opening up to public access. This change, made initially in the Finance Act of 1975 and then further enhanced in the Finance Act of 1976, served as a peace offering to country house owners. Notwithstanding the political point scoring that would be made over the case of Mentmore House, which came up for auction shortly afterwards, the foundations had been laid for a revival in country house fortunes in the decades that followed.[21]

CONCLUSION

In addition to being depicted in oils or watercolours, being brought to life in the pages of works of literature, and forming a gilded backdrop to film and television productions, this essay has sought to show how the UK country house has on occasion been rendered as an intellectual idea and through the medium of political rhetoric. This rhetoric has been prone to swinging from one extreme to another, depending on the political circumstances. Lord Montagu of Beaulieu

---

21 The Mentmore case led to the formation of the National Heritage Memorial Fund in 1980. The story of the revival of houses in the years that followed is traced in Ben Cowell, *British country house revival* (Woodbridge, 2024).

began by engendering a view of country houses as the motor forces of the post-war tourism economy, vying with each other for visitors in a popularity battle that was played out in the pages of the tabloid newspapers. By the early 1970s, however, the imminent threat of new levels of capital taxation encouraged a different perspective to be drawn: that of houses as the victims of successive governments' addiction to imposing ever more stringent fiscal penalties on the ownership of assets. The capital gains tax imposed in 1965 was only the start, since now a new wealth tax promised to raise funds not just from assets that had been sold but also from those simply held in the same family for generations. Would the nation's 'historic homes', previously so self-sufficient and resilient, soon become its latest 'roofless ruins'?

The essay has detailed the political contexts for the foundation of the Historic Houses Association in 1973 – among the most enduring of the various self-help groups established to represent houses in the second half of the twentieth century. The transformation of the BTA's Standing Conference of historic house owners into a fully independent and free-standing association in 1973 was, after all, a political act. The owners represented at the Standing Conference were alarmed by political developments and wanted the freedom to speak out. The formation of the HHA was about political representation – having the freedom to speak out in opposition to government policy. The association would be described by its own deputy president, George Howard, at its first AGM in October 1974 as 'a political pressure group with political origins'.[22]

Political campaigning for a cause – in this case the survival of a category of built heritage – often requires the mobilizing of public support. From the start, the Historic Houses Association was influential in shaping public perceptions of the country house. Whether or not these perceptions were necessarily wholly accurate misses the point. Lord Montagu, the HHA's founding president, understood instinctively the power of images, and their ability to shape attitudes and behaviours. The main message from the earliest years of the HHA was that country houses were on the brink of collapse. This idea was reinforced in multiple ways: in the pages of John Cornforth's report, in the black and white photography of the V&A's *Destruction* exhibition, and in the news reports of Marcus Binney's SAVE Britain's Heritage (founded in 1975).

Once the initial battle over the prospect of a new wealth tax had been fought, and won, the association could represent the country house in a much more positive cast. The *Treasure houses* exhibition hosted at the National Gallery of Art in Washington DC in 1985 was a bravura display of the opulence and success of British country houses. It involved more than 700 artworks, borrowed from more than 200 houses, transported across the Atlantic in a feat of logistical planning and artfully curated by J. Carter-Brown. The show was a sensation, and drew

---

22 HHA Archive, Minutes of the first AGM of the Historic Houses Association, 23 Oct. 1974.

international headlines thanks to the arrival of the prince and princess of Wales for the opening (at a gala dinner the night before, Diana famously danced with actor John Travolta).

Followers of the HHA might have been forgiven for thinking that the dark days of the *Destruction* exhibition had been left behind. But just seven years later, in 1992, the HHA sponsored another new publication – *The disintegration of a heritage*, based on a study by Michael Sayer and Hugh Massingberd.[23] Drawing on a comprehensive research exercise, the book highlighted the losses that had been sustained in the period since the V&A exhibition, and under the subsequent period of Conservative government (from 1979). The losses here were not dramatic demolitions so much as the insidious loss of family-owned estates, once the traditional rural properties proved less and less sustainable and families opted to sell. It was taking place at a rate of about twenty estates a year, with more than 250 sold since the Thatcher government had assumed office in 1979. A melancholy sense of loss hung over the presentation of these bare statistical facts.[24]

The intellectual idea of country houses in the post-war period has therefore been liable at times to swing between extremes; from boosterish enthusiasm for the competition for visitors, to despair at the losses incurred as a consequence of government policy; from bombastic and patriotic statements of how country houses were the treasure houses of the nation, to laments at how the owners of those houses were being supplanted by 'new' money as long-standing families could no longer afford to keep pace. Sometimes these views were presented simultaneously, seemingly without fear of contradiction.

To some degree these rhetorical gymnastics continue to be performed today. Given the competitive nature of modern politics, with different interest groups vying for ministerial attention, heritage as a political cause requires an element of jeopardy – it needs to be 'at risk' for it to attract political support. It is equally axiomatic that solutions are offered too. Historic houses now may be wrapped up in red tape, burdened with taxation and at the burning edge of the realities of climate change. But at the same time, they are entrepreneurially minded, able to generate significant levels of income, and can demonstrate a pathway to a net-zero future. They can be all these things at once, since the art of politics is rarely about resolving issues into a simple, singular truth. Instead, it is invariably a carousel of ideas and perspectives, which tend to vary in focus according to context and circumstance, and which can sometimes be sufficiently impactful to secure valuable concessions (as happened with the HHA in 1975/6).

---

[23] Michael Sayer with Hugh Massingberd (eds), *The disintegration of a heritage: country houses and their collections, 1979–1992* (Norwich, 1993). [24] Ibid., pp 5, 14, 20.

The painted decorations in the Long Gallery at Castletown House: new light on the intellectual lives of Thomas and Louisa Conolly

DEIRDRE CULLEN

The Long Gallery of Castletown House, Co. Kildare, is one of a small number of surviving examples of the neoclassical fashion for painted rooms '*all'antica*' in Britain and Ireland (fig. 2.1).[1] In vogue from the late 1750s to the 1780s,[2] these rooms were decorated in what was thought of as the 'antique taste'.[3] Their painted ornaments referenced the architecture and artefacts of the antique world – which might be observed during the course of a Grand Tour, examined in print in the antiquarian publications in the libraries of the elite, or perhaps collected as souvenir sculptures, vases and gems, and brought back from Italy. Such rooms provide a window into the mental worlds of their creators – the architects, patrons and artists who participated in their design.

The Long Gallery's painted decorations were executed from circa April 1775 to the end of 1776 during the tenure of Thomas and Louisa Conolly, and it could be argued that the Gallery contains one of the most complex iconographies to be found within the painted room genre. In many ways its decorations are typical of neoclassical decorative painting – a combination of figurative and grisaille panels set into an ornamental structure of grotesques and ancillary motifs, with visual sources chosen from illustrated antiquarian books and from engravings of the grotesques in the Vatican loggia, painted by Raphael's workshop in emulation of Roman fresco decoration.

But is the Long Gallery a celebration of the classical world by erudite patrons engaged in a scholarly exchange of antique references within an erudite social circle, or is it simply an arrangement of 'pretty ornaments'?[4] Focusing primarily

---

1 The foundational survey of these rooms and their typology is J. Wilton-Ely, 'Pompeian and Etruscan tastes in the neo-classical country-house interior', *Studies in the History of Art*, 25 (1989), pp 51–73. 2 Ibid., p. 70. From the 1780s, taste turned to decorations that were more archaeologically informed. 3 Horace Walpole's assessment that the grotesque ornaments in Lady Spencer's closet at Wimbledon were 'in good antique taste' provides an insight into contemporary understandings of 'antique': see Walpole's 'Book of materials', 1 (1759), p. 20 (Lewis Walpole Library, Yale University). For a reconstruction of Lady Spencer's closet, see K. Bristol, 'The painted rooms of "Athenian" Stuart', *Georgian Group Journal*, 10 (2000), p. 166. 4 Louisa Conolly was 'fond of pretty ornaments': see W. FitzGerald to his mother, 24 Feb. 1767, in B. Fitzgerald (ed.), *Correspondence of Emily, duchess of Leinster*, 3 vols (Dublin, 1949–57), iii, p. 459.

2.1 The Long Gallery, Castletown, Co. Kildare. Detail of the south wall showing a portion of the room's *all'antica* decorative painting, three of the eight marble busts, and the *Aurora* lunette. Courtesy of the Office of Public Works, photography by Davison Associates.

on the iconographies of two hitherto-unidentified figurative scenes in the Long Gallery and on the library at Castletown at the time that the Gallery was being decorated, this essay aims to demonstrate that in-depth consideration of relationships between text and image can throw new light on the Conollys' intellectual engagement with the antique subject matter with which they decorated one of the most important social spaces in their home.

I

An insight into the intellectual formation of Thomas Conolly's (*c*.1738–1803) is provided by Viccy Coltman's observation that neoclassicism was 'not an ahistorical decorative style' but 'a form of thought' that permeated the intellectual lives of upper-class men as a result of their classics-dominated public-school education.[5] Thomas is traditionally cast as an amiable country squire rather than an antiquarian,[6] and appears to have had little involvement in determining the Gallery's scheme.[7] Nonetheless his education and Grand Tour suggest that the possibility of his having had an input must not be entirely dismissed. He attended Westminster School in London, where he was admitted into the third class in January 1750 at the age of 12.[8] Assuming that he remained there until 1754, he must have received the classical education common to every elite young man at public school at that time.[9] The curriculum at Westminster during the eighteenth century is poorly documented,[10] but a 'poetical essay' from the *Gentleman's Magazine* in 1739, ten years before Thomas' admission, gives a glimpse of what he studied during his early years at the school:

> Look 'cross the school, the third employs your sight;
> There Martial sings, there Justin's works appear,
> And banish'd Ovid finds protection there.
> From Ovid's tales transferr'd, the fourth pursues
> Books more sublimely penn'd, more noble views:
> Here Virgil shines; here youth is taught to speak
> In different accents of the hoarser Greek.[11]

Thomas' education and travels are documented next in 1755, when his name was recorded in the Geneva Academy's special register of upper-class foreign students who attended lectures on a less regular basis.[12] Two letters (recently unearthed by the author) sent from Geneva and Naples in early 1757 by

5 V. Coltman, *Fabricating the antique: neoclassicism in Britain, 1760–1800* (Chicago, 2006), pp 11–13.   6 For example, see S. Tillyard, *Aristocrats: Caroline, Emily, Louisa and Sarah Lennox, 1740–1832* (London, 1994), pp 109–10.   7 Surviving family correspondence shows that Louisa Conolly played the leading role in commissioning the decorations: see A.M. Keller, 'The Long Gallery of Castletown House', *Bulletin of the Irish Georgian Society*, 22 (1979), pp 5–8.   8 Westminster Schools Lists, 1744–53 (Westminster School Archive, WS-02-reg-01-13).   9 Westminster School Archive does not hold a school list for 1754, but see G.F. Russell Barker and A.H. Stenning (eds), *The record of old Westminsters*, 2 vols (London, 1928), i, p. 208.   10 A general idea of the curriculum can be reconstructed: by the time he left Westminster, Conolly had studied Latin and some ancient Greek, and must have read texts by at least some of the ancient authors from a list that included Homer, Demosthenes, Polybius, Theocritus, Caesar, Virgil, Ovid, Martial, Juvenal, Justin and more. For this, see Lord Tavistock's school bill for 1756–7 (Westminster School Archive, A0019/D3DG8); see also the verses reproduced here from Walford.   11 E. Walford, 'Westminster School' in idem, *Old and new London*, 6 vols (London, 1878), iii, pp 462–83, https://www.british-history.ac.uk/old-new-london/vol3/pp462-483, accessed 5 May 2022.   12 S. Stelling-Michaud and S. Stelling-Michaud, *Le livre du recteur de l'Académie de Genève (1559–1878)*, 6 vols (Geneva, 1959–80), i, pp 10, 20, 22–3, 33–7, 303; ibid., ii, p. 551. Conolly's association with the Geneva Academy first came to light in A.P.W. Malcomson, 'The fall of the house of Conolly' in A. Blackstock and E. Magennis (eds), *Politics and political culture in Britain and Ireland: essays in tribute to Peter Jupp* (Belfast, 2007), p. 109.

2.2 The Long Gallery, Castletown, Co. Kildare. Thomas Conolly in Rome while on his Grand Tour (1757–8). (Anton Raphael Mengs' portrait, now in the National Gallery of Ireland, is replaced in Castletown by a photographic reproduction.) Courtesy of the Office of Public Works, photography by Davison Associates.

The painted decorations in the Long Gallery at Castletown House 17

2.3 The Long Gallery, Castletown, Co. Kildare. Stephen Catterson Smith, *Lady Louisa Conolly* (after Joshua Reynolds, *c*.1775). Courtesy of the Castletown Foundation and the Office of Public Works, photography by Davison Associates.

Thomas' tutor William Fraigneau to his uncle William Wentworth, 2nd earl of Strafford (who had taken charge of his education and Grand Tour), greatly extend our knowledge of Thomas' itinerary after he left Westminster and travelled to the Continent.[13] He remained in Geneva until early 1757, receiving private tuition in several subjects – including Latin, French and ancient history – and he took lessons in Italian in preparation for his tour in Italy. While in the city he found time to attend lectures in experimental philosophy at the Academy. By 23 April 1757 he was in Naples where he met the envoy and antiquarian Sir James Gray, who introduced him to the royal family and may well have facilitated viewings of artefacts from the ongoing excavations at Herculaneum and elsewhere. After Naples, Thomas was planning to proceed to Rome and onward to Turin, crossing the Alps before winter and finishing his travels in Brussels and then Holland by May 1758. If this plan was followed, then Thomas' undated Grand Tour portrait by Anton Raphael Mengs was probably painted in 1757 (fig. 2.2).[14] At some point on his tour, he spent enough time in Florence to take further lessons in Italian.[15] Thomas' itinerary was quite typical and does not indicate any specialist or antiquarian interest in what he saw on his travels. But his education and his Grand Tour experiences must have equipped him later to fully appreciate the Long Gallery's complex decorative scheme.

Lady Louisa Conolly (1743–1821) (fig. 2.3), third surviving daughter of the 2nd duke of Richmond, spent her childhood at Richmond House in London, Goodwood in Sussex and Carton in Co. Kildare. She did not make a Grand Tour – though she travelled regularly to England, went to France on several occasions, and later in life toured Holland and visited Brussels. If 'educated schoolboys were quite literally steeped in the classics',[16] this was rarely the case in the education of elite girls, who were generally schooled at home – though Richmond's daughters may have been an exception, as the duke is said to have ensured that they studied classics.[17]

Neoclassical painted rooms were typically created with architectural supervision. The Long Gallery diverges from this pattern in that no architect was involved in its design.[18] We know from correspondence that Louisa and her

---

[13] BL, Add. MS 72715; BL, Add. MS 72718. William Fraigneau (1717–78), regis professor of Greek at Cambridge 1744–50, took up employment as tutor and Grand Tour companion, first to Frederick St John, 2nd Viscount Bolingbroke, and secondly to Thomas Conolly: see J. Venn and J.A. Venn, *Alumni cantabrigienses*, part 1 (Cambridge, 1922), ii, p. 171; J. Ingamells, *A dictionary of British and Irish travellers in Italy, 1701–1800* (London, 1997), p. 103. [14] Most accounts date the portrait to 1758. M. Wynne, *Later Italian paintings in the National Gallery of Ireland: the seventeenth, eighteenth and nineteenth centuries* (Dublin, 1986), p. 74 gives the date as circa 1757–8.   [15] W. FitzGerald to his mother, 14 June 1767, in Fitzgerald (ed.), *Correspondence*, iii, p. 473. FitzGerald's Italian master in Florence, Abbé Pilloni, had taught Conolly ten years earlier.   [16] Coltman, *Fabricating the antique*, p. 12.   [17] R. Baird, *Mistress of the house: great ladies and grand houses, 1670–1830* (London, 2003), p. 17. This topic forms a component of the author's ongoing doctoral research.   [18] Most were created under the supervision of leading British architects James 'Athenian' Stuart, Robert Adam or James

sister Lady Sarah Bunbury played major roles in designing the Gallery's painted scheme. Louisa wrote to their sister Emily in June 1775 to say that the English artist Charles Reuben Ryley was 'now painting our gallery in a most beautiful way, Sarah's taste in putting the ornaments together, and mine in picking them out, so that we flatter ourselves that it must be charming'.[19] The content of the scheme is not discussed in surviving family correspondence, so to understand the Conollys' intellectual engagement with the antique visual motifs on the walls of the Long Gallery, we need to rely on circumstantial evidence.

II

One of the unresolved questions concerning the Long Gallery's iconography relates to an important pair of large oval paintings on the south wall, contained within gilded plasterwork frames and positioned above the niches on either side of the main entrance to the room. Their subject matter, their visual sources and their executant painter have long remained unidentified.[20] The author attributes these paintings to Charles Reuben Ryley,[21] and in this essay advances new identifications of the subjects of the two paintings as a prelude to a deeper investigation into their significance in the Gallery scheme.[22]

Ann Margaret Keller's essay 'The Long Gallery of Castletown House' (published in 1979 in the *Bulletin of the Irish Georgian Society*) is the foundational study of the Gallery's painted decoration and has remained, up to now, the only in-depth analysis of the room and its iconography.[23] Keller identified a substantial number of the Gallery's painted motifs and their engraved sources.[24] However, among the motifs that she did not identify are those in these two oval paintings. Considering the paintings to be out of place with the rest of the decoration in style, Keller argued that the first (fig. 2.4), to the left of the entrance, probably depicted a home-coming classical hero.[25] In the case of the second (fig. 2.5), on the right, she suggested that the river and landscape background might hint at its subject matter, but concluded that none of the well-known myths came to mind.[26] But, a fresh look at possible sources of inspiration suggests otherwise.

Wyatt. See, for example, Wilton-Ely, 'Pompeian and Etruscan tastes', pp 51–73. No architect is mentioned in family correspondence and accounts in connection with either the decorative painting or the general refurbishments in the Long Gallery in the 1770s. **19** Fitzgerald (ed.), *Correspondence*, iii, p. 141. **20** The English artist Charles Reuben Ryley (c.1752–98) has long been acknowledged as the author of a substantial portion of the Long Gallery's painted scheme, though it has been previously suggested that the oval paintings discussed here are by a different hand: see Keller, 'Long Gallery', pp 45–50. **21** This topic forms a component of the author's ongoing doctoral research. **22** A detailed investigation of the Long Gallery's decorative scheme is the subject of the author's ongoing doctoral research. **23** Keller, 'Long Gallery', pp 1–53. **24** Ibid., ch. 2. **25** Ibid., p. 30. **26** Ibid.

2.4 The Long Gallery, Castletown, Co. Kildare. Charles Reuben Ryley, the first oval painting: Apollo anoints Phaeton and places the sun crown on his head (1775–6). Courtesy of the Office of Public Works, photography by Davison Associates.

Ovid's story of the ill-fated youth Phaeton – whose hubris led to his disastrous flight across the sky in the chariot of his father (the sun-god Phoebus Apollo) – is one of the most colourful and substantial passages in *Metamorphoses*.[27] A review of these verses unveils Ovid's narrative as the source of the scenes in the Long Gallery's oval paintings. Perhaps the subjects of these two paintings have remained elusive because, in this case, the most obvious sources for the compositions are literary and textual rather than the more usual engraved visual sources discussed earlier.

Ovid's telling of the Phaeton myth can be summarized as follows:

> Phaeton, son of Phoebus Apollo, travelled to his father's palace to seek proof of his parentage. He was recognized and welcomed by his father but wanted a further token of proof and begged to be allowed drive the sun

27 Ovid, *Metamorphoses*, Bk I, 747–779, Bk II, 1–400.

2.5 The Long Gallery, Castletown, Co. Kildare. Charles Reuben Ryley, the second oval painting: the 'Western' nymphs discover the body of Phaeton beside the river Eridanus (1775–6). Courtesy of the Office of Public Works, photography by Davison Associates.

chariot for a day. Apollo, not wanting to grant such a dangerous wish, tried in vain to dissuade him and, seeing that Dawn was about to rise, ordered the Hours (goddesses of the seasons) to get the horses and golden carriage ready. He rubbed his son's face with ointment to protect him from the celestial flames and placed his own crown on Phaeton's head, bidding him steer a mid-way path between heaven and earth. But the chariot was soon out of control, creating chaos and setting fire to everything as it passed. Jupiter hurled his lightning bolt at Phaeton. The horses broke loose and escaped, and Phaeton shot from the flaming chariot like a falling star. His body landed in the waters of the Eridanus (traditionally identified with the river Po). The Western nymphs found his body and buried him.[28]

28 Referred to by Ovid as 'Naides Hesperiae', i.e., Western naiads, these nymphs are sometimes identified as Italian; see, for example, M.M. Innes, *The Metamorphoses of Ovid* (London, 1955), p. 58.

Based on this new identification of subject matter and literary source, it is now possible to conclude that the two oval paintings comprise an interconnected pair, each depicting a different episode in the tale of Phaeton.

The first painting is an almost literal visualization of Ovid's description of the final encounter between Apollo and Phaeton before the catastrophic chariot ride. As if to leave no doubt in the viewer's mind as to intended references, the artist has depicted Apollo rubbing the divine ointment onto his son's face while at the same time placing the rays-of-the-sun crown on his head. The chariot – with golden axles and wheels with rims of gold and silver spokes – conscientiously follows Ovid's description,[29] and likewise the Hours are shown preparing the horses. The painting's composition appears to be original, although the treatment of the Apollo and Phaeton grouping conforms to a tradition seen in illustrated editions of *Metamorphoses* from as far back as the sixteenth century.[30]

The subject in the second painting can also be identified from Ovid's recounting of the tale. Phaeton's body is shown lying on the banks of the river Eridanus. The four female figures, gesturing in alarm as they discover the dead youth, can be identified as the Western nymphs referred to by Ovid. In the background, the fiery sky alludes to Phaeton, shooting across the horizon like a falling star, lighting up the sky as his body hurtles in the direction of the edge of the painting to the right. The depiction of the dead Phaeton follows the tradition of Baroque (and earlier) representations.[31] Similar poses – albeit showing Phaeton in freefall – can be seen in many versions of Phaeton's fall, including those by Rubens, Sebastiano Ricci, and Giovanni Antonio Pellegrini.[32] Familiarity with this tradition – in which the youth is invariably dressed in a red garment, as he is in the Long Gallery painting – may well lie behind the composition of the second painting. It is notable that the 'falling Phaeton' pose is also seen in engraved illustrations in published editions of *Metamorphoses*, to be discussed shortly.

In the light of this assertion that the Long Gallery's oval paintings are in effect meticulous illustrations of the Phaeton myth in Ovid's *Metamorphoses*, questions arise about the choice of these scenes as important motifs within the overall painted scheme. As noted above, Thomas Conolly encountered 'Ovid's tales' as a 12-year-old schoolboy. But to understand the Conollys' route to the commissioning of the two Phaeton paintings, we need to know what sources they had to hand while the Gallery was being decorated, and if Louisa Conolly, the key author of the scheme, was familiar with *Metamorphoses* or with the Phaeton trope in general.

---

[29] See, for example, Ovid, *Metamorphoses*, trans. F.J. Miller, Loeb Classical Library (Harvard, 1984) I, 67–9.   [30] For example: Ludovico Dolce (trans.), *Le Transformationi* (Venice, 1553), p. 29; and Bernard Picart's illustration in A. Banier, *Les Métamorphoses d'Ovide: en latin, traduites en françois, avec des remarques, et des explications histories*, 2 vols (Amsterdam, 1732), i, p. 41.   [31] Baroque depictions of Phaeton's fall follow Renaissance and antique models.

III

The Castletown library is documented in a manuscript catalogue,[33] adjudged to have been compiled between 1781 and 1818.[34] Some pages are missing but cross-referencing with inventories and sales catalogues shows that the Conollys had thousands of books,[35] among them many important recently published antiquarian books of engravings, indicating that they kept up to date on archaeological matters and subscribed to the latest publications. The library contained numerous works of classical literature, one of which was a single folio volume recorded in the catalogue as 'Ovid's Metamorphoses by eminent hands'. This item can be identified as 'Garth's Ovid'.[36] The surviving records of the Castletown library do not list publication dates but given that 1781 was the start date for the compilation of the catalogue, we can be almost certain that the work was already at Castletown while the Gallery was being decorated.

Samuel Garth's *Ovid's Metamorphoses, in fifteen books, translated by the most eminent hands* was the standard English translation in the eighteenth century (fig. 2.6).[37] First published by Jacob Tonson in London in 1717, it brought together translations by Dryden, Addison, Congreve, Pope, Gay and Garth himself.[38] Much read, and much reprinted and republished into the nineteenth century, Garth's *Ovid* played a

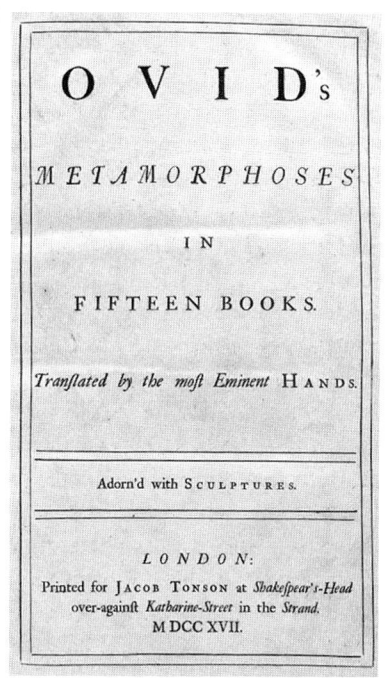

2.6 Samuel Garth, *Ovid's Metamorphoses in fifteen books, translated by the most eminent hands*, published by Jacob Tonson, London, 1717. Title page of the first edition.

---

32 For example, Peter Paul Rubens, *The Fall of Phaeton*, c.1604–5 (National Gallery of Art, Washington DC); Sebastiano Ricci, *Fall of Phaeton*, 1703–4 (Museo Civico, Belluno); Giovanni Antonio Pellegrini's Phaeton fresco in the dome at Castle Howard, where the original (1709–12) was recreated (1961–2) after an earlier fire.   33 TCD, Conolly papers, MS 3960.   34 E.J. Salholm, 'Library catalogue in the Trinity College Dublin Conolly manuscripts collection' (M.L.I.S. thesis, UCD, 1985).   35 Castletown inventory 1893–4 (IAA, 94/133). See also Jackson-Stops and McCabe, *An interesting sale … at Castletown House, Celbridge, Co. Kildare: Auction on Wednesday, 20th April, 1966 and the following days* (Dublin, n.d. [1966]).   36 Castletown inventory 1893–4, p. 363; Jackson-Stops and McCabe, *Interesting sale*, p. 27.   37 D. Hooley, 'Ovid translated: early modern versions of the *Metamorphoses*', in J.F. Miller and E. Newlands (eds), *A handbook to the reception of Ovid* (Chichester, 2014); Innes, *The Metamorphoses*, pp 21–4.   38 S. Garth, *Ovid's Metamorphoses, in fifteen books, translated by the most eminent hands* (London, 1717).

significant role in shaping the eighteenth-century understanding of the stories in *Metamorphoses*. The Phaeton passages relevant to the Long Gallery oval paintings were translated by Joseph Addison, and the paintings closely follow the descriptions in his verse. For example, the following lines correspond exactly with the first painting:

> A golden axle did the work uphold,
> Gold was the beam, the wheels were orb'd with gold.
> The spokes in rows of silver pleas'd the sight,
> The seat with party-colour'd gems was bright …
> From their full racks the gen'rous steeds retire,
> Dropping ambrosial foams, and snorting fire.
> Still anxious for his son, the god of day,
> To make him proof against the burning ray,
> His temples with celestial ointment wet,
> Of sov'reign virtue to repel the heat;
> Then fix'd the beamy circle on his head …

The scene in the second painting is described in the following passages:

> The breathless Phaeton, with flaming hair
> Shot from the chariot, like a falling star,
> That in a summer's ev'ning from the top
> Of Heav'n drops down, or seems at least to drop;
> 'Till on the Po his blasted corps was hurl'd,
> Far from his country, in the western world …
> The Latian nymphs came round him, and amaz'd,
> On the dead youth, transfix'd with thunder, gaz'd …

The two oval paintings commissioned by the Conollys scrupulously follow these two episodes in Ovid's version of the Phaeton myth and exactly match Addison's translation.

Early editions of Garth's *Ovid* were 'adorn'd with sculptures' – that is, illustrated with engravings on the opening pages of each of the fifteen books that comprise *Metamorphoses*, and the first edition was, like the Castletown copy, a single folio volume.[39] Therefore, it is likely that the Conollys' copy was an early and illustrated edition. Book two, which contains the episodes in the Long Gallery paintings, opens with a plate which, like the Gallery's depiction of the dead Phaeton, conforms to the established conventions for depicting his fall.

---

[39] See D. Hopkins, 'Dryden and the Garth-Tonson *Metamorphoses*', *Review of English Studies*, 39:153 (1988), p. 64. Later eighteenth-century editions of Garth's *Ovid* were sometimes published in two volumes.

While clearly not a visual source for the second painting in its entirety, an illustrated edition of Garth's *Ovid* may have influenced Phaeton's pose in this composition.

IV

Eighteenth-century translations of Ovid into English made *Metamorphoses* accessible to female readers, such as Louisa Conolly, who had not benefitted from a public-school education in the classics. The Print Room at Castletown, created by Louisa and completed circa 1769,[40] provides evidence that she was already familiar with Phaeton as a subject and decorative motif before the Long Gallery's paintings *all'antica* were executed. Print rooms, prolifically decorated with engravings and etchings, were fashionable in Ireland and England from the 1750s to the early nineteenth century. While some were commissioned from professional decorators, others were amateur creations, typically undertaken by women.[41] Like the Long Gallery, the Print Room is dense and complex in arrangement and required numerous aesthetic and iconographical choices, as well as intense engagement with subject. Its creation is, therefore, a significant precedent to Louisa's supervising role in the creation of the Long Gallery scheme and reveals a familiarity with episodes from Ovid's *Metamorphoses*.

An engraving after Richard Wilson's painting *Phaeton's petition to Apollo* was installed high on the room's east wall (fig. 2.7).[42] This print depicts the episode from *Metamorphoses* seen in the first oval painting, although in this case the composition is not a literal illustration. It is paired with a print after Wilson's *The destruction of the children of Niobe* – another story from *Metamorphoses* – which is positioned at the other end of the east wall.[43] The figures are difficult to discern now that the engravings are pasted high on the wall, but when handled at close quarters the prints would have presented Lady Louisa with the striking detail in Wilson's versions of the two stories. In preparation for installation, the prints were trimmed of their borders, thereby losing details of painter, engraver, publisher and date – and in the case of the *Niobe* engraving, the inscription 'See Ovids Metamorphos. Page 17' which identified the literary source of the scene. Louisa is likely to have read this information before cropping her prints.

Apollo and Diana can be seen in the upper right-hand corner of the *Niobe* print. It has been noted that the Apollo theme dominates the Long Gallery's iconographical programme, and that references to Diana are also present in the

[40] R. Johnstone, 'Revisiting the Print Room' (PhD, RMIT University, Australia, 2005), pp 31–2, 37.   [41] Johnstone, 'Print Room', pp 16, 18.   [42] Richard Wilson RA, *Phaeton's petition to Apollo* (1763), etched by William Woollett and published by John Boydell, London, 1763. See Johnstone, 'Print Room', p. 170.   [43] Richard Wilson RA, *The destruction of the Children of Niobe* (1760), etched by William Woollett and published by John Boydell, London, 1761. The *Phaeton* and *Niobe* prints may have been sold as a pair: see Johnstone, 'Print Room', p. 170.

2.7 William Woollett, *Phaeton*, etching and engraving after Richard Wilson, RA (1763).
© Victoria and Albert Museum, London.

decoration.[44] And while the *Phaeton* print is clearly a precedent for the Long Gallery oval paintings, it is conspicuous that Niobe is also present among the Gallery's surviving furnishings from the 1760s and 1770s. Ranged along the south wall is a set of eight marble busts, attributed to Simon Vierpyl,[45] one of which is a representation of Niobe, the only mythical figure among a cast of philosophers, poets and statesmen from ancient Greece and Rome. Among over a hundred prints chosen by Louisa for her Print Room, there are also depictions of Venus and Cupid, Clytie, Latona, Hercules, Marsyas, Helen of Troy, scenes from Roman history and popular sights on the Grand Tour. Clearly, the creation of the Print Room was in itself an education in antiquity.

[44] Keller, 'Long Gallery', pp 22, 34. [45] V. Brown, 'Catalogue' in E. Mayes (ed.), *Castletown decorative arts* (Trim, 2011), pp 206–7.

V

The identification of episodes from the Phaeton myth as the subject matter of the oval paintings adds an additional sub-theme to our understanding of the overall iconographical programme of the Long Gallery. This new interpretation is also supported by the fact that it continues and expands the Apollo theme, long acknowledged to permeate the Gallery's decorations.[46] It is now clear that the two oval paintings are thematically and visibly connected to the large canvas lunette after Guido Reni's *Aurora*,[47] placed over the main entrance to the Gallery on the south wall – Apollo, the Hours, and the chariot and horses appear in both the lunette and the first of the two paintings. The positioning of the oval paintings on the south wall to the left and right of the main entrance reinforces the subject of the lunette – Apollo in his sun chariot preceded by Aurora and the Hours – that dominates the Gallery's decoration from a centre-point on this wall (see fig. 2.1). It has been suggested that the lunette may have been the starting point for the planning of the painted decorations,[48] and if that is the case, then it may have determined the choice and position of the two Phaeton scenes.

VI

The neoclassical interior was an arena within which the eighteenth-century elite used a visual vocabulary derived from classical antiquity to demonstrate, not simply that they could afford the latest fashion, but to indicate privileged access to education and the Grand Tour, and quite often to convey meanings and messages through the iconographies of the interiors they commissioned.

An important mechanism underlying the neoclassical programme has been articulated by Adriano Aymonino: most of the visual motifs are ultimately derived from specific, identifiable, antique sources, and their use within elite eighteenth-century circles was motivated by the desire to visually 'cite' or 'quote' antiquities which would, in turn, be recognized by one's peers.[49] Even if not especially erudite, one needed to understand a decorative scheme created for public display. The textually accurate Phaeton paintings commissioned by the Conollys were a visual quotation of an antique *literary* source, in this case Ovid's well-known verses from *Metamorphoses*, familiar within elite circles from schooldays and country house libraries. The subject matter contained in the painted decorations on the walls of the Long Gallery would have provided a

46 Keller, 'Long Gallery', pp 16, 22, 34, 48–9; F. O'Kane, *Landscape design in eighteenth-century Ireland* (Cork, 2004), pp 59–60. 47 Guido Reni, ceiling fresco of Aurora, 1614 (Casino of the Palazzo Rospigliosi Pallavicini, Rome). 48 Keller, 'Long Gallery', pp 48–9. 49 See, for example, A. Aymonino, '"The true style of antique decoration": Agostino Brunias and the birth of the Adam style at Kedleston Hall and Syon House' in C. Thom (ed.), *Robert Adam and his brothers: new light on Britain's leading architectural family* (Swindon, 2019), p. 104.

topic of conversation with visitors and, no doubt, the pleasure of explaining the scheme to those less knowledgeable.

A precise knowledge of Ovid's version of the Phaeton myth is displayed in the oval paintings. Armed with Garth's *Ovid*, either of the Conollys, or perhaps both together, could have provided a detailed brief to their artist. For Thomas, the Long Gallery and the Castletown library would have been experienced as a natural extension of a mental world formed by his classical education at public school and reinforced by his Grand Tour. Louisa had not gone through the rigours of a public-school education. Nonetheless, she played a leading role in commissioning the Long Gallery's complex scheme of *all'antica* decorative painting – showing a familiarity with the history and mythology of antiquity and a certain degree of erudition.[50] Access to a library of books containing translations of classical works into English and antiquarian books of engravings, her Print Room, Grand Tour correspondence, conversations with her husband and with visitors to the Gallery, and the visual culture and literary world of her time would have provided a sort of alternative classical education.[51]

Further interrogation of the intersection between text and image on the walls of the Long Gallery of Castletown is likely to unlock additional insights into its iconography and has the potential to reveal the richer cultural significance of the classical world for the Irish Ascendancy class.

---

50 Keller, 'Long Gallery', p. 44, asserts that the Long Gallery's iconography is 'surprisingly learned'. 51 The topic of Louisa Conolly's education as a girl (and whether it included the classics) forms an important component of the author's ongoing doctoral research. For an earlier example of female engagement with the classical world, see Lady Calverley's Virgilian needlework in D. Arnold, *The Georgian country house* (Stroud, 2003), p. 92. For an example of female patronage of a neoclassical painted scheme with similar literary sources, see M. Whinney, *Home house* (London, 1969), passim.

'An effect rather than a reality'? The place of the country house in the Irish gentry's perception of their world

IAN D'ALTON

Writer Elizabeth Bowen once captured the concept of the gentry's houses as half-real, half-dream when she wrote that their size 'like their loneliness, is an effect rather than a reality'.[1] The idea of 'effect' catapults the house away from mere reality into another realm, and according to John Banville in his subversive Big House novel, *Birchwood*, 'We imagine that we remember things as they were, while in fact all we carry into the future are fragments which reconstruct a wholly illusory past'.[2] While the Irish country house may have been a receptacle for the history and transmission of ideas, it was itself an *idea*.[3] It was never just 'a kind of fever of bricks and mortar handed on from father to son', a passive backdrop to the gentry's world, as supposed by Dorothea Conyers.[4] And if the country house had lost most of its purpose by the early twentieth century, it was nevertheless 'reborn in Irish literature'.[5] A cascade of novels, plays and poetry offer this opportunity, then, to reinterpret the Irish country house as an imaginative scaffolding around the gentry's perception of themselves.

The country house was a place of permanence, embodying notions of perfection and flaw. It complemented its inhabitants' roles as parent, guardian, child and nurturer of their families. A house was also a psychological space that encouraged theatre, liaison and intrigue, and, like its occupants, was an alien presence in unwelcoming and uncomprehending territory. A house could imprison its occupants, even if that prison was an open one. Sometimes its fate was to be a funeral pyre, but many houses also had a stubborn afterlife. These varying perceptions meant that the house had a transcendental significance as in the Anglican formulation, it was 'the outward and visible sign of an inward and spiritual grace'. This was central to the gentry's sense of what their world was – or was not.

---

[1] E. Bowen, 'The Big House' in Bowen, *Collected impressions* (London, 1950), pp 195, 196. [2] J. Banville, *Birchwood* (London, 1984), p. 12; I. d'Alton, 'Remembering the future, imagining the past: how southern Irish Protestants survived' in F.M. Larkin (ed.), *Librarians, poets, and scholars: a festschrift for Donall Ó Lúanaigh* (Dublin, 2007), pp 212–30. [3] G. Bachelard, *La poétique de l'espace* (Paris, 1957), pp 24, 51–78 explores the psychology of houses. [4] D. Conyers, *Some happenings of Glendalyne* (London, 1911), p. 2. [5] Quoted in V. Kreilcamp, *The Anglo-Irish novel and the Big House* (Syracuse, 1998), p. 2.

PERMANENCE IN AN UNSTABLE GENTRY WORLD

The most obvious characteristic of the country house was its relative permanence. It is tempting to place the history of the Irish gentry in a corresponding state of being – that they were always there, too. But, this is not the whole story. The Irish gentry in the round exhibited perhaps much less security and permanence than the narrative often implies. For example, in the second half of the nineteenth century up to a quarter of estate-owned lands changed hands as a result of the operations of the encumbered estate and land courts, even if a significant proportion of such land was bought up by more solvent landlords.[6] To take an instance: Waterford landed society exhibited a significant 'churn' from the second half of the nineteenth century onwards, and only a little over one-third of these appear to have still been resident there in 1918.[7] Only eleven families out of thirty-four identified in the period 1837–1919 stayed the course, and these were the larger and more prominent landlords – including Beresfords, Devonshire, Villiers Stuart, Keane, Musgrave, Bagge, Chearnley and Smyth – who were a constant during the period. Thus, if we are searching for a more fixed gentry presence, it may have resided in the house more than in the family. Through its permanence the house had its own dynamic – in Bowen's phrase, 'living under its own spell'.[8] That spell could also exhibit an almost sinister manipulative force, as in Lennox Robinson's play *The Big House*, wherein Ballydonal House ensures that, through the agency of a drunken butler, its titular owner, St Leger Alcock, has been prevented from going down to his wine-cellar for six months.[9]

PERFECTION AND FLAW

The gentry invested a great deal of emotional capital in their houses, not least because these were the visible signs of their own self-fashioning. The Irish gentry's passionate attachment to their Big Houses is well-documented – particular examples can be found in Lady Gregory's devotion to Coole, Edith Somerville's embrace of Drishane, and Elizabeth Bowen's desperate quest to keep Bowen's Court going in her straitened 'fifties'. Indeed, over the course of the nineteenth century it could be said that the house grew ever more important, as the gentry began a troubled search for identity in a changing Ireland. Usually regarding Ireland as 'a country, rather than as a nation',[10] the gentry 'turned to geography in the attempt at patriotization'.[11]

---

[6] K.T. Hoppen, *Ireland since 1800: conflict and conformity* (London, 1999), p. 87.   [7] L. Proudfoot, 'The estate system in mid-nineteenth-century Waterford' in W. Nolan and T. Power (eds), *Waterford history and society* (Dublin, 1992), pp 521, 534–5, fig. 20.2.   [8] Bowen, 'Big House', p. 195.   [9] C. Murray (ed.), *Selected plays of Lennox Robinson* (Gerrard's Cross, 1982), pp 144, 149.   [10] J.M. Hone, 'Five Strains', *The Bell*, 2:6 (Sept. 1941), 26.   [11] D. Kiberd,

The place of the country house in the Irish gentry's perception of their world   31

Houses were often placed on pedestals of perfection. Thus, Aragon in Molly Keane's novel (a mix of Villiers Stuart's Dromana with a dash of Devonshire's Lismore Castle) was sinuous and serpentine, entwined with land and water. The house

> ... stood high above a tidal river. So high and so near that there was only a narrow kind of garden between house and water. It was almost a hanging garden: as Spanish as the strange name Aragon ... Beauty so correct and satisfactory since then there has never been; nor so much dignity with so little heaviness ... It was the quietest, most solemn garden. The parliaments of rooks in the woods below, only an echo here, a ring for the circle of the quiet.[12]

Likewise, Gillian Bence-Jones's paean of love for the Somerville house Drishane puts warm flesh on stone bones:

> The house rang, in cuckoo-clamour;
> He sang all evening; a blacksmith
> Beating our worries to better shape.
> With the power of Spring he spelled out
> That the frail hold on the old house
> Would nevertheless be strong enough ...
>
> ... The double cuckoo, carolling
> Somewhere in curtain trees disclosing view;
> Plays orchestra to perfection;
> Lawn, haven and point. The house solidly
> Attends; weather-slated, fanlighted,
> Wrapped in a gentle Georgian dream.[13]

By contrast, Bowen's own house was flawed, unfinished, one corner missing, and that missing symmetry was countered by the representations of perfection in Bowen's other writings, as in her 1929 novel about the last days of a Big House, *The last September*, where Gerald Lesworth's affections are 'rare and square – four-square – occurring like houses in a landscape, unrelated and positive'; and further reflected in her last novel, *Eva Trout*, where the house, Larkins, was also 'Square, two-storeyed, five sash windows in front (three above, two below) with a door in the middle' and 'its gaze was forthright'.[14] For Bowen,

---

Inventing Ireland (London, 1996), p. 107.   **12** M.J. Farrell [Molly Keane], *Two days in Aragon* (1941; repr. London, 1985), pp 16–17.   **13** Gillian Bence-Jones, 'Drishane' in Bence-Jones, *Ostrich Creek: Tom and other survivors* (n.p., 1999), p. 23; see also Francis Warner, 'Castle Leslie' in *Poetry of Francis Warner* (Philadelphia, 1970), p. 41.   **14** E. Bowen, *The last*

fictional houses could supply symmetry, perfection and completion, qualities lacking in the real world.

PARENT, GUARDIAN, CHILD AND NURTURER

Anthropomorphizing the Irish Big House is nothing new. At the very end of *The last September*, Bowen characterized Danielstown's destroyers as its 'executioners'. This is more than a literary device; it speaks to Carl Jung's theories of the persona and our use of archetypes – mental frameworks to interpret and explain the world around us.[15] As mother and matriarch, country houses were, in Max Deen Larsen's words, 'essentially female structures that embody the principles of order, security, and stability and create meaningful space for birth, nourishment, sleep and death'.[16] Molly Keane's Aragon 'was a very female house both within and without and wore the more exquisite moments of the year with a wonderful grandeur and quietness … there was a calm and kindness about its lines …'.[17] When a mother is lost, as Bowen's was to cancer when Elizabeth was thirteen, then houses – memorably termed 'pavilions of love' by Bowen[18] – could be seen in a different light.[19] 'I was the child of the house from which Danielstown derives', she wrote in 1942.[20] And yet Bowen's 'portraits of empty but claustrophobic houses challenge our stereotypical associations of family homes with a nurturing and beneficent female essence'.[21] Perhaps they become more like austere, desiccated, touchy maiden aunts, or barren spinster than broad-bosomed matronly smiling mothers? Equally, the Big House might be something other than a maternal figure: it could be masculine too, as a protector or guardian. With its 'formidable sinister stillness', the house Rathblane in Iris Murdoch's novel about the 1916 Irish Rising, *The red and the green*, is almost sentiently policing its inhabitants.[22] Likewise in her Irish gothic novel *The unicorn* she establishes Gaze Castle as a 'big, self-absorbed house' yet also a dangerous one, with its 'staring windows'.[23] In *The last September*, two visitors to Danielstown drive out, and the house watches; 'looking longest after them, like an eye, a window glittered.'[24] Bowen's Court, which faced south-west, had lots of glittering windows.

September (1929; repr. London, 1998), p. 40; E. Bowen, *Eva Trout* (London, 1999), p. 16. **15** I am indebted to Dr Patricia Orr for a stimulating conversation about this aspect. **16** Max Deen Larsen, 'Saints of the ascendancy: William Trevor's Big House novels' in O. Rauchbauer (ed.), *Ancestral voices: the Big House in Anglo-Irish literature* (Dublin, 1992), p. 261. **17** Farrell, *Two days in Aragon*, pp 16–17, 94. **18** E. Bowen, *Pictures and conversations* (London, 1975), p. 29. **19** Rauchbauer (ed.), *Ancestral voices*, p. ix. **20** Quoted in V. Glendinning, 'Introduction' to Bowen, *Last September*, p. 2. **21** P. Lassner, *Elizabeth Bowen* (London, 1989), p. 160. **22** J. Cronin, *The Anglo-Irish novel* (Belfast, 1990), pp 2, 126; I. Murdoch, *The red and the green* (1965; repr. London, 2002), p. 185. **23** I. Murdoch, *The unicorn* (1963; repr. London, 2000), pp 16, 30. **24** Bowen, *Last September*, p. 65.

For Bowen, her own house may have been much more than just as ancestor, nurturer or protector. Bowen's marriage was childless.[25] Yet, Bowen's Court can be seen as the child she never had – wayward, expensive, exasperating, but also loved and loving, a point of hope.[26] While Kate Alcock in Robinson's play may declare that the house Ballydonal once was but 'bricks and stones',[27] it is the only time in which the house is treated in such a brusque, inanimate way. More typically she fiercely claims that Ballydonal '… is life, our life'; the house is her world, her life, her faith, her country. The loss of a house is not just that of wood, stone and mortar, paintings and silver. In the last sentences of *The last September* the door of burning Danielstown may have 'stood open hospitably upon a furnace';[28] but its owners, the Naylors, were witnessing much, much more than red-hot stones.

THE PSYCHOLOGICAL SPACE

In these fictional or imagined houses atmosphere was never in short supply – an atmosphere built out of space as well as time, such as Danielstown with its 'pellucid silence … distilled from a hundred and fifty years of conversation'.[29] Bowen's 'Big House' has to have a 'Big Garden' too; its demesne land is an integral part of it, established in the very first pages of *The last September*.[30] These are the spaces that defined the gentry's psychology, the private kingdoms where 'high on a hill behind two white gates we were a world and a law unto ourselves'.[31] As a reflection of the gentry's precarious existence in a hostile land the house encompasses uneasy spaces. On the one hand there could be too much space, the inhabitants dwarfed by it scale, creating an emptiness; at Danielstown 'in the dining-room, the little party sat down under the crowd of portraits … spaced out accurately round the enormous table … each so enisled and distant that a remark at random, falling short of a neighbour, seemed a cry of appeal.'[32] On the other it could be crowded with the spirits of the departed, unable to accommodate emotionally all those who seek shelter in it, as recorded by Bowen in a later novel, 'Life works to dispossess the dead, to dislodge and oust them. Their places fill themselves up; later people come in; all the room is wanted.'[33]

25 I. d'Alton, '"My name is Alan Charles Cameron …": the Farahy Address, 9 September 2007', *The Irish Review*, 40–1 (Winter 2009), 171–6.   26 S. Osborn (ed.), *Elizabeth Bowen: new critical perspectives* (Cork, 2009) and a review article, I. d'Alton, 'Courting Elizabeth Bowen: *Elizabeth Bowen: new critical perspectives*, ed. Susan Osborn (Cork, 2009); *Love's civil war: Elizabeth Bowen and Charles Ritchie: letters and diaries 1941–1973*, ed. V. Glendinning, with J. Robertson (London, 2009)', *The Irish Review*, 42 (Spring/Summer 2010), 128–36. 27 Murray, *Selected plays*, p. 196.   28 Bowen, *Last September*, p. 206.   29 Ibid., p. 20. 30 Ibid., p. 7; Bowen, 'Big House', pp 195–6.   31 J.M. Hone, *Duck soup in the Black Sea* (London, 1988), p. 238.   32 Bowen, *Last September*, p. 24; Murray, *Selected plays*, p. 184. 33 The quotation is from Bowen's 1955 novel *A world of love*, quoted in H. Lee, *Elizabeth Bowen* (London, 1999), p. 190; d'Alton, '"My name is Alan Charles Cameron"', p. 4.

THEATRE, LIAISON AND INTRIGUE

It is no coincidence that so many novels and plays are set in the country house. As 'a place of isolation, exclusion and enclosure',[34] it stands as an island, a ship at sea, supplying an internalized place where characters can bounce off each other without external distractions. Its essential unreality plays to a sense of illusion, of the house being almost outside the control of the puny human actors who inhabit their halls, walks and gloomy rooms – even if many may have felt like St Leger Alcock, the owner of Ballydonal in Robinson's *Big House*, 'for so many years like a bad actor cast for a part far too heroic for his talents.'[35] Here is the ideal backdrop for a 'representative if miniature theatre', as Bowen wrote of her own Bowen's Court.[36] Here, in the introverted Lilliputian worlds of Somerville's & Ross's *The Irish RM* and *The real Charlotte*, the landed classes weave an intricate social filigree and indulge, among themselves, in a variant of Freud's 'narcissism of small differences'.[37]

Labyrinthine and light-starved corridors, passageways and rooms were the perfect backdrops for desire to flourish. Historian Adrian Tinniswood has a somewhat more earthy formulation, 'The great nocturnal pastime of the country-house party was sex'.[38] The geography of the house and its capaciousness facilitated the making and unmaking of assignations. In the fiction, youthful liaisons – such as those of Elizabeth Bowen's Lois in *The last September* (1929), Iris Murdoch's Marian Taylor in *The unicorn* (1963) and Molly Keane's Nicandra in *Loving and giving* (1988) – are counterpoints to the house as something that always seemed to have a miasma of age, decay and weariness about it.[39] Intrigue was equally in the warp and weft of the house, illustrated by an episode in Bowen's Court in 1936 when Elizabeth's plans to seduce a younger man went horribly awry.[40]

ALIEN CO-CONSPIRATOR

There were those who thought the house as not part of their Ireland at all – or if so a very dark part, captured in Michael Hartnett's *A visit to Castletown House* –

---

[34] G. Cronin, 'The Big House and the Irish landscape in the work of Elizabeth Bowen' in J. Genet (ed.), *The Big House in Ireland: reality and representation* (Dingle, 1991), p. 147. [35] Murray, *Selected plays*, p. 192. [36] E. Bowen, *Bowen's Court & seven winters* (London, 1984), p. 455. [37] Bowen, *Bowen's Court*, pp 259, 436; M. Bence-Jones, *Twilight of the Ascendancy* (London, 1987), passim; D. Akenson, *Small differences: Irish Catholics and Irish Protestants, 1825–1922* (Montreal, 1988), p. 149, using the term from S. Freud, 'The taboo of virginity' (1917). [38] A. Tinniswood, *The long weekend: life in the English country house between the wars* (London, 2018), p. 284. For similar behaviour in Irish country houses, see Molly Keane's novels *Devoted ladies* and *Loving and giving*. [39] E. O'Brien, 'Abjection and Molly Keane's "very nasty" novels' in E. Walshe and G. Young (eds), *Molly Keane: essays in contemporary criticism* (Dublin, 2006), p. 101. [40] S. Hastings, *Rosamond Lehmann* (London,

> … I went into the calmer, gentler hall
> in the wineglassed, chattering interval:
> there was the smell of rose and woodsmoke there.
> I stepped into the gentler evening air
> and saw black figures dancing on the lawn.
> *Eviction, Droit de Seigneur, Broken Bones*,
> and heard the crack of ligaments being torn
> and smelled the clinging blood upon the stones.[41]

For Maurice Farley in his poem 'Stately home', the demise of the house signals a sense of payback by the dispossessed:[42]

> We follow guides through rooms and galleries,
> Stare at ancestors' portraits in the hall,
> Remembering how long ago they took
> Our weeping daughters from their wedding feasts,
> Chattels to be used and given back,
> Droit de seigneur.
>
> To-day their heir must bolt connecting doors,
> And wait in patience till closing hour
> Restores his house, made stale by breath of crowds,
> And cigarette butts ground into the floor,
> Something we have used and given back,
> Droit de seigneur.

From these poets' perspectives, the house comes across as alien, a co-conspirator, always on the same side – the wrong side in the eyes of the less privileged – as its inhabitants.[43] In Anthony Coleman's words 'Formidable, reasonable, stately, the Big House spoke in a strange accent; it did not speak to the Gaelic heart'.[44] When it could, though, it was still powerful; it is said that when raiders arrived to torch Lord Waterford's house Curraghmore, they fled when the flitting moon shone suddenly on the gilded cross on a coat of arms over the door.[45] Perhaps the rebels had to work hard to overpower the Big House; Ernie O'Malley recounted carrying out manoeuvres in demesne lands to rid his volunteers of 'their inherent

---

2002), pp 172–3; V. Glendinning, *Elizabeth Bowen, portrait of a writer* (London, 1993), pp 113–16; Lee, *Bowen*, p. 116. **41** M. Hartnett, *Collected poems*, ed. Peter Fallon (Oldcastle, 2001), pp 136–7. **42** M. Farley, 'Stately home', *Poetry Ireland Review*, 8 (1983), p. 45. **43** See J. Dorney, 'The Big House and the Irish revolution', at http://www.theirishstory.com/2011/06/21/the-big-house-and-the-irish-revolution/#.Vxy98XiDpHg, accessed 19 May 2023. **44** A. Coleman, 'The Big House, Yeats and the Irish context' in Rauchbauer (ed.), *Ancestral voices*, p. 124. **45** H. McDowell, 'The Big House: a genealogist's perspective and a personal point of view' in Rauchbauer (ed.), *Ancestral voices*, p. 286.

respect for their owners'.[46] Their actions were a deliberate violation and in Gemma Clark's words, 'a symbolic purging of the historic enemy',[47] something made easier by what Elizabeth Bowen characterized as the almost innocent welcoming qualities of the Irish Big House – 'the gates', she wrote, 'stood wide open with an expression of real Irish hospitality'.[48]

Rather piquantly, the gentry understood that their houses, like themselves, were essentially intruders in a strange land. Elizabeth Fingall wrote of her house with 'windows staring across the country like blind eyes … looking out across the country which they possessed but never owned'.[49] In Murdoch's *The unicorn*, Gaze Castle is 'belonging yet not belonging' to the landscape of which it is part.[50] As Bowen wrote of Danielstown, 'The house seemed to be pressing down low in apprehension, hiding its face … It seemed to gather its trees close in fright and amazement at the wide, light, lovely unloving country, the unwilling bosom whereon it was set.'[51]

AN OPEN PRISON?

Most of the time, the gentry were in harmony with their houses and took care of them. For Everard Gault in William Trevor's novel *The story of Lucy Gault*, 'There was no other place he might more happily have lived than beneath the slated roof of its three grey storeys'.[52] However, even if 'the physical precincts were … central to identity', it was not always a wanted one.[53] Captured by their genealogy, prisoners of their futures, the relationship between house and owner was not universally benign. There were reasons enough for owners to let go of the house; it gobbled up resources both material and emotional. Among the multiple personalities, the house might assume it could be akin to a tyrannous invalid aunt forever banging on the bedroom floor for attention; the spoilt child always demanding sweets; or the complacent, all-too-visible sentry in a hostile territory. In Jennifer Johnston's novel *The gates*, the wreck of the Major rails against *his* Big House, exclaiming 'I hate it. I've always hated it'.[54] In Robinson's *Big House*, St Leger Alcock has a dark perspective too: as one smoking ruin slumped in the midst of another, he recognizes that his feelings for the house were moribund long before it was burnt down – 'I'm just damned glad it's all over and there's no reason to make an effort any more.' Ballydonal may have attracted Kate Alcock back from London but it repels her English-born mother

---

46 G. Clark, *Everyday violence in the Irish civil war* (Cambridge, 2014), p. 75.   **47** Ibid., p. 68.
48 E. Bowen, 'The back drawing-room' in *The collected stories of Elizabeth Bowen* (Princeton, NJ, 1981), p. 205.   **49** Elizabeth, Countess of Fingall, *Seventy years young* (London, 1937), p. 29.   **50** Murdoch, *Unicorn*, p. 15.   **51** Bowen, *Last September*, p. 66.   **52** W. Trevor, *The story of Lucy Gault* (London, 2002), p. 4.   **53** O. MacDonagh, *States of mind: a study of the Anglo-Irish conflict, 1780–1980* (London, 1983), p. 28.   **54** J. Johnston, *The gates* (London, 1974), p. 172.

who never took to 'this white elephant of a house'.[55] In truth the senior Alcocks are quite ambivalent about it. For many characters the house is a type of open prison; they may come and go but psychologically and culturally they are incarcerated in it:

> The door, that shadowy door
> Closes. And the mind is closed.
> A disembodied eye
> Roves through the big house …[56]

THE FUNERAL PYRE

The colours of the *The last September* are orange and red and russet and yellow and rust-brown: all autumnal shades, but also those of fire, the ultimate symbolic cleansing agent.[57] Fire was to the Big House as kryptonite was to Superman. Accidental fires were almost endemic[58] – seventy-six outbreaks are recorded in Munster and Connacht from the late eighteenth to the mid-twentieth centuries.[59] The question remains, of course, as to how many of these were wholly accidental? In John Hughes's ambiguous poem:

> … Was it chance or choice which brought her
> To the big house on the hill?
>
> Each morning she'd light the only fire in the house –
> That is until I set the whole place ablaze
> With ninety-nine parts carelessness
> To one part malice aforethought.[60]

Outsider Scottish poet George MacBeth well catches the careless animosity of those who destroyed these houses in turbulent times:

> … Yes, I'm sorry
> For those bricks and mortar, crashing joists
> And ancient floorboards. Houses don't have feelings,
> Do they? Lucky for us that they don't.

---

55 Murray, *Selected plays*, pp 153, 164, 192–3. **56** M. Davitt, 'Third draft of a dream', trans. P. Muldoon, in Tim Pat Coogan (ed.), *A special issue of Literary Review Ireland and The Arts* (London, 1982), pp 161–3. **57** Clark, *Everyday violence*, p. 61. **58** Irish Unionist Alliance, 'The defence of Irish country homes' (1913), a practical guide on the steps to be taken to prevent fire (PRONI, D/989/C/1/17). **59** http://www.landedestates.ie/, accessed 30 Nov. 2019. **60** J. Hughes, 'The Big House on the hill' in Hughes, *Negotiations with the chill wind*

> Ruining two centuries' handwork, Irish masons
> Laid the stones. Irish work and Irish genius
> Pissed on for a night of spite.[61]

For J.G. Farrell as the Majestic Hotel is destroyed by fire in *Troubles*, the flames open it 'to the Irish sky',[62] and enables the landscape to reclaim what was its own, through the agency of those other fundamental elements of water, wind and earth.[63]

In times of conflict targets are chosen for their real as well as their symbolic importance, and during the Irish revolutionary periods, houses featured in terms of military strategy. But there were other reasons why they were singled out: political animosity, sectarian conflict, the stubborn re-emergence of historical grudges over land, the settling of slights, and so on.[64] But even then the seemingly unreal intrudes. While Danielstown is a victim of the local war of independence, Ballydonal's killing is a reprisal for a Civil War execution far away in Dublin, and unfathomable for all that: 'Is that why we're to be burnt!' is the Hampshire-born Mrs Alcock's futile cry of incomprehension.[65]

The ritual of destruction often required the occupants to watch the funeral-pyre.[66] In the fictional *Two days in Aragon*, Sylvia Fox suffers humiliation as she is tied to a laurel tree and forced to witness the house as it is consumed by fire, 'so that she might watch her own soul burning'. In the world of real burning, Lord and Lady Bandon in June 1921 had to watch the destruction of Castle Bernard; the feisty elderly countess defiantly sang *God save the king* in her nightdress on the lawn as the castle behind her burned.[67] Lady Castlemaine and her daughter were provided with armchairs to watch Moydrum Castle go up in flames.[68] Some souls, though, were immune, or just joyous. At Kimmage, Dublin, Beatrice, Lady Glenavy exhibited a similar sense of release as that of the fictional St Leger Alcock and Jennifer Johnston's Major:

(Oldcastle, 1991), p. 33. **61** George MacBeth, 'A conversation with grandfather' in MacBeth, *Trespassing: poems from Ireland* (London, 1991), pp 44–5. **62** J.G. Farrell, *Troubles* (London, 1970), p. 446. **63** Clark, *Everyday violence*, p. 92. **64** Specifics can be identified, with the targeting of Anglo-Irish senators' houses by anti-Treaty forces being an example: Clark, *Everyday violence*, pp 70–85; see also Terence Dooley *Burning the Big House: the story of the Irish country house in a time of war and revolution* (London, 2022), p. 240. **65** Murray, *Selected plays*, p. 186. **66** For the early Danes, high flames at a funeral pyre were a mark of high status – see https://sciencenordic.com/archaeology-denmark-history/high-flames-gave-status-to-ancient-funeral-pyres/1443438, accessed 19 May 2023. **67** Farrell, *Two days in Aragon*, p. 253; M. Elliot, 'Molly Keane's Big Houses' in Genet (ed.), *The Big House in Ireland*, p. 195 ('her nails sunk into the very body of Aragon'); *Irish Times*, 22 June 1921; http://lordbelmontinnorthernireland.blogspot.com/2013/07/castle-bernard.html; http://www.irishmasonichistory.com/james-francis-bernard-4th-earl-of-bandon-grand-secretary-1875—1895-and-provincial-grand-master-of-munster.html (accessed 10 Nov. 2023). **68** https://www.westmeathindependent.ie/2009/10/21/the-burning-of-moydrum-castle/, accessed 19 May 2023.

The place of the country house in the Irish gentry's perception of their world   39

> I went round to the garden at the back of the house and stood in the wind and the rain in an ecstasy of relief – no one had been shot or burnt. As I watched the flames in the bedroom windows I had a most wonderful moment feeling that everything that I owned was being destroyed. No more possessions – I experienced an extraordinary sense of freedom.[69]

Far from being traumatized, which is the culmination of most fictional accounts of Anglo-Irish tragedy (as in *The last September*), Beatrice is freed from *her* open prison by the hand of the very forces that had made her Big House existence so beleaguered.

Thus, while at the last some houses awaited destruction, most cowered in the countryside thankfully unnoticed, lucky to survive, living on, dying in their beds.[70] Of those that were fired some, like Lord Mayo's Palmerstown in Kildare, were rebuilt; but not many were. Kate Alcock's ambition for the destroyed Ballydonal – 'We'll build it up again' – was a futile wish.[71] In a quasi-sequel to *The Big House, Killycregs in twilight* (1937), Lennox Robinson, with the awful 1920s and 1930s behind him, recognized the folly and impracticality of rebuilding: 'I wish we'd been burned out in the Troubles … I wouldn't have behaved like that fool-girl in the play, The Big House. I would never have rebuilt Killycregs. I'd have thanked God to be quit of it.'[72]

In the post-independence world many houses accepted their fate, purging their apostasy and guilt, seeking salvation by 'submitting to Rome' in the shape of the Catholic religious orders who purchased them for use as convents of nuns or houses for priests and brothers. Many others simply died of old age and neglect, such as Pallastown, near Kinsale, home of the Heard family, knocked down in the 1960s after significant deterioration; or Woodlawn in Galway.[73] Some had later near-miraculous resurrections as new money moved in, such as Castle Hyde and Ballynatray House, both on the Blackwater in Co. Cork.[74]

AFTERLIFE

In Bowen's novel *A world of love*, she avoided the death throes altogether; the house Montefort becomes almost a ghost in the landscape that it once

---

69 Beatrice Lady Glenavy, *Today we will only gossip* (London, 1964), p. 115.   **70** Elizabeth Bowen was haunted by images of Bowen's Court burning: Glendinning, *Elizabeth Bowen*, pp 40, 68. It is reckoned that some 300 or so were destroyed deliberately between early 1920 and mid-1923, representing some 20% of the total: T. Dooley, *The decline of the Big House* (Dublin, 2001), pp 171–97.   **71** Murray, *Selected plays*, p. 196.   **72** Ibid., p. 17.   **73** F. Browne, 'The death of the Pallastown heir: Lt Robert Heard, Irish Guards' in T. Dooley and C. Ridgway (eds), *The country house and the Great War: Irish and British experiences* (Dublin, 2016), pp 27–8; for Woodlawn, 'Challenging restoration awaits in Big House', *Irish Times*, 30 Aug. 2001.   **74** Castle Hyde, near Fermoy, was restored by dancer Michael Flatley in the 1990s. Further

dominated. 'Montefort? Pity that place has gone' remarks a neighbour who should have known better; and a casual visitor has 'No idea there was anyone living here'.[75] To all intents and purposes this miniature mansion is already gone, taking its inhabitants with it. And if the Big Houses always sheltered their quota of ghosts, the revolutionary burnings turned many of the houses themselves into nothing but ghosts, like Kilbarran in Bowen's short story, 'The back drawing-room'.[76] If occupants are defined by their houses, so the buildings themselves are personifications of their owners, they become living beings. At times it is hard to separate this mutual identity, and determine which is threatened or saved, alive or dead.

And yet the house renews its life by drawing in the spirits of the dead, as the son Ulick, killed three days before the Armistice, is in Robinson's play, or from the spectral republican who brushes past Lois in the garden of Danielstown. Bowen's Court turned into a sort of ghost, too. Ozymandias-like, only a few stones are left today, as in a ruined graveyard. What is there now is not necessarily a ghost, but rather a preservation of memory – Bowen's 'livingness' of these houses. In an afterword to *Bowen's Court* three years after the demolition of the house she wrote that 'it is part of the character of Bowen's Court to be, in its silent way, very much alive',[77] and elsewhere she remarked 'when I think of Bowen's Court, there it is'.[78] And indeed there it still is – it remained on the maps of north Cork for many years after it had been razed; it exists in the book *Bowen's Court*; and in an imaginative sense continues to be brought to life again every last September at a commemorative Anglican evensong in the little Bowen church at Farahy. Bowen's Court, preserved in the aspic of memory, has had a long finish. The gentry's world has all but gone, but their houses still stubbornly carry the echoes of a lost life –

> In revolutionary moments we attacked them,
> And now that time has conquered them,
> And, paying guests, we pass through halls and libraries,
> Our pride resents the counted silver spoon,
> The railed-off carpet space.
> The empty drawing-rooms still keep us in our place ...[79]

---

down the Blackwater, near Youghal, Ballynatray was a near-ruin in the early 1980s but since has been restored as a commercial venture: see P. Cockburn, *Figure of eight* (Dingle, 1989), p. 20. For more examples, see Dooley, *Decline of the Big House*, pp 250–60. 75 E. Bowen, *A world of love* (1955; repr. New York, 1978), pp 37, 80. 76 E. Bowen, 'The back drawing-room' in Bowen, *Collected stories*, pp 209–10. 77 Quoted in Spencer Curtis Brown, 'Foreword' to Bowen, *Pictures and conversations*, p. xxxv. 78 Bowen, *Bowen's Court*, p. 459. 79 M. Farley, 'Ascendancy', *Poetry Ireland Review*, 1 (Spring 1981), p. 25.

Mary Delany and the mental and creative world of Delville

KRISTINA DECKER

'I have been sorting my mosses and ores, and am going to new arrange my shells, and to *cover* two large vases for my garden'[1]

For those interested in eighteenth-century decorative arts, the artist Mary Delany (1700–88) needs little introduction. Unsurprisingly, much attention has been given to her 'paper mosaicks', a collection of botanically-accurate flower collages that she commenced making in her seventies, creating nearly 1,000 until her eyesight began to fail. Held in the collections of the British Museum, these floral collages were the culmination of a lifelong engagement with art, design, craft and Enlightenment thought, yet comparatively little attention has been devoted to the earlier germination of these interests. Particularly important to her intellectual and creative development was the period when she lived in Ireland, from 1744 to 1767, at Delville in Glasnevin, Co. Dublin, during her marriage to the Irish clergyman Patrick Delany. Yet, the distinctions of Mary Delany's Irish life have largely been subsumed within her longer biography.[2]

While Delville can be listed among Ireland's many lost eighteenth-century landscapes, it is possible to recreate its intellectual and creative world and explore its importance for Mary Delany by examining her written and artistic works. Through these, this essay will place Delville at the heart of Delany's networks, essential to her experience of the Enlightenment, the intellectual movement that was prominent within elite circles during the long eighteenth century. It will investigate how common intellectual interests were pursued through relationships that crossed the Irish Sea, and how these interests shaped the landscape of Delville. In this way, this essay will explore the mental world of Delville during Mary Delany's residence there and examine the role that it played in her experience of the Enlightenment during this time, themes that can be seen throughout her later botanical artwork.

---

1 Mary Granville Delany to Anne Granville Dewes, 22 Oct. 1745, in *Autobiography and correspondence of Mary Granville, Mrs Delany*, ed. Augusta Hall, 6 vols (Cambridge, 2011), ii, p. 395. Hereafter cited as *Correspondence*. 2 Some exceptions being: Angélique Day, *Letters from Georgian Ireland: the correspondence of Mary Delany, 1731–68* (Belfast, 1991); Katherine Cahill, *Mrs Delany's menus, medicines and manners* (Dublin, 2005).

MARY DELANY'S INTELLECTUAL NETWORKS

Mary Delany is well known for her extensive correspondence. Rarely does such a large collection of women's correspondence remain intact, and historians regularly mine her letters for anecdotes and details of everyday life in eighteenth-century Ireland and England. Yet, while there is often a Delany quotation for every occasion, it is important to remember that her voice is not the voice of the eighteenth-century everywoman. It is necessary to examine her correspondence within her own very specific context and place her within a large network of educated, cultured women and men.

Mary Delany's list of acquaintances reads like an eighteenth-century *Who's who*, including King George III and Queen Charlotte. But, perhaps most interesting are her friendships with like-minded individuals known for their intellectual and creative activities. Among the prominent intellectual figures she could count as her correspondents were: Jonathan Swift; Margaret Cavendish Bentinck, the duchess of Portland; and Elizabeth Montagu, dubbed the 'Queen of the Blues' – that is, the Bluestockings. Jonathan Swift's association with Delville predated Mary Delany, as he was great friends with her husband, Patrick Delany, who was an active member of Swift's literary coterie. They moved in similar circles during her first visit to Ireland in 1731–3, when she also met Swift's 'triumfeminate' of female 'wits': editor, poet and scholar Constantia Grierson; literary critic Elizabeth Sican; poet Mary Barber; and poet and memoirist Letitia Pilkington.[3] Mary Delany's earliest encounters with her future husband occurred within this intellectual context during this trip. Patrick Delany hosted weekly gatherings that Mary Delany (then still known as Mrs Pendarves) recorded attending,[4] later describing the attendees as 'those of the best learning and genius in the kingdom'.[5]

After her return to England, Mary Delany wrote to Jonathan Swift, inquiring about the gatherings, while simultaneously seeking to maintain her connections with his and Patrick Delany's Irish circle: '[t]he cold weather, I suppose, has gathered together Dr Delany's set: the next time you meet, may I beg the favour to make my compliments acceptable?'[6] But these weekly gatherings seem to have waned after Patrick Delany's marriage to Margaret Tennison (whom he had married during Mary's visit to Ireland), and Swift complained that 'Dr Delany lives entirely at Delvill [*sic*], the town air will not agree with his lady, and in winter there is no seeing him or dining with him but by those who keep coaches, and they must return the moment after dinner'.[7] Swift was attempting to

---

[3] Mary Pendarves (Delany) to Anne Granville (Dewes), 9 Oct. 1731 in *Correspondence*, i, p. 301; Mary Pendarves (Delany) to Anne Granville (Dewes), 5 Apr. 1733 in *Correspondence*, i, p. 407.   [4] Mary Delany, 'Letter XVII: autobiography' in *Correspondence*, i, p. 296.   [5] Mary Pendarves (Delany) to Anne Granville (Dewes), 24 Jan. 1733 in *Correspondence*, i, pp 396–7.
[6] Mary Pendarves (Delany) to Jonathan Swift, 24 Oct. 1733 in *Correspondence*, i, pp 420–1.
[7] Jonathan Swift to Mary Pendarves (Delany), 22 Feb. 1734 in *Correspondence*, i, p. 523.

maintain this coterie, in which he included the then Mary Pendarves, as he added: 'But I have chid him into taking a house just next to his, which will have three bed-chambers, where his winter visitants may lie, and a bed shall be fitted up for you.'[8] Mary Pendarves replied some months later: 'I am sorry the sociable Thursdays, that used to bring together so many agreeable friends at Dr Delany's, are broke up: though Delville has its beauties, yet it is more out of the way.'[9] This was a repeated theme, as Swift observed the following year that 'Dr Delany hath long ago given up his house in town. His Dublin friends seldom visit him till the swallows come in. He is too far from town for a winter visit, and too near for staying a night in the country manner; neither is his house large enough.'[10] Although she was far away in England, the breaking up of the regular meetings mattered less to Mary Delany, who could only nurture her Irish connections through correspondence, as is evident in her postscript to a 1736 letter to Swift: 'I beg my compliments to all friends that remember me, but particularly to Dr Delany.'[11]

Despite the distance, Mary Delany clearly maintained her Irish friendships well and nearly a decade after her first visit to Ireland, she married Patrick Delany. When she took up residence at Delville in 1744, the weekly meetings had long since ceased, and Swift died in 1745 after many years of illness. Yet, while the Delville of the 1740s was somewhat quieter without Swift and regular meetings 'among the wits', as Mary Delany might have termed it, the house had not lost its position as an intellectual centre. The Delanys had a wide acquaintance of like-minded individuals throughout Ireland, and Mary Delany's correspondence as chatelaine of Delville ensured that she and her husband remained connected to wider networks of scientific discovery and exchange.

Through Mary Delany, two major intellectual groups overlapped at Delville: the intellectual coterie around Jonathan Swift in Ireland and the extended Bluestocking circle in England. Mary Delany was friends with the duchess of Portland and Elizabeth Montagu, and regularly stayed at the duchess's Bulstrode Park, Buckinghamshire. A 1743 letter from Elizabeth Montagu to Mary Delany after her marriage to Patrick Delany emphasized the importance both women placed on creative and intellectual matters through her discussion of important elements of the Delanys' characters. On Patrick Delany, Montagu wrote: 'In his imagination I could perceive the *poet*, in his reflections the *philosopher*, and *in both the divine*.'[12] Later in the letter Montagu gave similar attributes to her friend: 'Dr Delany is happy in a companion like you, who take a philosopher's and an artist's part in the natural world; to a *mind* that *comprehends* you have a *hand that records* and represents its beauties.'[13]

8 Jonathan Swift to Mary Pendarves (Delany), 22 Feb. 1734 in *Correspondence*, i, p. 523.
9 Mary Pendarves (Delany) to Jonathan Swift, 16 May 1735 in *Correspondence*, i, p. 539.
10 Jonathan Swift to Mary Pendarves (Delany), 29 Jan. 1736 in *Correspondence*, i, p. 552.
11 Mary Pendarves (Delany) to Jonathan Swift, 22 Apr. 1736 in *Correspondence*, i, p. 555.
12 Elizabeth Montagu to Mary Delany, 1 Dec. 1743 (?) in *Correspondence*, ii, p. 232.   13 Ibid.

Unfortunately, in comparison to other correspondents, only a sampling of letters between Mary Delany and the duchess of Portland or Elizabeth Montagu have survived from this period. However a 'friendship box' featuring four enamel likenesses by the German miniaturist Christian Friedrich Zincke that was commissioned by the duchess of Portland in the early 1740s, just prior to Delany's second marriage and subsequent move to Ireland, provides an insight into the relationship between these women that echoes the sentiments expressed by Montagu in the letter discussed above. This small gold box features the portraits of Mary Delany (then Pendarves), the duchess of Portland, Elizabeth Montagu (then Robinson) and a fourth woman who it has been suggested might be Mary Howard, Lady Andover.[14] This small, but intricately detailed item, was a token of their friendship, grounded in mutual intellectual and creative interests.[15] Although Mary Delany might have been living in Delville, during the approximately twenty-year period that she lived in Ireland, her friendships allowed her to keep abreast of affairs in England, learning about Bluestocking salons and the ever-extending collections and intellectual inquiries associated with Bulstrode Park, where people such as naturalist Daniel Solander and scholar Elizabeth Elstob found patronage.[16]

On the peripheries of these networks was Anne Granville Dewes, Mary Delany's younger sister. The majority of Delany's extant correspondence from the period that she lived in Ireland was written to her sister and, after her sister's death in 1761, her niece Mary (Ann) Dewes.[17] While Anne lived a much quieter life than her older sister, spending much of her life in provincial England, she was also acquainted with many figures within Mary Delany's circles. She knew the duchess of Portland, who wrote to Anne, mentioning shell collections, their many mutual acquaintances and news of the Bentinck children.[18] The duchess's children also seemed to be well acquainted with Mary Delany's sister, for Elizabeth Elstob remarked on them several times in letters to Anne. In a 1740 letter Elstob commented 'how much you are in Lady Harriett's favour', and that Lady Betty 'has as great an affection for you as her sister has', sentiments that

---

[14] Elizabeth Eger, 'Paper trails and eloquent objects: Bluestocking friendship and material culture', *Parergon* 26:2 (2009), p. 115.   [15] Eger, 'Paper trails and eloquent objects', pp 113–23.   [16] For more on the duchess of Portland and Bulstrode Park, see Beth Fowkes Tobin, *The duchess's shells: natural history collecting in the age of Cook's voyages* (New Haven, CT, 2014); Madeleine Pelling, 'Collecting the world: female friendship and domestic craft at Bulstrode Park', *Journal for Eighteenth-Century Studies* 41:1 (Mar. 2018), pp 101–20. [17] Anne Granville Dewes's daughter Mary received the benefit of both her mother and aunt's interest in her education, and Mary Delany's correspondence to her niece followed similar themes as that to her sister. Anne Dewes clearly attempted to pass down their interests in natural history and prior to her death wrote of her intention to leave to her daughter, in addition to jewellery and pictures, her shells: see Anne Dewes, 23 Mar. 1756, in *Correspondence*, iii, p. 633. Mary Dewes is alternately referred to in Delany's correspondence as Mary or Mary Ann and in later life used the name Georgianna.   [18] Margaret Cavendish Bentinck to Anne Granville Dewes, n.d. in *Correspondence*, ii, pp 175–6.

were echoed in a later letter where Anne becomes a focal point for the children's activities, make believe, and play: 'Lady Betty often talks with pleasure of writing to you, and Lady Harriette is *Miss Pip* [a nickname for Anne] almost every day, and pays me visits under that name; the sweet little Marquis ... takes horse to carry you my compliments'.[19] Elstob was then employed by the duchess of Portland to educate her children, a position that both Mary Delany and Anne Granville Dewes had hoped she would attain.

Anne Granville Dewes, Mary Delany and the duchess of Portland shared similar interests in natural history, especially botany. Despite the lasting association between Mary Delany and flowers, in their letters it is apparent that Delany deferred to her sister's botanical expertise and knowledge. She would ask her younger sister for advice and help identifying plants, and Delany sent botanical specimens that she collected in Ireland and while travelling in England to Anne.[20] Furthermore, Anne obtained plants for the duchess's collections at Bulstrode Park, with plant exchange acting as a means through which they reinforced their friendship. The duchess wrote to Anne in a 1737 letter: 'Pray accept my thanks for the roots of the bee-flower; I shall take great care of them, for I will plant them myself.'[21] In the same letter she wrote detailed descriptions of plants and insects, comparing them to items in Anne's own collection with the clear expectation that her reader had a shared interest in, and knowledge of, natural history:

> I have looked all over my collection of moss, and can't find any kind like yours, that which most resembles it is the *small flowering green stone moss*, and the *beard of brier*, – but the first is a deeper green and not scarlet, and the other is not near so beautiful as yours. I found to-day a very odd fly – the body black, the legs red, and a tail half-an-inch long, the whole fly rather larger than a gnat.[22]

While letters between Mary Delany and Anne Granville Dewes are familiar family letters, they must equally be viewed as existing on the peripheries of the wider Bluestocking circle and the intellectual hive of Bulstrode Park. In this way,

---

19 Elizabeth Elstob to Anne Granville (Dewes), 6 May 1740 in *Correspondence*, ii, pp 85–6; Elizabeth Elstob to Anne Granville Dewes, 1740, in *Correspondence*, ii, p. 99. **20** See, for example, Mary Delany to Anne Dewes, 2 Aug. 1748 in *Correspondence*, ii, p. 491; Mary Delany to Anne Dewes, Dec. 1754 in *Correspondence*, iii, p. 308, and ibid., iii, p. 499; Mary Delany to Anne Dewes, 2 Sept. 1758 in *Correspondence*, iii, pp 508–9. **21** Margaret Cavendish Bentinck to Anne Granville (Dewes), 24 Aug. 1737 in *Correspondence*, i, p. 617. This was not an isolated incident. Mary Delany also facilitated plant discussion exchanges between her sister and the duchess of Portland: see, for example, Mary Delany to Anne Dewes, 26 Nov. 1749 in *Correspondence*, ii, p. 525; Mary Delany to Anne Dewes, 10 Dec. 1749 in *Correspondence*, ii, p. 531; Mary Delany to Anne Dewes, 28 Dec. 1753 in *Correspondence*, iii, p. 263; Mary Delany to Anne Dewes, 16 Dec. 1757 in *Correspondence*, iii, p. 474. **22** Margaret Cavendish Bentinck to Anne Granville (Dewes), 24 Aug. 1737 in *Correspondence*, i, p. 618.

when discussing Delany's correspondence from Delville, it is essential to remember that she was writing for this very specific audience and that this correspondence is part of an exchange that connected Delville to important intellectual networks in England.

MARY DELANY AND DELVILLE

The first year after the Delanys' marriage in 1743 was spent in England, where they maintained Mary's wide-ranging networks by visiting family and staying with friends like the duchess of Portland, while simultaneously trying to secure an ecclesiastical position for Patrick. Through Mary Delany's connections, they were successful, and he was appointed dean of Down, which prompted their removal to Dublin. Upon their arrival in Ireland in June 1744, Mary Delany immediately wrote to her sister, Anne Granville Dewes. With each stroke of her pen Delany took ownership of the house and gardens,[23] a theme that developed through these early letters. In the first, she described her voyage across the Irish Sea and arrival at her new home: 'I have traversed the house and gardens … and I have now the joy of seeing the kind and generous owner of it perfectly well, and well pleased to put me in possession.'[24] This sense of possession grew: by the end of the letter, she described Delville as 'my house' and asserted her new ownership by designating the room usage, identifying one room as that in which her sister would stay when she visited.[25]

Delany had also already begun to denote her ownership of her new home through physical alterations to the space. In part, this came through arranging her personal possessions. She had brought so many items with her that, she wrote to her sister: 'I wish I had sent you more, for this house is so full it will hardly hold what I have brought.'[26] But the important elements clearly found space in her new home; she described 'settling shell and papers', items central to her interests and sense of identity. She also had begun to make changes to features that were already there. She had an upholsterer visit and asserted that 'my new apartment will be very handsome'.[27] Of course, this sort of alteration to a new marital home was not unusual. A woman's involvement in the interior decoration of the Georgian home could be seen as an extension of wifely housekeeping responsibilities,[28] but, for Delany, there was a particular importance to having a sense of autonomy over her space and, to echo Virginia Woolf, 'a room of one's own'.

---

[23] Of course, under common law, Mary Delany had no legal right to ownership of Delville, and the property belonged to her husband Patrick Delany.   [24] Mary Delany to Anne Dewes, 28 June 1744 in *Correspondence*, ii, p. 306.   [25] Ibid., pp 305–7.   [26] Mary Delany to Anne Dewes, 19 July 1744 in *Correspondence*, ii, p. 313.   [27] Mary Delany to Anne Dewes, 12 July 1744 in ibid., p. 308.   [28] Amanda Vickery, *Behind closed doors: at home in Georgian England* (New Haven, CT, 2009).

Mary Delany and the mental and creative world of Delville 47

4.1 Mary Granville Delany, 'View of Dublin Bay from the bow window in the artist's closet', 1759, ink, graphite, and wash on paper, from *An album of 91 mounted drawings*. National Gallery of Ireland, Dublin, NGI.2722.64.

One such place was Mary Delany's closet. The closet was used as a place of sociable intimacy and retreat,[29] and Delany's closet at Delville fell into both of these categories. It provided her with a space in which to receive and entertain select guests, as well as one in which she could pursue her intellectual and creative interests, which ultimately extended beyond the walls of her closet to her wider network of friends.[30] It is possible to recreate the world of Mary Delany's closet, with the physical space long lost, through her visual and written depictions. Contained within an album of Delany's drawings held by the

29 Danielle Bobker, *The closet: the eighteenth-century architecture of intimacy* (Princeton, NJ, 2020); Robert Blair St George, 'Reading spaces in eighteenth-century New England' in John Styles and Amanda Vickery (eds), *Gender, taste, and material culture in Britain and North America, 1700–1830* (New Haven, CT, 2006), pp 81–106; Karen Lipsedge, '"Enter into thy closet": women, cross culture, and the eighteenth-century English novel' in Styles and Vickery (eds), *Gender, taste, and material culture*, pp 107–24. **30** Kim Sloan, 'Mrs. Delany's paintings & drawings' in Mark Laird and Alicia Weisburg-Roberts (eds), *Mrs Delany and her circle* (New Haven, CT, 2009), pp 113, 126; Maria Zytaruk, 'Epistolary utterances' in Laird and Weisburg-Roberts (eds), *Mrs Delany and her circle*, p. 131.

National Gallery of Ireland is a 1759 sketch, inscribed 'a view of the Port of Dublin Harbour and Delville Garden from the bow window in Mrs Delany's closet' (fig. 4.1).[31] This ink, graphite and wash drawing provides a glimpse of the edge of Delville's garden in the foreground, planted with a variety of trees and separated from the surrounding countryside with a stone wall. Across a series of fields lie several buildings with the sea beyond and a series of hills rise in the background. This happily corresponds with a 1744 letter where Delany described the view from her closet in her new home, confirming the location of the drawing. She wrote: '*the closet* within it is most delightful, I have a most extensive and beautiful prospect of the harbour and town of Dublin and a range of mountains of various shapes'.[32] Here, it is possible for the viewer to imagine themselves in Mary Delany's closet, with drawing materials strewn across the table by her bow window. Moreover, they can sit in her place, seeing with her eyes, and look across Delville's garden and the surrounding country to Dublin Bay beyond.

This drawing and other creative and intellectual activities were central to Delany's sense of ownership over her new home. Delany briefly mentioned two closets and a dressing room in her early catalogue of Delville in 1744, but this written description is primarily focused on the view of Dublin and its harbour from the windows and little mention is made of its interior.[33] At this point, she was still in the process of inhabiting the space and making it her own, its interior had yet to be filled.[34] Later, as Delany sketched views from her Delville closet window, the space became important for her creative endeavours that engaged with the external world. As Kim Sloan has observed, 'Mary continued to refer to her closets as inner sanctums from which she often enjoyed verdant views'.[35] Closet spaces can be understood as extensions of the inner self and Delany's Delville closets were invested with meaning and interest through her use of them.[36]

Delany put her stamp on these spaces by adding brackets of shellwork on which to stand items from her China collection, as well as other items from her collection.[37] The brackets are lost but Delany's correspondence enables us to reconstruct the shellwork that adorned her closet and their wider intellectual and creative contexts. Maria Zytaruk has identified Delany's organization of bedroom and closet space as in the 'architectural tradition of the virtuoso cabinet' of which the 'interplay between art and nature' was characteristic, and

31 Mary Granville Delany, 'View of Dublin Bay from the bow window in the artist's closet', 1759, Ink, graphite and wash on paper, 32.2 x 43.6cm, in *An album of 91 mounted drawings*, National Gallery of Ireland (NGI.2722.64). 32 Mary Delany to Anne Dewes, 12 July 1744 in *Correspondence*, ii, p. 309. 33 Ibid. 34 This process was repeated upon her arrival at Hollymount, the Delany's rented house in Co. Down, when Mary Delany's letter focused again on the view from the window of her closet: Mary Delany to Anne Dewes, 11 June 1745 in *Correspondence*, ii, p. 360. 35 Sloan, 'Mrs Delany's paintings & drawings', p. 126. 36 Lipsedge, '"Enter into thy closet"', pp 119–20. 37 Mary Delany to Anne Dewes, 25 Jan.

has further described Mary Delany's collecting and curating as a form of production.[38] In this way, Delany's natural history collections – including shells, fossils, mosses and other plant specimens – became part of her overall creative output, further transforming space in Delville.

In the end, one closet was not enough to accommodate all of her interests and in 1750 she found the need to expand into a second space. This new closet was designed as a workroom for the untidier creative pursuits, which would enable her to keep her other closet for collections, books, writing and work such as embroidery. When discussing this new 'working closet', she planned 'to have a dresser, and all manner of working tools, to keep all my stores for *painting, carving, gilding, &c.*' and identifying 'a deep nitch [*sic*] with shelves, where I shall put whatever china I think too good for common use'. While she mentioned 'a pleasant window that faces the garden', the focus of this room was inward rather than outward. This time the discussion of exterior view was secondary, and she considered it in terms of how it affected the room's interior and her use of it: its east-facing prospect meant that it was 'dry and warm' and with a morning light source to aid painting and other creative work.[39] The following year, Delany expressed similar views when she advised her sister on the design and functionality of her workroom, emphasizing light, convenience and comfort as all necessary elements of her own work space.[40] Contrary to Delany's 1744 descriptions of Delville's closets, by 1750 the rooms were undeniably stamped with her identity. They had become embodied spaces in which she could devote herself to creative and intellectual activities. In turn, these spaces had been physically altered by the very activities that they supported. In offering a place that could be improved through the production of crafts, her Irish home also became a space that contributed to her self-improvement.

DELVILLE AS CANVAS

Delany's collections and creative output were not to be confined within her closet walls. All of Delville became in effect a canvas, the possibilities inherent within its walls and gardens further nurturing her creative endeavours. After years of designing shellwork grottoes for family and friends, she was finally able to design her own. The addition of a chapel also provided an opportunity for Mary Delany to imbue the space with her particular brand of creativity. An ongoing project, the chapel was ostensibly the realm of Dean Patrick Delany as, after it began to take shape, she initially referred to it as 'his chapel'.[41] Later references were

---

1746 in *Correspondence*, ii, p. 415.   **38** Zytaruk, 'Epistolary utterances', pp 131–2, 135.   **39** Mary Delany to Anne Dewes, 6 Oct. 1750 in *Correspondence*, ii, pp 600–1.   **40** Mary Delany to Anne Dewes, 7 Nov. 1751 in *Correspondence*, iii, p. 56.   **41** Mary Delany to Anne Dewes, 20 Aug. 1748 in *Correspondence*, ii, p. 500.

primarily to 'the chapel',[42] but in one letter of 1750 she wrote: 'I am now copying a large Madonna and Child after Guido, for our chapel.'[43] Although a letter written ten days later again refers to it again as 'his chapel',[44] this designation of it as 'our chapel' is significant, as it appears to be intimately connected to her artwork and she appears to lay claim to the space through her creative process. This is reflected in a 1759 letter, when she wrote: 'I have laid aside my scheme of the *roses* for my chapel cushions as *too gay for the purpose*'.[45] The objects of Mary Delany's making were undeniably hers, and she asserted a sense of ownership through items of her own creation. Thus, the chapel became a joint space intimately connected to vocations of both Mary and Patrick Delany, reflective of their sympathetic partnership founded on mutual intellectual interests and 'perfect friendship'.[46]

Indeed, any visitor to the chapel would find it hard to escape Mary Delany's influence. In addition to supplying the religious iconography of the Madonna and Child, she copied a painting of Christ after Carlo Dolci for the chapel.[47] Despite their religious content these copies were secondary features in comparison to the shellwork that adorned the walls and ceilings. The chapel was a long-term project. In 1750 she noted that she'd already 'made 86 large flowers, and about 30 small ones',[48] but things had progressed considerably by 1759:

> My chief works have been the ceiling of the chapel ... done with cards *and shells* in imitation of stucco. In the chancel are four Gothic arches, two on each side, made *also of shells* in imitation of stucco, the arches no deeper than the thickness of the shells, to take off the plain look the walls would have without them.[49]

It certainly would have been an immersive experience: shell upon shell carefully combined into a gothic arch, pulling the eye heavenwards and to the shell-adorned ceiling, evidence of Mary Delany's touch everywhere. Thus, her creations enveloped the visitor or worshipper. Perhaps she considered shells a particularly fitting decoration for the chapel given her assertion that 'the beauties of *shells* are as *infinite as of flowers*, and to consider how they are inhabited enlarges a field of wonder that leads one insensibly to the great Director and Author of these wonders'.[50] The study of natural history ultimately offered an opportunity to consider the 'natural order' of things, eventually elevating

---

[42] See, for example, Mary Delany to Anne Dewes, 14 Dec. 1751 in *Correspondence*, iii, p. 67.
[43] Mary Delany to Bernard Granville, 18 Dec. 1750 in *Correspondence*, ii, p. 629.   [44] Mary Delany to Anne Dewes, 28 Dec. 1750 in *Correspondence*, ii, p. 633.   [45] Mary Delany to Anne Dewes, 3 Nov. 1759 in *Correspondence*, iii, p. 572.   [46] Patrick Delany to Mary Pendarves (Delany), 23 Apr. 1743 in *Correspondence*, ii, pp 210–11.   [47] Mary Delany to Anne Dewes, 14 Dec. 1751 in *Correspondence*, iii, p. 67.   [48] Mary Delany to Anne Dewes, 10 Dec. 1750 in *Correspondence*, ii, p. 626.   [49] Mary Delany to Anne Dewes, 15 Sept. 1759 in *Correspondence*, iii, pp 564–5.   [50] Mary Pendarves to Anne Granville, 30 June 1734 in *Correspondence*, i, p. 485.

thoughts to God.[51] In this way, the chapel is emblematic of her particular mode of Anglican Enlightenment where scientific and religious interests were compatible and could be explored through creative practices.

In the end, Delville was transformed through Delany's intellectual and creative pursuits. Although a comparatively small historic house, it was at the centre of overlapping networks that encouraged intellectual development and kept the Delanys at the forefront of Irish discussions and discoveries of the Enlightenment. The wider interests of these circles, and Mary Delany's involvement within them, were reflected in the changing visual landscape of Delville. Mary Delany's collections spilled out of her meticulously organized cabinet and closet spaces and into creative shellwork that adorned and altered the visual landscape of Delville, acting as a material record of her engagement with the Enlightenment. It was at her Glasnevin home that she was finally able to dedicate time and space to developing the themes and artistic practices that ultimately culminated with her famous 'paper mosaicks'. While Delville was one of the many Irish historic houses lost to development in the twentieth century, through the correspondence and artwork of Mary Delany, it is possible to recreate its mental world, enabling it to take its place among the intellectual hubs of eighteenth-century Ireland.

---

[51] Felicity Roberts, '"Idleness never grew in my soil": Mary Delany's flower collages, gender and the moral authority of "nature" in eighteenth-century England' in Jennifer G. Germann and Heidi A. Strobel (eds), *Materializing gender in eighteenth-century Europe* (London, 2016), pp 142–3.

Frances Power Cobbe, daughter of the Irish country house

CATHAL DOWD SMITH

INTRODUCTION

Frances Power Cobbe (1822–1904) is one of Ireland's foremost political, social and religious thinkers of the nineteenth century. Her contributions to society can be framed in many ways, as writer and journalist, or theologian, philosopher, reformer, feminist, social activist or animal rights campaigner. Regardless of through which lens of activism she is discussed, her confident, witty and personable voice is an inescapable aspect of her character. Writing on the emancipation of women she riposted:

> It is always amusing to me to read the complacent arguments of despisers of women when they think to prove the inevitable mental inferiority of my sex by specifying the smaller circumference of our heads. In this line of logic an elephant should be twice as wise as a man. But in my case, as it happens, their argument leans the wrong way, for my head is larger than those of most of my countrymen, – Doctors included.[1]

Frances' satirical, self-lambasting rhetoric enlivened Victorian debate of the women's movement. She engaged with the arguments of men, challenged them, showed her readers (who included all sexes and many social classes) the weaknesses and, at times, outright foolishness of the opposing argument. A gifted orator as well as writer, a talk given by Frances on suffrage was described as 'full of force and fire, and glittering with the satire which she knows how to use upon illogical opponents'.[2]

While much has been written on the Irish country house as a place of social, cultural, sporting and artistic happening, little ink has been spent on the intellectual life of the Irish country house, particularly that of its female occupants. An examination of Frances' early life spent within the walls of an Irish country house (Newbridge House, Co. Dublin) reveals how it was a place of spiritual and intellectual invocation for the nascent feminist and philosopher.

[1] Frances Power Cobbe, *The life of Frances Power Cobbe, as told by herself*, 2 vols (London, 1894), i, p. 4. [2] Sally Mitchell, *Frances Power Cobbe, Victorian feminist, journalist, reformer* (Charlottesville, 2004), p. 281.

The mental stimulation, or lack thereof, often felt by the women who dwelt in this nineteenth-century Irish country house context was not something that hindered the growth of Frances in later becoming a suffragist, social reformer, animal rights campaigner and journalist.

Heretofore, biographers of Frances have placed their protagonist in a context of Victorian England's activism circles, among campaigners and thinkers of the day like John Stuart Mill, Harriet Martineau and Mentia Taylor.[3] Intellectually, Frances rates among fellow theologian Theodore Parker, and other great minds such as Charles Darwin and Sir Charles Lyell, all of whom she knew well. Sally Mitchell and other feminist historians' work have presented Frances' activism, writing and theorizing in the context of these 'great men' and to the biographers' merit, on an equal footing. As Frances lived and worked for most of her adult life in England, it is appropriate to consider her career in that context. While all biographers deal with Frances' early years at Newbridge House, and the Cobbe family's position in post-union nineteenth-century Ireland and some in a wider imperial context, few have specifically looked at the formative impact of Ireland, the Irish country house, as well as Frances' own dominant Anglo-Irish identity, as influencing her outlook and work.[4] This pervasive influence came from Frances' experiences of early life spent in Ireland during the 1830s and 40s, observing the social disparity in rural Ireland. Her charitable work in the community, and her social and familial duty as the landlord's daughter and later chatelaine of a country house, is not without its traces through her work.

'A LONELY, DREAMING GIRL'[5]

The youngest and only daughter of five children, Frances' early years at Newbridge were overshadowed by the attention devoted by her father on her brothers' education.[6] Newbridge was filled not just with siblings, but periodically home to many cousins, as her father was guardian to some and for others Newbridge acted as a base while parents were abroad in colonial service.[7]

---

3 The incomparable biography is Mitchell, *Frances Power Cobbe*; see also Lori Williamson, *Power and protest: Frances Power Cobbe and Victorian society* (London, 2005); Deirdre Raftery, 'Frances Power Cobbe (1822–1904)' in Mary Cullen and Maria Luddy (eds), *Women, power and consciousness in nineteenth-century Ireland* (Dublin, 1995), pp 89–123. 4 For imperial context, see Barbara A. Seuss, 'Colonial bodies and the abolition of slavery: a tale of two Cobbes', *Slavery & Abolition: A Journal of Slave and Post-Slave Studies*, 37:3 (2016), pp 541–60. More recent scholarship looking at Frances through an Irish lens, see Maureen O'Connor, *The female and the species: the animal in Irish women's writing* (Bern, 2010); Maria José Carrera, 'Frances Power Cobbe on brutes, women, and the Irish (human) landscape: ethics, environment, and imperialism', *Estudios Irlandeses*, 15:2 (2020), pp 31–41. 5 Cobbe, *Life*, i, p. 84. 6 Mitchell notes that in thirty-four years of diary keeping, Charles Cobbe only mentions his daughter twenty-five times in comparison to the multiplicities of mentions of sons and nephews; Mitchell, *Frances Power Cobbe*, p. 35. 7 Between 1810 and 1840, the

5.1 East elevation of Newbridge House, *c.*1856. Courtesy: Cobbe Collection.

Unsurprisingly, Frances was continuously sidelined as her father fretted over the education and future occupations for the Cobbe sons and nephews: Sandhurst or Oxford to be followed by either military commissions, clerical orders or a legal qualification; oftentimes petitioning relations for help with postings. At most, the female cousins were sent to finishing school in England, while some were sent home to parents in India.

Newbridge was a house at times (mostly in summer and at Christmas) overflowing with relations and playmates, contrasting with periods of emptiness and the oft-commented 'solitary childhood', which led to a 'self-sufficiency as a child'; this helped in 'shaping the independent woman' Frances was to become.[8] In her autobiography, Frances paints a detailed picture of her childhood. As the sole infant in a sprawling country house, it was the Irish servants Mary Malone and Martha Jones, nicknamed 'Nanno' and 'Joney' respectively, who were her instructors and playmates. This is not to underplay the role of Frances' mother in her upbringing. Rather the prominence given to the staff in her childhood

combined total of Charles Cobbe and Frances Conway's nieces and nephews were some twenty-seven children, all dependent on Newbridge, in addition to their own five children.
8 Mitchell, *Frances Power Cobbe*, p. 34; also Valerie Sanders, *The private lives of Victorian women: autobiography in nineteenth-century England*, as quoted in Williamson, *Power & protest*, p. 10.

5.2 Frances Power Cobbe, Newbridge House *c*.1856. Courtesy: Cobbe Collection.

establishes ground for the later sympathy Frances was to have with the working classes, particularly servants, and shows her fructifying at an early stage an understanding of the Irish character, important for her later work.

Beyond these servant figures, Frances is vocal on the devoted love and care received from her mother. She recorded in her memoirs how her mother 'fulfilled that sacred duty of motherhood [breastfeeding] to all her children', presumably something oft mentioned for the youngest child to know. She remembers her mother's 'low, gentle voice, her smile, her […] arms, the atmosphere of dignity which always surrounded her, – the very odour of her clothes and lace, redolent of dried roses'.[9] From the perspective of her later views of womanhood, her mother reflects something of a bygone era, an almost helpless generation of women who epitomize maternal virtue and delicacy as the apex of female genteel life. While the Irish servants performed important duties in her upbringing, nothing substituted the presence of maternal love for Frances.

9 Cobbe, *Life*, i, p. 34.

5.3 Florence Graham, Portrait of Frances Power Cobbe, 1897, crayons on paper.
Courtesy: Cobbe Collection.

Her mother is idealized femininity juxtaposed against that of her daughter who was described variously as a 'merry, witty, Falstaffian personage', a 'fat Turkish Sultana' with 'mannish ways' and 'a fine intellectual head'.[10]

Despite this submissive view, Frances expressed a love for the shadowy spectre of her mother, who died following a long illness when Frances was just twenty-three years old. Frances believed nonetheless in achieving more than her mother had done and suggests in her writing this was also a view accepted by her mother. According to Frances, she recognized her difference and 'was aware of something' and looked with 'a little wonder, blended with her tenderness', while Frances indulged her unusual fancies of reading and serious study.[11] As Frances later struggled with her own religious conversion, she recalled 'there were great and terrible perturbations in my inner life, and these perhaps I did not always succeed in concealing from the watchful eyes of my dear mother'.[12]

In 1881, Frances published *Duties of women*, which rearticulated the idea of feminism in the wake of the growing suffragette movement. She encouraged a type of feminism in which women first and foremost remained true to their own moral autonomy. Frances advocated the rejection of what she called the 'vice of a servile sex' or subjugation on the basis of gender. She rallied against women who appeared 'little better than slaves [...] under the notion that it is a duty to husband or father'.[13] She argued that women foremost must have a duty to themselves. This fantastically radical sentiment was followed by a warning against the danger of a vocal and militant feminist movement. Frances saw woman's entry into the public sphere as an extension of the civility, morality and dutiful work already done in the home. The preface of the *Duties of women* articulated Frances' belief in the importance of womanly virtue for society:

> I will only add that, greatly as I desire to see the enfranchisement and elevation of women, I consider even that object subordinate to the moral character of each individual woman. If women were to become less <u>dutiful</u> by being enfranchised, – less conscientious, less unselfish, less temperate, less chaste, – then I should say: 'For Heaven's sake, let us stay where we are! <u>Nothing</u> we can ever gain would be worth such a loss.'[14]

EDUCATION TO SELF-EDUCATION

Frances recounts specific tales from her youth, which present her from a young age as being on a particular life path, as well as being rebellious and outspoken against inequality. Whether running away from home aged five to the cottage of

---

10 Williamson, *Power & Protest*, pp 1, 91. 11 Cobbe, *Life*, i, p. 84. 12 Ibid., p. 31.
13 Frances Power Cobbe, *The duties of women; a course of lectures* (London, 1881), p. 28.
14 Ibid., p. 11.

her retired nursemaid, or eavesdropping as her father read *Pilgrim's progress* to her brothers, her youth at Newbridge was a place of mischief, merriment and education.

A succession of resident governesses in the nursery attended to Frances' early education. But on 21 October 1836, approaching her fourteenth birthday, Frances left with her mother and elder brother for England. At 32 Brunswick Terrace, Brighton, she attended the school of Miss Runciman and Miss Roberts. An expensive finishing school with a small number of pupils, Frances would remain critical of the substance, or rather lack thereof, in the curriculum for the rest of her life. She described how 'the education of women was probably at its lowest ebb' during the 1830s: 'Infinitely more costly' and 'more shallow and senseless than can easily be believed' with dancing, music and languages taking precedence over religion, English, history, or science. While its social make-up was typical for an Anglo-Irish gentry household looking to send a daughter to be 'finished' in England, the substance of Frances' education at Brighton left much to be desired. Frances revelled in the thought that her later accomplishments as a writer would have been seen by her tutors 'as a deplorable dereliction'.[15]

Upon the completion of her formal education in 1838, Frances returned to Newbridge to continue her self-education. This period of her life lasted for the next two decades, as she lived in her family home occupying roles as daughter, spinster sister and chatelaine. Most importantly, however, for herself, Newbridge offered Frances the stability, support and comfort to learn and develop. 'I came home at sixteen, and then, once more [was] able to enjoy the solitude of the woods and of my own bedroom and its inner study where no one intruded'. She read widely in philosophy, history and theology, and studied Greek with the help of the local clergy. Such study was easily undertaken in a house whose library was richly populated from the classics to the more contemporary religious thinkers of the day, albeit of a certain conservative and evangelical hue. She found in the library works from which she learned, as well as writings with which she fundamentally differed. Frances described from a young age her 'strange fancy for reading the most serious books in my playhours', and recorded how in her seventeenth year the summer was spent with 'endless Bible readings to myself', rising early 'in the summer dawn and read a whole Gospel before I dressed'.[16] Reading Heroditus, Horace, Euripides and Aristotle undoubtedly inspired Frances' later travels through Italy, Greece, Constantinople and Egypt.

Frances' sure and deep knowledge of these books is shown in the library catalogue she produced in September 1852. This catalogue is one of her many contributions to what are now the important family archives at Newbridge House. While the library catalogue is more housekeeping prowess than academic pursuit, Frances' passion for history and genealogy produced other valuable

---

15 Cobbe, *Life*, i, pp 58, 64. **16** Ibid., pp 88, 84.

Frances Power Cobbe, daughter of the Irish country house

5.4 Illustrated genealogical tables of Charles Cobbe's ancestry by Frances Power Cobbe. Courtesy: Cobbe papers, Alec Cobbe division.

outputs (today important archive treasures). Her interest was mainly in her own illustrious ancestors, as she noted herself: 'I have enjoyed through life the advantages of being, in the true sense of the words, "well born."'[17] In addition to a well-researched picture catalogue, completed in 1868 with biographical accounts of ancestors, Frances had previously occupied herself with making an illustrated manuscript of genealogy which charted her descent from the Plantagenet kings and the Gaelic clans of O'Brien and McCarthy (fig. 5.4). Assembled from 1842, her genealogical research project was aided with visits to London in 1847 and in 1851 to the British Museum, which enabled Frances to inspect manuscripts that recorded the arms and heraldry of her ancestral families.[18] At the time, evolutionary biology was the cutting-edge of science, and Frances' genealogical research bears out a Darwinian fascination with exploring her antecedents. She identified certain characteristics as attributable to her royal Plantagenet or Gaelic clan bloodlines. This led her to identify with a Norman-Gaelic lineage rather than Anglo-Irish.[19] Yet, this multifaceted sense of heritage

17 Ibid., p. 3.   18 Thomas Cobbe to his father, Charles, 5 Oct. 1842 (Newbridge House, Dublin, Cobbe papers); Account book of Charles Cobbe, 11 Mar. 1847 (ibid.).   19 See also Frances Power Cobbe, *Darwinism in morals and other essays* (London, 1872).

has not always been identified by historians, as Frances herself would identify differently (English 'Saxon', Irish or British) as the argument required. This populates her self-description throughout her writings on Irish matters, particularly when addressing the English audiences of her later life.[20] Frances' own understanding of this Norman-Gaelic heritage is a lot more nuanced than recognized. Of this, she was 'proud to be accepted' but rather to be liked 'on the strength of my own talk and books, not on that of my father's acres'.[21] This time of independent research allowed Frances to hone the skills she would rely on in her professional career. As her biographer noted her work was famed for 'careful research, concrete details and a biting edge that compelled public attention'.[22]

SENSE OF DUTY

Frances' solitude at Newbridge would end during the summer holidays and Christmas, when her brothers and 'a regiment of young cousins, male and female' would descend upon Newbridge.[23] They all grew up under the shadow of her strong-willed and authoritarian father, Charles Cobbe, a man of 'narrow religious creed', with a 'fiery temper' and a 'despotic will'.[24] Despite his faults, he was a devoted husband and father, a tireless landlord and a man of intense faith and good charity, known for being prone to acts of unparalleled philanthropy. She describes him as having an 'upright, honourable, fearless nature' and, most potently of all, a 'strong sense of duty'.[25] It was this sense of duty that defined, for Frances, her father's generation of evangelical Protestants, which she juxtaposed against her own youthful love of God. She later wrote: 'my good father and mother performed their religious exercises more as a duty, – whereas to me such things, so far as I could understand them, were real pleasures'.[26]

The bookshelves of Newbridge extrapolate the strong creed and devotional faith demonstrated by Charles Cobbe. The sermons of William Jay (published in Bath, 1802), a preacher regularly attended by Cobbe, include one where Jay discusses 'them that walk uprightly' and whose 'external service arises from inward principle'.[27] On 23 November 1823, Cobbe wrote in his diary: 'Went to hear Mr Jay at Argyle St Chapel, I seldom hear him preach without receiving instructions. Grant I God [sic] that what I hear maybe grafted in my heart & bring forth the fruits of good living to the praise of thy name.'[28] Another author, Samuel Horsely, bishop of St Asaph, preached a sermon in 1796 (published in

---

20 O'Connor, *Female and the species*, p. 55. **21** Cobbe, *Life*, ii, p. 83. **22** Sally Mitchell, 'Florence Graham, portrait of Frances Power Cobbe (1822–1904)' in Alastair Laing (ed.), *Clerics and connoisseur: an Irish art collection through three centuries* (London, 2001), p. 49. **23** Cobbe, *Life*, i, p. 43. **24** Ibid., p. 206. **25** Ibid. **26** Ibid., p. 84. **27** William Jay, *Sermons of William Jay* (Bath, 1802), pp 343, 345. **28** Diary of Charles Cobbe, 1823–24

1827) in which he spoke of how Jesus Christ fulfilled the ancient prophecies as his duty, by performing the miracles as expected. The bishop talked of 'a man who executes that which by his calling and profession it is his proper task to do', and that in doing such and 'everything in the most perfect manner which we had a right to expect that he should do', it is he 'who shall come to us assuming the character of the Messiah'.[29] Perhaps even more apt for the work of Charles Cobbe as improving landlord, Horsley made reference to the vices of the late eighteenth century, to 'a voluptuous nobility' who 'squander on base and criminal indulgences'.[30] It was exactly in opposition to the behaviour of this earlier generation that Charles Cobbe fashioned his life, not as his grandfather did, imbibing and collecting art, but adjusting his love toward his fellow man, 'to the measure and example of Christ's love'.[31] Growing up among this library of theological, evangelical and doctrinal writing, it is no wonder that Frances' first publication dealt with religion, especially intuitive morals and non-sectarian moral principle derived not from religious doctrine or scripture but rather from individual innate morals.[32] *An essay on intuitive morals*, published in 1857 after her father's death, presents Frances' belief in a 'universal nondoctrinal theism', which emerges as a result of progress in all religions.

Charles Cobbe's staunch evangelical Protestantism translated into positive actions. To enable improvements to the lives of his fellow man, namely his tenants, when Frances was fourteen, her father sold a large chunk of the Wicklow estate not simply to generate capital, but to focus his attention more concentratedly and, thus, more dutifully on the tenants who needed it the most – namely those on the poorest lands. Three years later, he sold two paintings, jewels of the Newbridge collection, to reconstruct, repair and build new tenants' cottages on his estate.[33]

It was this keen sense of duty, morality and selflessness that Frances was to inherit from her father. During her time at Newbridge as spinster daughter and sister, Frances' role was to aid and help her brothers. In spring 1846, Frances journeyed to Armagh, where her brother was curate of a busy parish, Grange, located on the road to Belfast. Her role there was presumably to keep house and provide support in administering famine relief in the parish. At this time, Frances' financial habits and dependence can be carefully traced through her father's account books. When Frances was aged eighteen, her father had increased her quarterly allowance from £2 to £12. This saw Frances taking on responsibility for paying for her own clothes and writing materials, with

(Cobbe papers). **29** Samuel Horsley, *Sermons* (London, 1827), p. 117. **30** Ibid., p. 123. **31** Ibid., p. 124. For more, see Peadar Bates, *The life of Charles Cobbe, 1781–1857* (Dublin, 2007). **32** Frances Power Cobbe, *Essay on intuitive morals, being an attempt to popularise ethical science* (London, 1855). **33** See Arthur K. Wheelock Jr and Alec Cobbe, '"A better picture to the Christian eye": the sale of Meindert Hobbema's Wooded Landscape from Newbridge' in Laing (ed.), *Clerics and connoisseurs*, pp 87–9.

additional funds occasionally given by her father. By 1842, aged 20, her quarterly allowance was £25 but interestingly by 1846 it had decreased to £20, perhaps inflation brought on by the worsening famine meant cutbacks, or possibly Charles Cobbe had realized that his twenty-four-year-old daughter was increasingly less likely to marry and so rationalized this expense that would be borne indefinitely. By this time, however, Frances had taken on greater responsibility in the household as her mother's health failed. As a friend recalled, 'Beautiful Newbridge with its splendid hospitality [...] what a gentleman's estate and country home could be in those days when ancient race and noble family traditions were still of some account'.[34]

After the breakdown of her other brother Thomas' marriage, it was Frances who was given £20 'for her expenses to London'.[35] When Thomas retreated to the quiet glens of Donegal during the publicity of the divorce case, it was Frances who travelled north to keep him company and offer comfort. It was under the guise of familial duty that Frances gained her first experience of travel. The railway and steam packet ships facilitated travel, bringing escape and also a taste of the world beyond the demesne walls of Newbridge. Later, when her father died in 1857, after a decade spent nursing and keeping house for him, Frances returned to travel with a hunger for the independence and responsibility it brought. Europe, North Africa and the Middle East were visited, albeit at the sacrifice of leaving her family home. As her elder brother and his wife took their place at the centre of Newbridge, the middle-aged Frances no longer had a role to play. She regarded her womanly duty as fulfilled in her home-making and caring for her elderly parents. Regardless of her desire to achieve something in life, and her refusal to be betrothed and to raise her own family, a love of home-making and a sadness at leaving her family home stayed with her:

> It is one of the many perversities of woman's destiny that she is, not only by hereditary instinct a home-making animal, but is encouraged to the uttermost to centre all her interests in her home [...] Yet when a young woman takes thoroughly to this natural home-making, when she has, like a plant, sent her roots down into the cellars and her tendrils up into the garrets and every room bears the impress of her personality, when she glories in every good picture on the walls or bit of choice china on the tables and blushes for every stain on the carpets, when, in short, her home is, as it should be, her outer garment, her nest, her shell, fitted to her like that of a nurex, then almost invariable comes to her the order to leave it all, tear herself out of it – and go to make (if she can) some other home elsewhere.[36]

---

34 Felicia Skene, quoted in Cobbe, *Life*, i, p. 27.   35 Account book of Charles Cobbe, 1840–56 (Cobbe papers).   36 Cobbe, *Life*, i, p. 203.

Talking of the difficulty of some of her spinster contemporaries whose fathers survived late into their lives and, in middle age, were forced to uproot and resettle, she declared her own luck that her father died while she was still 'in full vigour and able to begin a new existence with spirit and make new friends'.[37]

A 'NEBULA OF FENIAN BOASTING'

Despite heartache at departure, Frances retained her close ties with home, and continued to visit Newbridge until her elder brother's remarriage in 1883 when she was sixty-one. Her early experiences remained with her and frequently informed her writing, nowhere less so than in her article, 'The Fenians of Ballybogmucky', published in 1866; this was in response to the Young Irelanders' rebellion some years earlier and the more recent founding of the Irish Republican Brotherhood and the Fenian Brotherhood in America, or what Frances termed 'the very large nebula of Fenian boasting'.[38]

Her writing reveals her tightrope station as a 'well-born' Anglo-Irish child of the 'squirearchy'. She remained sceptical of any 'insane attempt' or belief that it 'was possible to wrench Ireland from the grasp of England's strong right arm'.[39] Yet, her belief in reason, and that Irish political happenings were not without causation is clear when she stated: 'It will surely not be amiss for us in England to pause a little and study the state of some millions of our fellow-subjects'. She observed the jealousy of the Irish, and how their mistreatment was leading them to become a 'social powder-magazine', which was 'ready to be exploded by the first weak hand that applies the torch of some wildfire project'.[40]

Frances' interpretation of the 'Irish problem', namely absenteeism, was also coloured by a desire not to judge the character of the Irish by the colonizer's values. She considered Irish blood was made of 'the largest share of the milk of human kindness', but that the Irish could be both 'docile', 'mild', 'religious' and also 'predisposed towards occasional outbursts of insane violence, fanaticism, and treachery', a trait that she identified in the Irish blood as a 'drop of intensest gall'.[41]

In the article, Ballybogmucky is presented as a fictional place but is in fact based entirely on the reality of famine life in the village of Ballisk, which neighboured her native Newbridge. Ballisk, like Ballybogmucky, was owned and neglected by the absentee landlord Lord Trimbleston of Turvey House.[42] In

---

37 Ibid.   38 Frances Power Cobbe, 'The Fenians of Ballybogmucky', *The Argosy* (Jan. 1866), 80.   39 Ibid.   40 Ibid.   41 Ibid., p. 81.   42 The 'good' landlord is Mr Norton of Knockillsassenach – undoubtedly a trope of her father. Norton being her father's great-great-great-grandmother's maiden name, while Knockillsassenach being a bastardization of the Gaeilge for Englishman 'Sasanach' (referring to the Cobbe name being of English origin as opposed to Barnewall's Norman lineage), with the prefix 'Knock' commonly used in placenames such as the townland and estate near Newbridge, Knocksedan.

Ballisk/Ballybogmucky, inhabitants occupied cabins 'one, two and a few three roomed, made of mud, thatched and with earthen floors', scantily filled with furniture and 'a door, over and under and round which all the winds and rains of heaven find their way'.[43] It was in these poorest of conditions that the milk of human kindness was found, alongside the poverty, starvation and disease of famine. This essay reads as an early iteration of the chapter in her memoirs that describes Ballisk in exactly the same vein, leaving the reader of both in no doubt as to where she derives inspiration. As described in her memoirs, Ballisk was 'a centre of fever and misery' as a result of absenteeism.[44] Her argument was that the plight of the Irish explained the rise in Fenianism: 'wrongs inflicted by England upon Ireland are probably as bad as ever disgraced the history of conquest!'[45] As has been written of Frances' abolitionist campaign, at Newbridge she 'acquired the understanding that a body, by virtue of the immutability of its genealogical constitution, should not be made to bear the violence of cultural and economic denigration'.[46] Showing an awareness of Irish nature, Frances highlighted how social improvements, such as those enacted by her father on his estate, could create more stable communities. In this brief foray into Irish politics, just as in her campaign for female enfranchisement, Frances advocated social reform over militant action.

CONCLUSION

Frances Power Cobbe's place in the pantheon of nineteenth-century female writers is by now well established. She was one of the leading feminist voices of Victorian Britain and beloved by many. Arguably, she is deserving of a greater place in the historiography of Irish writing, much maligned by her commentary on social issues across both sides of the Irish sea, her complex political voice, her genteel upbringing and her middle-class readership. She is difficult to pigeon-hole into one category, on account of championing causes as broad as animal rights, servants' working conditions and higher education (to name a few). The legacy of her writing continues most notably in campaigns still being fought.[47]

Her writing provides a greater depth to our understanding of post-union Anglo-Irish identity, both socially, politically and culturally. For her, the Irish country house was a setting of intensive maternal love and attention. While her early education in her father's evangelical library informed her non-doctrinal theological view and the moral philosophy which permeates her work, Frances

---

43 Cobbe, 'Fenians', p. 82. 44 Cobbe, *Life*, i, p. 137. 45 Quoted in O'Connor, *Female and the species*, p. 57. 46 Suess, *Colonial bodies*, p. 544. 47 Two societies she founded remain active today: the Society for the Protection of Animals Liable to Vivisection (now the National Anti-Vivisection Society), established in 1875; and the British Union for the Abolition of Vivisection, founded in 1898.

5.5 Frances Power Cobbe in her library at Hengwrt, her home in Wales.
Courtesy: Cobbe papers, Alec Cobbe division.

in her own way significantly contributed to the history of the country house in Ireland. The return to Newbridge after school was critical in shaping her, and the qualities of life in the Irish country house, often isolated yet well-resourced, offered her the space to grow and develop intellectually. Her self-educated early years, in the halls of her ancestors, were informed by dutiful Irish servants and her loving mother. Outside of the confines of the country house, the experience of encountering and understanding the plight of the labouring poor and sufferers on absentee estates were formative and directive experiences. In her later writing, she was unafraid to take on the prejudices of English audiences and to correct them, using her first-hand knowledge of Ireland, its culture and its people. Frances campaigned to make a male-dominated world more equitable through the betterment and enfranchisement of women, thereby creating a more moral and just society. She formed a key part of a school of nineteenth-century women who would advocate for equal opportunities as long as it was not to the detriment, or abandonment, of familial responsibilities or societal duties. She lived as she preached. An elitist who respected the few moral values to be found in the status quo, while not shying away from calling out inequality.

> Had I been a man, and had possessed my brother's facilities for entering Parliament or any profession I have sometimes dreamed I could have made my mark and done some masculine service to my fellow creatures. But the woman's destiny which God allotted to me has been … the best and happiest for me; nor have I ever seriously wished it had been otherwise.[48]

Her life shows that ladies in the Irish country house were far more nuanced in their intellectual development. A deep observationist, keen-eyed and honest, her writings have much to offer us as a view into the nineteenth century, not least her wit which runs through much of her writing, making her works enjoyable to read centuries later. Throughout her work, whether writing on animal torture or domestic abuse, Cobbe believed ethics and morals were sacrosanct. The instillment of the sense of duty from her parents pervaded Frances' life, a life which, spent inside the Irish country house in the 1830s and 40s, helped to create one of the Victorian age's most formidable campaigners and loved feminists.

---

48 Cobbe, *Life*, i, pp 4–5.

Safe and unsafe houses: architecture, politics and the Irish cultural imagination

ROY FOSTER

A 'safe house' has a specialized but well-known meaning, signifying somewhere that a dissident or rebel can hide out: a particularly cogent issue in Irish history. But I want to apply the term in another way, and discuss the insecure status of Irish houses, especially Irish country houses. Some of my preoccupations reflect an era before the transforming work of Terence Dooley, Christopher Ridgway and this conference. But the feelings and reactions aroused by Irish country houses remains a potent subject, partly because it involves taking a moral line. Architecture and ideology are inseparably linked, as illustrated by the messages encoded in, for instance, Victorian public buildings, Fascist cultural artefacts, and post-modern 'revivalist' skyscrapers incorporating jokey details from Sheraton furniture.

Thus, in 1977, David Watkin's manifesto *Morality and architecture* stirred up several intellectual and aesthetic beehives.[1] In his polemic, Watkin took on what he saw as the modernist establishment, tracing it back to Pugin, Viollet-de-Duc, le Corbusier and others who claimed that their chosen style had to be truthful and rational, reflecting society's needs; opponents, in Watkin's view, were written off as anti-social, reactionary and immoral. The ensuing arguments heralded an era where issues of reproduction, pastiche and authenticity were battled over, along with the inheritance of post-war brutalism and the questions of conservation, innovation and sustainability. It also, I think, announced the fight-back of an unashamedly conservative and even reactionary tone in English public discourse, represented by, *inter alia*, the philosophical writings of Roger Scruton, the history-writing of John Vincent and Maurice Cowling, the popular journalism of Paul Johnson, and the politics of Enoch Powell and Margaret Thatcher, but that is a subject for another day.

Controversies over architecture were fought out in the British world of urban development and starchitect practices, but they were also reflected in the debates over the role and future of historic country houses. This subject had already been floated in the book produced by Roy Strong, Marcus Binney and John Harris in 1974, *The destruction of the country house*, and the accompanying exhibition in the

---

[1] David Watkin, *Morality and architecture: the development of a theme in architectural history and theory from the Gothic revival to the Modern movement* (Oxford, 1977), and published in a revised edition by John Murray in 2001.

Victoria and Albert Museum (of which Strong was then director).[2] As David Cannadine has brilliantly demonstrated, the situation in Britain, given a very different social history of landholding and, above all, the existence of the National Trust, seems far removed from that in Ireland. But, fourteen years later, in 1988, the Knight of Glin, David Griffin and Nicholas Robinson published *Vanishing country houses of Ireland*.[3] In its pages, William Laffan has written, 'each [Irish] county offered up the spoils of an internecine war fought on social, political, cultural and economic fronts'.[4] It is true, as the authors pointed out, that some Irish country houses were inevitably doomed through sheer scale and impracticality; but, others were the victims of an uncaring and implicitly disapproving attitude, epitomized by the Land Commission's attitude towards the history and artefacts of the Ascendancy. Thus, the intertwining of 'morality' (or ethics) and 'Architecture' remained relevant, and carried a special weight and heft in the Irish case.

This had been quintessentially articulated in 1930 by the Cumann na Gaedheal minister for finance, Ernest Blythe, when the then-owner of Russborough House offered it to the Irish nation. William Cosgrave, head of the Cumann na nGaedheal government, was attracted to the idea, but Blythe threw it out of court. A secretarial memo from his department read:

> So far as the minister has been able to gather, neither Russborough House nor the family connected with it has ever been associated with any outstanding events or personalities in Irish history ... Accordingly, the interest which the place possesses is only its interest to connoisseurs of architecture plus whatever interest it has as illustrating a certain phase of social life in Ireland. Opinions differ as to the aesthetic merits of the Georgian as a style of architecture, but, the period being relatively modern, good specimens of it are sufficiently numerous in this country and in England to render state action to preserve this one superfluous. He is informed, however, that Russborough is not the best specimen in the Saorstát of Georgian country house architecture, that it is only the central block which has real architectural distinction, and even there distinction belongs to the interior rather than to the exterior. Even if this house were the best specimen of Georgian country house architecture in the Saorstát, which it is not, ... Georgian is not a style of Irish architecture ... there seems no point in an Irish government preserving as a national monument a building not distinctly Irish.[5]

---

[2] Roy Strong, Marcus Binney and John Harris, *The destruction of the country house, 1875–1975* (London, 1974). [3] Desmond FitzGerald [the Knight of Glin], with David J. Griffin and Nicholas K. Robinson, *Vanishing country houses of Ireland* (Dublin, 1988). [4] Kevin Mulligan, *Vain, transitory splendours: the Irish country house and the art of John Nankivell* (Dublin, 2018), p. 9. [5] William Laffan and Kevin Mulligan, *Russborough: a great Irish house, its families and*

As Laffan and Mulligan's absorbing history of Russborough shows, this does scant justice to the complicated and interesting history of the house and its owners, let alone the beauty and impact of its architecture and setting, but the implications are clear. These attitudes were still expressed three decades later in the battles over the destruction of Dublin's Fitzwilliam Street and the campaign to preserve Hume Street. These epics were essentially bound up, as Erika Hanna has shown, with Dublin's urban history and theories of urban development, as well as sensitive issues of national history; but, the rhetoric was familiar, from Kevin Boland's attacks on 'belted earls' to the dismissal of the Fitzwilliam streetscape by another Fianna Fáil luminary as 'Fine Gael architecture' (Ernest Blythe would have heartily disagreed).[6]

Dublin was in some ways a special case. The city remained a curiously intimate and familiar space, and the campaign for preservation of its Georgian streets was couched, by spokespeople such as Terence de Vere White, in terms of 'character' rather than historical importance. Trying to persuade the government that two houses in Kildare Place were worth preserving in 1957, de Vere White wrote:

> these houses have no particular historical associations; they form a part of a great heritage which was allowed go to waste in the last century and which, if every effort is not made in the present, will be dissipated. The preservation of a few historical buildings do not keep a city's character; it is the total effect of the houses such as these which made Dublin unique.[7]

Another argument used by urban conservationists was based on the Irishness of the people who both built and lived in these dwellings. In 1964 the TD, Maurice Dockrell, employed this argument in the Dáil, regarding Fitzwilliam Street, asserting that:

> These houses in Lower Fitzwilliam Street, far from being the homes of an unwanted and unwelcome aristocracy, were in fact the habitations of Dublin professional people ... in the 1830s ... the houses were occupied by families named Hughes, Darley, Daly, O'Hagan, Murphy and Driscoll. Another was Alderman Tom Makinney, Lord Mayor of Dublin ... Did you ever hear of aristocrats with names like that? These were Irish names of Irish people at that time ... There is no reason to think it is in any way perpetuating a part of Irish life which now, in a new state, some people wish to forget.[8]

collections (Russborough, 2014), pp 228–9. **6** Erika Hanna, *Modern Dublin: urban change and the Irish past, 1957–73* (Oxford, 2013), p. 197. **7** Terence de Vere White et al. to Éamon de Valera, 19 June 1957 (re: Kildare Place), quoted in ibid., p. 73. **8** *Dáil Éireann deb.*, vol. 212, no. 2, 4 Nov. 1964, quoted in ibid., p. 103.

This was astute for its purposes (and its audience), but the implications of this argument were not good for the circumstances of a big country house, where the themes of settlement and expropriation lay easily to hand as rationalizations for neglect or destruction. Here, 'morality' was rapidly employed to condemn 'architecture'.

So, in Ireland, the literary reflections of dwelling-houses carry a powerful historical charge, involving especially possession and dispossession. I do not want to re-trace the Ascendancy self-image as reflected in the literary treatment of country houses, since Ian d'Alton has done it so vividly and effectively elsewhere in this book. Rather, I want to trace the political and even moral implications of architecture and historical memory in Ireland, which the literary record helps to illuminate. In the early nineteenth century, houses represented contested history in the Gothic imaginations of Charles Maturin and Sydney Owenson; later they represented privilege insecurely held, and money running out, in the fictions of Sheridan Le Fanu, Somerville and Ross, William Trevor and J.G. Farrell. Perhaps, the Irishman Bram Stoker even imagined Dracula's castle, with its rapacious landlord, absent servants, secret rooms and threatening architecture as an Irish rather than Transylvanian Big House.

The opening of Lord Dunsany's novel *The curse of the wise woman* is particularly redolent. A boy sits with his father before a fire in the library of a big house in Ireland on a winter's evening. 'Of the date of the house' the narrator tells us,

> I can tell you nothing accurate. It was built by a forbear of ours who was a historical character, but it is just about that time that the history of Ireland begins to be fabulous, so that it is truer to tell you merely that the house was very old.

They are alone in the house except for a couple of servants. The father has secured every door and window because 'You never know who might come over the bog'. Nonetheless, the house is invaded by assassins, miraculously evaded by the father; the last the son will ever hear of him is the sound of a horse being walked softly across the stable yard and finally trotting down the avenue.[9] The novel was published in 1933 and, interestingly, one of the would-be assassins, who gives the boy sage advice on shooting both geese and men, later turns up in the plot as a Free State politician. I instance it here because its opening distils the essence of the Anglo-Irish Big House novel: loneliness, uncertainty, an implicitly threatening countryside, unknown natives, the threat of death and a house which is certainly unsafe.

By contrast, novels reflecting the lives of an established Catholic bourgeoisie in the pre-revolutionary period, such as Katharine Cecil Thurston's *The fly on*

---

[9] Lord Dunsany, *The curse of the wise woman* (London, 1933), pp 14–15.

Architecture, politics and the Irish cultural imagination

the wheel (1908), Kate O'Brien's *The ante-room* (1934 but set in 1880) or Michael Farrell's *Thy tears might cease* (written by 1937 but not published till 1963), were set in precisely realized and appropriately solid *haut-bourgeois* houses, based on an expectation of an assured future. The Irish revolution reversed this and created a powerful new image: the burning Big House. As Ian d'Alton has shown, the theme of conflagration is emblematically used by Elizabeth Bowen and Molly Keane. More recently, it has been invoked retrospectively in Colm Tóibín's first two novels, *The south* (1990) and *The heather blazing* (1993).

In both Tóibín's books, the image of 'burning out' a family from their country house is powerfully portrayed. The house that the central figure in *The south*, Katherine Proctor, runs away from in the 1950s is not a Big House in the usual Irish-novel sense; built by her father thirty years before, it is large-windowed, yellow-painted, eventually to be made cheerful with cane furniture and floral prints by her son's breezy Catholic wife. But, it has been built anew because an earlier house was 'burned out': a realization that comes to Katherine later on. It is only possible to put this historical memory into words when she has herself left Ireland to make a new life as a painter. She writes to her mother:

> There is something else that has been on my mind and I will say it to you now. We were burned out during the Troubles in Ireland. You and I have never talked of this, which is odd, as we have spoken frankly of other things. We were burned out during the Troubles. I put it bluntly down now and I hope that you're still reading. This is how I put it. But it isn't exactly what happened, is it?
>
> We weren't burned out because we didn't leave, we built a new house which still stands and we built it fast. But you were burned out because you left then and you've never been back; no matter what my father said about how safe we were, you stayed in London. I am your only child. I saw you for holidays and we never talked about what happened that night in all the years.
>
> The locals turned on us. That's what happened. That's what the Troubles were for us. The time the locals turned on us. That was what happened in Ireland in 1920. I don't remember a fire but I remember a sound, like a big wind, and being carried. I don't remember seeing the fire, I must have been three years old. I remember staying in Bennett's Hotel in Enniscorthy. I'll never forget the sound of the wind. What do you remember? Please tell me what happened. How did you get out? How did I get out? How many of them came? Why did you leave and never come back?
>
> I always believed that what happened to us was an act of evil, something vicious done, that when tension was high it was us they would go after – they would round on us, the locals. No good came of it. Did it? I want to

know about it, so I can think about it. It has become important. If you want me to write to you, I'm afraid you'll have to take me seriously. It's not easy to write like this.[10]

The distancing of Katherine from her country's past as well as her own is one of the novel's tropes and is central to its obliqueness. This obliqueness, and the sense of fracture which it conveys, is strongly reminiscent of Henry Green's Irish novel, also set in a Big House, *Loving* (1945); the closure of Tóibín's book, with the shadow of illness hanging over the middle-aged lovers, carries a particularly strong echo of the finale to Green's book, but so do the conversations Katherine's mother instigates about 'the Irish'. Another novelist implicitly evoked is Molly Keane, whose own family house in Wexford was burned during the Troubles: a scene she puts into *Two days in Aragon* (1941). House-burning has been the subject of pioneering historical analysis by Gemma Clark, Terence Dooley and Robert O'Byrne;[11] Dooley in particular explores the varied contexts and motivations of arson, linking it to local circumstances and long-established patterns of disputes and resentments over landownership. As for Irish literary history, Colm Tóibín has both defined house-burning as a recurring theme in Irish fiction and contributed to that tradition himself, identifying it as an intrinsic, inescapable part of the history of his native Wexford-like colonization.[12]

Tóibín's second novel, *The heather blazing*, takes its title from a rebel ballad, and the revolutionary history of Wexford is established with corresponding precision. After a Fianna Fáil election meeting, the young Eamon Redmond sits with his father and uncle in his grandmother's house. Their conversation counterpoints and answers Katherine Proctor's letter in the earlier novel.

> 'You couldn't just burn a house, you see,' Uncle Tom said. 'You'd have to get permission from Cathal Brugha in Dublin. You'd have to present him with all the facts; any of the houses that entertained the Black and Tans, had the officers for dinners and parties, they'd be on the list. Your father'd go up, he was young enough and he pretended to spend the day in the National Library, but he'd slip out to see Brugha, or one of Brugha's men, and then permission would come back and we'd do the job.'
> 'Burn the house?' Eamon asked.

---

10 Colm Tóibín, *The south* (London, 1990), pp 90 ff.   11 Gemma Clark, *Everyday violence in the Irish Civil War* (Cambridge, 2014); Terence Dooley, *Burning the Big House: the story of the Irish country house in a time of war and revolution* (London, 2022); Robert O'Byrne, *Left without a handkerchief* (Dublin, 2022).   12 See Colm Tóibín, *The Penguin book of Irish fiction* (London, 2001), p. xxi, and an interview with Lynne Tillman, *BOMB* (1992), 22: 'For me that Wexford landscape is resonant. It's where I'm from, where history has taken place that, in some way, has been fundamental for me; and for Katharine Proctor [in *The south*], it's not the case.'

Architecture, politics and the Irish cultural imagination 73

> 'We gutted a good few of them all right,' his uncle sipped his drink. 'Wilton, old Captain Skrine, the Proctors on the Bunclody Road, Castleboro. I have a book upstairs I took from Castleboro the night we went out there. They had a great library. It's a pity I didn't have more time. I still have it upstairs. It has a note inside saying '*Ex Libris Lord Carew*'. What's it called? Cranford by Mrs Gaskell. I must look for it. I'm sure it's up there somewhere.'
>
> 'Were they all Protestants?' Eamon asked.
>
> 'They were,' his uncle said. 'And they were all up to their neck in the British Army who were on the rampage here, and the British Legion, and the King and Queen. It's all gone now. At least we got rid of that, whatever else we did.'[13]

This is history as much as fiction (Captain Skrine was Molly Keane's father, and Wilton and Castleboro indeed met their end in this manner). Some of the autobiographical transference in *The heather blazing* is equally exact. Tóibín's uncle took just such orders from Cathal Brugha. More significantly, Tóibín's own father, like Eamon's, was a schoolteacher and local historian, and founded the Wexford County Museum in the ancient castle, as well as writing a book on the town's history.[14] In a long and passionate introduction to the lavish and comprehensive *History* of Enniscorthy which Tóibín edited, he remembers visiting the castle as a child, the atmosphere of the place as it was taken over and the sense of ghostly inhabitants.

> My father, who wrote about the history of the town, and Father Ranson, who had lived in Salamanca and edited an edition of the ballads of the Wexford coast, were acutely conscious of what it meant to acquire Enniscorthy Castle, open it to the public, and dedicate some rooms to the history of the struggle for independence. As it was being restored, old ghosts must have wandered in its rooms, the shadowy shape of figures such as Edmund Spenser and Lodowick Bryskett must have asked themselves or each other what new outrages, or indeed civilities, were being committed in the name of history by the descendants of the barbarians.[15]

It is an interesting transposition of the haunted Big House theme familiar to Irish fiction. But, there are ambivalences. In *The heather blazing*, the protagonist is possessed by the past and its elusive certainties. But country-house libraries feature elsewhere in this volume and the image of a burning library is a symbol of the destruction of a civilization, from Alexandrian times to the present. The

---

13 Colm Tóibín, *The heather blazing* (London, 1992), pp 171–2.   14 Michael Tóibín, *Enniscorthy: history and heritage* (Dublin, 1998).   15 Colm Tóibín and Celestine Rafferty (eds), *Enniscorthy: a history* (Wexford, 2010), pp 15–16.

removal of a book from the conflagration might be, not so much an indication of 'civilized values', as the kind of trophy a serial killer selects and keeps, after dispatching his victim. We might remember that in *The last September*, Elizabeth Bowen gives highly personalized, human names to houses like Danielstown and Mount Isabel, and refers to them being 'executed'. And two engrossing books which deal with Irish history as reflected through the lives of a family and their house – William Magan's *Ummamore* and Sara Day's *Not Irish enough* – end with the house (Rathrobin, Co. Laois and Derrylahan Park, Co. Tipperary) being burned out and the family displaced to England.[16]

Also reflecting the Troubles of the early 1920s, Yeats' symbolic manipulation of threatened dwellings in his greatest collection, *The tower* (1927), mobilized architectural motifs to invoke a history of violence and 'bitterness' – a favourite word of the poet's. For independent Ireland, the appropriate dwellings emblematized in the cultural imagination were either the idealized cottages beloved of de Valera or – much more mordantly – the confined spaces of city suburbs conjured up by Maeve Brennan in *The springs of affection*, posthumously published in 1997, but dealing with Dublin in the 1930s and 1940s: tidy, cramped, uncomfortable places with their front gardens imprisoned by railings and the rear areas dominated by a coal store. The symbolism is achingly precise.

But, these are urban dwellings. In the countryside, John Banville detonated the Big House stereotype in his first novel *Birchwood* (1973), described by Colm Tóibín as the most seriously revisionist text of the 1970s: a parody where 'Irish history was an enormous joke, a baroque narrative full of crackpot landlords and roaming peasants and an abiding sense of menace and decay.'[17] More prosaically, William Trevor and Jennifer Johnston returned to the theme of real-life decay and insecurity, in novels where the historic antipathies conjured up by country houses lie only just below the surface, and are even exacerbated by the reawakened violence happening in the north.

Times have changed. By the end of the twentieth century, the spectacular upswing in Ireland's economic circumstances was apparently accompanied by a change in the fate of some country houses at least. While the good times lasted, new money was poured by individual owners into houses such as Castletown Cox, Lyons, Ballyfin, Humewood, Castle Hyde, Ballynatray and others; while Castletown in Celbridge, Emo Court, Doneraile Court, Annes Grove and Russborough found new roles under versions of public ownership. There is now a growing record of source-material and commentary on the Irish country house – books, articles and theses stemming from all that Terry Dooley and his team have established at Maynooth; the great achievement of the Irish Architectural

---

16 William Magan, *Ummamore: the story of an Irish family* (Salisbury, 1985); later republished as *The story of Ireland: a history of an ancient family and their country* (Salisbury, 2000); Sara Day, *Not Irish enough: an Anglo-Irish family's three centuries in Ireland* (Washington, DC, 2021).   17 Tóibín and Rafferty (eds), *Enniscorthy*, p. 3; see also *Penguin book of Irish fiction*,

Archive; the scholarly and vividly-detailed volumes of the *Buildings of Ireland* series published by Yale University Press; and substantial volumes on individual houses such as Russborough, Abbey Leix, Ballyfin and Townley Hall.

Nonetheless, in an underlying way, it seems to me that in the Irish imagination historic architecture retains some of its political and moral/ethical charge, if no longer as crudely employed as in the rationalizations of 'colonial architecture' used by those who destroyed Dublin's streetscapes and wrote off country houses as un-Irish. It is striking that one of the most absorbing books on Irish country houses, by the Knight of Glin and James Peill,[18] took as its rationale houses that were still lived in by families who had been established there for generations. The result produced a fascinating profile of lesser-known houses, but also made a quiet statement about authenticity and Irishness. This suggests an intention to step carefully. The era when country houses either fell down or were preserved by religious orders may have passed, but in recent years the publications of the 'Aubane Historical Society' in north Cork still took an ostentatious and obsessive pleasure in the destruction of Bowen's Court and denounced its famous owner as a British spy.

This is an extreme and eccentric example. But, as recently as 2014 a director of the National Museum asserted that ancient prejudice against the heritage bequeathed from the era of British rule still existed in the Department of Finance, and similar attitudes can be discerned in the reaction to planning applications which threaten demesne landscapes.[19] It is more cheering to reflect that the belated development of appreciating Ireland's great architectural traditions has been enabled, not only by the annual CSHIHE Conference and its predecessors, and a welcome proactive involvement by the Office of Public Works, but by the rise of conservation movements such as the Irish Georgian Society; the achievements of the Irish Architectural Archive; and by pioneering scholars such as Maurice Craig, Jeanne Sheehy, the Knight of Glin and architect-scholars such as the late Niall McCullough and his partner Valerie Mulvin. Their book, *A lost tradition: the nature of architecture in Ireland*, published in 1987, almost contemporaneously with *Vanishing country houses of Ireland*, not only celebrated the unique forms and shapes of Irish vernacular and institutional architecture, but incorporated these traditions into the study of Irish country houses, including the very grand (such as Eyrecourt and Summerhill), as well as more modest adaptations of Palladian themes and idioms.[20]

When this beautiful book first appeared thirty-five years ago, it suggested not only a new kind of architectural history, but a new kind of Irish history. The

pp xxi–xxxii.   **18** The Knight of Glin and James Peill, *The Irish country house* (London, 2010).   **19** See 'National Library warns of cut in services', *Irish Times*, 3 Nov.: 'Former National Museum director Dr Pat Wallace said ... the cultural institutions were "loathed" by some officials within the Department of Finance "because our origins come from the British Days. There is a residue of that still within the Department of Finance."   **20** Niall McCullough and Valerie Mulvin, *A lost tradition: the nature of architecture in Ireland* (Dublin,

buildings so sympathetically analysed over centuries of habitation and colonization are often very far from grand: corbelled clochans, vernacular cottages, modest farmhouses, little churches, national schools. But the splendour of Augustan classicism is also given its due, and the forward projection of Georgian style into later Irish architectural modes is enticingly delineated. The domestic typography of the classical Irish house echoes ahead through mills and alms-houses and charter schools. The architectural legacy of military forts from the era of conquest and plantation is tamed and tempered into other uses and forms. Continuity of architectural tradition projects forward from eighteenth-century formality into rural schools, fire stations, cinemas and handball alleys. This is an expanded history that addresses context, accretion and palimpsest rather than imposing a retrospective and inimical morality on architecture.

This reflects the change in attitudes towards Ireland's architectural heritage which was encouraged by joining the EU and by drawing UNESCO's attention to Irish buildings. In McCullough's and Mulvin's interpretation, Irish architectural modes are similarly vitalized by international connections: not just via the Palladian sub-wings of farmhouses, or the Italianate grandeur of the baroque forecourt at Curraghmore, Co. Waterford, but by comparison to colonial streetscapes in Macao, Lima and Quebec. Historically sensitive to the 'sullied image' of institutional buildings imposed throughout Ireland (barracks, jails, workhouses), they remind us that, despite bitter associations, such relics survive as well-proportioned, dignified works of architecture. And they can be redeemed and repurposed. Birr Workhouse has been colonized by small workshops and houses so that it feels stripped of its repressive stigma, revealed only as a set of beautiful stone courtyards. The adaptation of the Royal Hospital Kilmainham into the Irish Museum of Modern Art, and the conversion of Collins Barracks into a National Museum might also be instanced.

But, this is not a route open for country houses, and ruination remains a dominant theme. The sculptural ruins that typify so much of the Irish landscape still persist as an 'architecture of perpetual fragments': while that key volume, *Vanishing country houses of Ireland*, has been joined by Tarquin Blake's two-volume *Abandoned mansions of Ireland*, Duncan McLaren's and Simon Marsden's *In ruins*, and, most recently, Robert O'Byrne's vivid and informative *Ruins of Ireland*.[21] This reminds us that Ireland's stock of heritage buildings continues to decline at a depressing rate, exacerbated by the lack of government resources available for conservation and also the failure of official retribution when the owner of a 'protected structure' allows it to fall down, despite the terms of the Planning and Development Act (2000). Another book, charting Irish ruins through the beautiful drawings of John Nankivell and scholarship of Kevin

---

1987). Also see Niall McCullough, *Palimpsest: intervention and change in Irish architecture* (Dublin, 2014). **21** Tarquin Blake, *Abandoned mansions of Ireland* (Cork, 2011); Simon Marsden and Duncan McLaren, *In ruins: the once great houses of Ireland* (London, 1980);

Mulligan, eloquently makes the same point.[22] There is the question of an underlying attitude here and we are reminded, yet again, of Yeats emblematizing the history of his own medieval tower-house in Co. Galway as reflecting the brutal vicissitudes of history, but surviving to celebrate later lives lived there: 'these stones remain their monument and mine.'

Looking on the brighter side, McCullough Mulvin, O'Donnell Tuomey, de Blacam and Maher, the Grafton practice and other innovators have over recent decades inaugurated a great age of Irish architecture in public buildings, at home and abroad. This is less true of Irish domestic architecture; the historic glory of Irish dwelling-houses remains the Palladian-derived country houses (of all sizes) of the eighteenth and early nineteenth centuries, and the urban streetscapes of the same period. The Office of Public Works has been transformative in recent years and the Heritage Council is an important and welcome development, but defines 'heritage' in such a wide-ranging and scatter-gun way that domestic architecture is implicitly overwhelmed by archaeological remnants, flora, fauna, wildlife habitats, wrecks, inland waterways and other valuable national possessions declared worthy of attention and conservation. There is also an implicit nervousness in the council's mission statement that it wants to 'take heritage out of the past and into the present' – implying that 'history' is a dangerous and antagonistic arena, from which we should avert our faces.

Around the same time as that mission statement (the late 1990s), a Bord Fáilte market research report presented Ireland as 'a saved country and culture undisturbed by European history … a destination that can offer escapism and freedom'. Though tourism is inevitably one of the routes whereby Irish country houses may be enabled to survive, this approach to the history which created them indicates the deliberate avoidance of an awkward subject. Interestingly, the study of country houses in Britain has recently taken a contentious turn, thanks to research into the exploitative and slaver economies that funded so many of them.[23] As Ireland tries to de-toxify attitudes to historic houses, Britain is heading in the other direction – a new twist in an old pattern.

Thus, the 'safety' of Irish country houses implicitly continues to be connected to considerations of morality and architecture. Perhaps, we should not be surprised that the subject remains, at one level, sensitive in political terms – as is clearly seen when a historic house such as Lissadell or Westport comes on the market, and the idea of public ownership is mooted but too often evaded or dismissed. For all the great work done by the conference from which this volume emanates and its offshoots over the last twenty years, perhaps some of Yeats' 'bitterness', for better or worse, will always remain encoded in Ireland's cultural DNA.

Robert O'Byrne, *The Irish aesthete: ruins of Ireland* (London, 2019).   22 See footnote 4 above.
23 See Margot C. Finn, 'Material turns in British history, iv: empire in India, cancel cultures and the country house', *Transactions of the Royal Historical Society*, 31 (2021), 1–21.

'A persevering proclamation of gospel truth': the 3rd earl of Roden and evangelical Christianity at Tollymore Park and Dundalk House, *c*.1820–70

JAMES FRAZER

Many country houses had an extensive collection of books in their library, but for evangelical occupants the most important book in their lives was the Bible. Evangelical Christianity is an international and interdenominational Protestant movement that emerged from the British Puritanism and German Pietism of the seventeenth century, and its expansion can be attributed to Protestant missions, itinerant preaching and religious revivals during the eighteenth century.[1] Like most mainstream forms of Protestantism, evangelicalism emphasizes the depravity and sinfulness of humanity that leads to the just punishment of eternal damnation. The individual can only be redeemed by God's grace through faith alone in the atoning death and resurrection of Jesus Christ.[2] David Bebbington argues that evangelicals are defined by four theological attributes. First, a conviction that one must undergo a personal conversion in order to depart from sin and trust in Christ as their saviour, or the concept of being 'saved' or 'born again'. Second, a call to be actively engaged in evangelism, which is the spreading of the Christian message, known as the gospel. Third, a strong regard for the authority of the Bible as the inspired word of God. Fourth, a focus on the redemptive sacrifice of Christ on the cross.[3]

This religious outlook was not particularly widespread among the Irish landed class in the nineteenth century, but the work of historians such as Irene Whelan and D.H. Akenson has shown that evangelicalism took root among a small, yet profoundly, influential network of aristocratic families. This group included the Rodens of Down and Louth, Gosfords and Manchesters of Armagh, Farnhams of Cavan, Powerscourts of Wicklow, Mountcashells of Cork and Lortons of Roscommon.[4] Using the case study of Robert Jocelyn, 3rd earl of Roden, this essay highlights the importance of evangelicalism in the Irish country house and argues that these buildings often allowed the occupants to express their spirituality in a way that may not have been acceptable in the parish church.

---

[1] W.R. Ward, *The Protestant evangelical awakening* (Cambridge, 1992).   [2] Ian Bradley, *The call to seriousness: the evangelical impact on the Victorians* (London, 1976), pp 15–16.   [3] D.W. Bebbington, *Evangelicalism in modern Britain: a history from the 1730s to the 1980s* (London,

Robert Jocelyn, 3rd earl of Roden, was born in 1788 and after inheriting the family estates in 1820, he became widely respected as a benevolent and efficient landlord. He had two Irish residences: Tollymore Park was located in the Mourne Mountains of south Co. Down in the province of Ulster, and Dundalk House in Co. Louth, Leinster, in a large enterprising port and market town. Roden gained the reputation of a titan of Irish ultra-Protestantism by championing the Protestant establishment as a Tory in the House of Lords and engaging with popular loyalism during the 1830s and 1840s. He joined the Orange Order in 1831 and, infamously, he was dismissed from the magistracy for hosting on 12 July 1849 an Orange procession at his Tollymore estate that was subsequently involved in a sectarian skirmish at Dolly's Brae, near Castlewellan. Despite the negative publicity he received for his connection to the affray, he continued to be an important advocate of the Protestant cause until his death in 1870.[5]

Like most of the Irish landed class, Roden was a member of the established Church of Ireland and his understanding of religious duty and piety throughout the early years of his life was focused on being a good churchman: someone who believed in the Thirty-nine Articles of Anglicanism, regularly prayed and attended church, respected the clergy's authority, and supported the integral place of the Church of Ireland in the Irish Protestant establishment. He was exposed to several evangelical influences during his upbringing and early career, until he eventually experienced a deeply personal and emotional evangelical conversion in 1817 after attending, out of curiosity, the annual meeting of the Hibernian Bible Society in Dublin.[6] This organization was established in 1806 to assist with Bible distribution in Ireland, and evangelicals dominated the membership.[7] Roden's spiritual transformation not only reinforced his commitment to the established church, but also reorientated his priorities towards glorifying God in all aspects of his life, public and private. As Ian Bradley notes, 'a regenerate man could have no pleasure in anything but striving to please his new Lord'.[8]

Alan Acheson argues that Roden was one of the most high-profile aristocrats who identified with the evangelical revival in the Church of Ireland, and he was an integral member of what Whelan terms the 'Bible gentry'.[9] This was a

1989), pp 2–17.   **4** Irene Whelan, *The Bible war in Ireland: the 'Second Reformation' and the polarization of Protestant-Catholic relations, 1800–1840* (Dublin, 2005); Irene Whelan, 'The Bible gentry: evangelical religion, aristocracy, and the new moral order in the nineteenth century' in Crawford Gribben and A.R. Holmes (eds), *Protestant millennialism, evangelicalism and Irish society, 1790–2005* (Basingstoke, 2006), pp 52–82; D.H. Akenson, *Discovering the end of time: Irish evangelicals in the age of Daniel O'Connell* (London, 2016).   **5** James Frazer, 'The public life of Robert Jocelyn (1788–1870), 3rd earl of Roden: landlord, Conservative, evangelical, and Orangeman' (PhD, Queen's University Belfast, 2023).   **6** Ibid.; *Inverness Courier*, 13 May 1824.   **7** Alan Acheson, 'The evangelicals in the Church of Ireland, 1784–1859' (PhD, Queen's University Belfast, 1967), p. 94.   **8** Bradley, *The call to seriousness*, pp 15, 21.   **9** Alan Acheson, 'Roden, (third) earl of [Jocelyn, Robert]' in D.M. Lewis (ed.), *The Blackwell dictionary of evangelical biography, 1730–1860*, 2 vols (Oxford, 1995), ii, p. 950;

network of elite Irish families that became influenced by evangelicalism during the early decades of the nineteenth century. Their shared understanding of religious responsibility and commitment to a pious lifestyle meant that they frequently visited each other's country houses – families such as the Rodens, Farnhams and Powerscourts were regularly in each other's company. Marriage and other ties further embedded them in what Whelan describes as 'a distinctly aristocratic evangelical culture'.[10] For example, four of Roden's relatives married into the Powerscourt family, and he was a political ally of evangelicals in the houses of parliament, such as the 5th Baron Farnham and Lord Mandeville (afterwards 6th duke of Manchester).

Bradley argues that 'Evangelicalism was above all else the religion of the home', and the evangelical elite attempted to fashion their households according to what God commanded in holy scripture.[11] This affected everyday life in the country house for all occupants. For instance, H.F. Kearney notes that the shift towards religious sensibility contributed to 'a break with the prevailing social ideal of aristocracy' – activities such as drinking, dancing and playing cards were exchanged for a more puritanical lifestyle that emphasized the individual's obligation to glorify God, such as praying, singing psalms or hymns, keeping a diary for spiritual accountability, and reading material of a devotional nature.[12] The Bible was, of course, the book of choice for evangelicals and their sense of religious duty meant that they usually read a portion of it every day. Biblical commentaries were also common reading material, as were books that emphasized the importance of piety, such as John Bunyan's allegory, *The pilgrim's progress* (1678), or William Wilberforce's *A practical view* (1797), the latter being described by Bradley as 'the handbook of the Evangelicals'.[13] Roden's reputation in evangelical circles for Christian integrity meant that he eventually became the subject of a children's story book, *Lord Roden and the servant girl* (1857), which taught the importance of honour, duty and humility in the Christian life.[14] These qualities had no role in the evangelical interpretation of salvation because Protestantism emphasized that the sinner could only be justified in God's eyes by their faith alone. However, evidence of such characteristics in an individual's life were regarded as important signs that they had experienced a genuine conversion.[15]

Family prayer was a central aspect of life in the evangelical country house. This occurred twice a day – morning and evening – and lasted for about an hour.

Whelan, 'The Bible gentry', p. 52.   **10** Whelan, 'The Bible gentry', p. 61; Akenson, *Discovering the end of time*, pp 5–6, 19–20.   **11** Bradley, *The call to seriousness*, p. 179.   **12** H.F. Kearney, 'The estate as social community: Armagh in the early 19th century', c.1971, p. 2 (PRONI, Tandragee estate papers, D1248/O/25).   **13** Ibid., p. 3; John Bunyan, *The pilgrim's progress from this world, to that which is to come* (London, 1678); William Wilberforce, *A practical view of the prevailing religious system of professed Christians, in the middle and higher classes in this country, contrasted with real Christianity* (London, 1797); Bradley, *The call to seriousness*, pp 19, 182.   **14** *Lord Roden and the servant girl* (London, 1857).   **15** Bradley, *The*

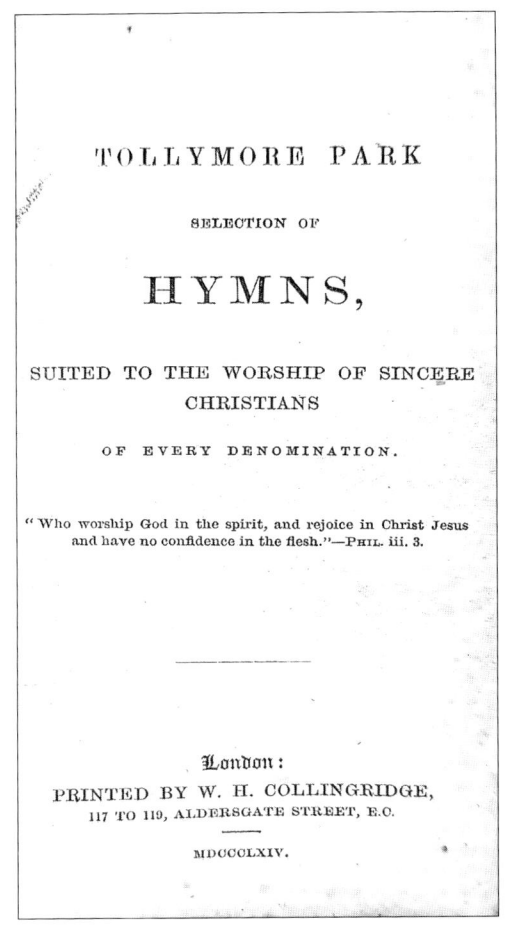

> TOLLYMORE PARK
>
> SELECTION OF
>
> # HYMNS,
>
> SUITED TO THE WORSHIP OF SINCERE CHRISTIANS
>
> OF EVERY DENOMINATION.
>
> "Who worship God in the spirit, and rejoice in Christ Jesus and have no confidence in the flesh."—PHIL. iii. 3.
>
> London:
> PRINTED BY W. H. COLLINGRIDGE,
> 117 TO 119, ALDERSGATE STREET, E.C.
>
> MDCCCLXIV.

7.1 Title page of the second edition of the Tollymore Park selection of hymns. By kind permission of Downpatrick Library (County Down Collection, Heritage Services, Libraries NI).

It was typically conducted by the head of the family, and every member of the household was required to attend, including the servants.[16] Roden's family prayers were held in a purpose-built room, unlike other country houses where it may have been held in the drawing room. When he inherited the estates in 1820, he converted a room in both residences into a private chapel to provide a dedicated place for prayer, capable of holding approximately forty people. The English author, Charlotte Elizabeth, described the domestic chapel of Tollymore Park during her visit in 1837 as, 'A plainer apartment I have not seen: it is an oblong square, of a good size and height, the windows just under the ceiling,

call to seriousness, p. 21.   16 Ibid., pp 179–80.

white walls, and benches with good backs ranged transversely throughout'.[17] The simplicity of the chapel's design and furnishings was typical of most Protestant places of worship that had a plain style to avoid distractions from the preaching of God's word and to ensure that scripture alone was the foundation of teaching, not imagery.[18]

Prayer was almost regimental in Roden's households; as Charlotte Elizabeth explained, 'We are called by beat of drum, the butler striking the great drum in the hall at nine o'clock, morning and evening, to this modest place of prayer [...] A hymn is sung, a portion [of scripture] read and commented on, and prayer offered.'[19] The hymns were a notable feature of the meetings because, as Mark Noll recognizes, hymn singing provided an important link between individual and collective expressions of evangelical spirituality.[20] Roden published in 1831 his own selection of hymns for use in the chapel, and he reflected in the preface of the second edition in 1864 that he was 'very thankful' to God 'for the opportunities we have had in using these songs of praise for so many years' (fig. 7.1).[21] Roden's prayer meetings were unique in that they were open to anyone, not just his family and servants. He welcomed everyone to join him and his household from the outset, including friends, guests, neighbours, tenants and strangers of all denominations who always had access to the private chapels through a door leading to the demesne.[22] Roden remembered that 'this was thought a very strange act and much spoke of on it'.[23] Clearly, he had a unique sense of pastoral responsibility to promote the spiritual welfare of others – reinforced by his position as a landlord – and the prayer meetings indicate the cross-class dimension to the transmission of religious ideas in his country houses and on his estates.

Sunday, or the Lord's Day, was the most important day of the week for evangelical piety in the country house because it was consecrated as a day of rest and worship.[24] The household would have attended the parish church, morning and evening, and the remainder of the day was dedicated to prayer, reading the Bible, or catechizing, a method of instruction using question and answer. Members of the family refrained from recreation and all other activities that had the potential to distract them from their devotion to God, such as writing letters or dining out with friends. Children were prohibited from playing with toys or participating in games, which were considered a profanation of the Sabbath. Instead, they attended the local Sunday school where they were taught passages

---

[17] Charlotte Elizabeth, *Letters from Ireland, 1837* (London, 1838), p. 237. [18] David Brett, *The plain style: Protestant theology in the history of design* (Cambridge, 2005). [19] Elizabeth, *Letters from Ireland*, p. 238. [20] Mark Noll, *The rise of evangelicalism: the age of Edwards, Whitefield and the Wesleys* (Nottingham, 2004), pp 260–9. [21] Robert Jocelyn (ed.), *Tollymore Park selection of hymns, suited to the worship of sincere Christians of every denomination* (2nd ed. London, 1864). [22] Elizabeth, *Letters from Ireland*, p. 238. [23] Roden's reminiscences from memory, 1868 (PRONI, Farren Connell papers, D3835/D/4). [24] John Wolffe, *The expansion of evangelicalism: the age of Wilberforce, More, Chalmers and Finney* (Nottingham,

of scripture or catechisms.[25] Unlike other landlords, Roden was a Sunday school teacher, which was an example of his distinctive personal involvement in promoting an environment of religious improvement on his estates.[26]

A unique event in Roden's country houses on Sundays was the Sabbath evening lecture, which he established when he inherited the family properties in 1820. The lectures, which were essentially sermons or biblical expositions to which all comers were invited, were held in the private chapels following the evening service in the parish churches at Tollymore and Dundalk.[27] Although a clergyman or a domestic chaplain occasionally preached, Roden typically delivered the lecture himself and frequently did so extempore. This was unusual because the Church of Ireland did not permit lay preaching until 1866, and it was contrary to the predominant view of apostolic succession within Anglicanism, which emphasized that preaching was the preserve of the ordained clergy of the established church.[28] Furthermore, praying or preaching extempore were uncommon in Anglican worship.[29] Despite these factors, Roden felt a spiritual calling to preach, which he explained in 1824 in a letter to the Revd Elias Thackeray, vicar of Dundalk, following criticism of the lectures. He wrote:

> I find nothing in God's word which forbids our evening lectures, but on the contrary, everything that should encourage me in them, and when I reflect upon the wonderful change which the reception of Christ […] with my heart has produced in my views, and when I look back to the darkness in which I was involved formerly, when I bear in mind the comfort which I have received from the view of Christ's finished work, I cannot but anxiously desire to testify to others of him, wherever an opportunity is given me.

Referring to passages from Numbers 11 and Philippians 1 as 'Scripture grounds for my anxiety', he declared that 'whether it be in our own Church or amongst the Dissenters, whether it be by priests or by laymen, so [long] as Christ is preached I rejoice, yea, and will rejoice'.[30] Therefore, not only were Roden's country houses organized around Scripture and worship, but they became spaces from which the gospel itself was proclaimed. Roden's talent for biblical expositions further embedded him in the network of elite evangelical families

---

2006), pp 97–9.   **25** Bradley, *The call to seriousness*, pp 44, 182–3.   **26** *The Warder*, 12 Apr. 1856.   **27** Dundalk House and Tollymore House were both demolished in the twentieth century along with their chapels.   **28** Peter Garner, 'The reader: an explanation of the history and present place of reader ministry in the Church of England' (PhD, University of Leeds, 2010), p. 59; Peter Nockles, 'Church or Protestant sect? The Church of Ireland, high churchmanship, and the Oxford Movement, 1822–1869', *The Historical Journal*, 41:2 (1998), 475.   **29** William Gibson, 'The British sermon 1689–1901: quantities, performance, and culture' in K.A. Francis and William Gibson (eds), *The Oxford handbook of the British sermon 1689–1901* (Oxford, 2012), p. 16.   **30** Roden to Elias Thackeray, 13 Sept. 1824 (PRONI,

because he was invited to preach in other domestic chapels, including the one in Tandragee Castle, Co. Armagh, the duke of Manchester's Irish residence.[31]

The Sabbath evening lectures and daily prayer meetings in Roden's country houses allowed him and other evangelicals to come together to express their spirituality and sense of Christian fellowship in a way that would not have been acceptable in the parish church. As John Wolffe notes of similar evangelical gatherings, such meetings 'played a crucial part in the spread and maintenance of evangelical convictions and devotion'.[32] The lectures and prayer meetings were not problematic at Tollymore because the local clergymen were evangelicals and often attended. However, in using his home to shape religious ideas, Roden caused tension with the vicar at his Dundalk estate, the Revd Elias Thackeray. Appointed to the parish by Roden's father in 1803, Thackeray held to a tradition of churchmanship that emphasized the exclusive ministry of the ordained clergymen of the established church and the need for formality in public worship.[33] Thackeray explained his objections in a polite protest in 1824:

> The collecting together those who are not members of your house has a tendency to pervert family prayer [...] to draw persons from the evening service of the church – to make it a doubtful question how far the public liturgy and worship in the church is more a duty than extemporary prayer out of it – how far people may regard or neglect the service performed and the expositions given by an appointed and ordained ministry, when their taste may lead them to private prayer meetings and lectures in private houses.[34]

Roden, on the other hand, saw no contradiction in promoting evangelicalism outside the structures of the established church because he believed his lectures and prayer meetings were supporting the work of the church, not hindering it. In addition, the evangelical community of Dundalk appear to have been dissatisfied with Thackeray's preaching because his sermons stressed the necessity of upholding God's moral law, but neglected the doctrine of justification by faith alone in Christ's atoning sacrifice on the cross.[35] Evangelicals recognized the importance of the moral law, but they yearned for sermons that proclaimed Christ's death for all sinners and of their need for personal conversion, which were essential characteristics of evangelicalism.[36] Roden's lectures and prayer meetings in the country house filled that void by providing local evangelicals with a Christocentric message supplementary to what they heard in the parish church.

Roden papers, MIC147/5).   **31** Roden to Lord Mandeville, 29 June 1841 (Huntingdonshire Archives, Manchester papers, M10/11/6–7).   **32** Wolffe, *The expansion of evangelicalism*, p. 107.   **33** Nockles, 'Church or Protestant sect?', pp 457–93.   **34** Elias Thackeray to Roden, 9 Sept. 1824 (PRONI, Roden papers, MIC147/5).   **35** Roden to Thackeray, 13 Sept. 1824.   **36** Bebbington, *Evangelicalism in modern Britain*, pp 2–17.

Although the country house created opportunities for expressing individual spirituality, the evangelical elite continued to seek the extension of the established church and demonstrated their commitment as supporters of the so-called 'Second Reformation'. This was a Church of Ireland movement that emerged at the start of the nineteenth century that aimed to achieve the wholescale conversion of Roman Catholics to Protestantism by means of preaching and evangelism.[37] It contrasted with earlier attempts to extend the state church during the previous century that had involved coercive penal legislation.[38] The movement was initially marked by a moderate form of evangelism that promoted scriptural education and Bible distribution. However, it intensified from $c.1820$ when more direct methods were adopted, such as open evangelism among the Catholic population and public debates with the Catholic clergy.[39] Roden and other members of the evangelical elite supported the Second Reformation because of their religious concerns that were rooted in the activist and conversionist hallmarks of evangelicalism. To varying degrees, all evangelicals felt a responsibility to convert their unsaved countrymen out of a sincere anxiety for what would happen to their souls when they died, and at the same time to share the sense of assurance that God had given them following their own conversions. This sentiment was extended to people living outside of Ireland, which accounts for the rise in overseas missions at this time.[40] Secondary to this concern was the conviction that secular benefits would inevitably flow from the spread of Protestantism. The Bible gentry held the Roman Catholic church responsible for Ireland's pervasive poverty, agrarian crime and immorality by keeping the majority of the Irish people in a state of spiritual ignorance, superstition and subservience to the papacy. They argued that a new moral order could only be achieved by the growth of Protestantism, which they associated with characteristics such as temperance, deference, industry and loyalty to the established order in church and state.[41]

The evangelical elite engaged with the movement nationally as patrons of evangelical societies. Roden, for example, was president of the Sunday School Society for Ireland from 1822 and vice-president of a plethora of other agencies, such as the Hibernian Bible Society, the Religious Tract and Book Society, and the Irish Society, to name but a few. The Bible gentry also helped to implement the Second Reformation locally by using their position as landlords to establish

---

[37] David Hempton and Myrtle Hill, *Evangelical Protestantism in Ulster society, 1740–1890* (London, 1992), p. 84. [38] S.J. Brown, 'The New Reformation movement in the Church of Ireland, 1801–29' in S.J. Brown and D.W. Miller (eds), *Piety and power in Ireland, 1760–1960: essays in honour of Emmet Larkin* (Belfast, 2000), pp 182, 184–6. [39] Whelan, *The Bible war*, pp 139, 156, 160. [40] Alan Acheson, *A history of the Church of Ireland, 1691–2001* (2nd ed. Dublin, 2002), p. 164; Wolffe, *The expansion of evangelicalism*, pp 157–9. [41] Whelan, *The Bible war*, p. 267; Whelan, 'The Bible gentry', pp 68, 70; Desmond Bowen, *The Protestant crusade in Ireland, 1800–70: a study of Protestant–Catholic relations between the act of union and disestablishment* (Dublin, 1978), p. xii; S.J. Brown, *The national churches of England, Ireland,*

7.2 Glacial erratic at Tollymore Park. The inscription was commissioned by Roden and is a reflection on John 1:3: 'Stop. Look around and praise the name of Him who made it all'. Photograph by James Frazer, 2023.

branches of the evangelical societies, promote scriptural education schools and encourage evangelism on the estates.[42] Roden's tenantry at both Tollymore and Dundalk were overwhelmingly Catholic.[43] Therefore, he had a clear reason for supporting the movement at his properties because he believed most of the people under his authority as a landlord were destined for hell. Some landlords, such as the 5th Baron Farnham, reformed their estate management by employing a so-called 'moral agent' who was responsible for promoting the moral, spiritual and physical well-being of the tenantry. The agent's duties included, for example, ensuring that parents sent their children to the estate's schools, reading scripture to tenants, and reporting to the landlord or his land agent on tenant living conditions.[44] Roden, on the other hand, endeavoured to be the moral agent himself on his estates.[45] He was superintendent of scriptural education schools on his properties, some of which he established at his own expense, and he made regular visits to his tenantry to enquire of their spiritual state and to distribute Bibles and tracts. His visits to the poor were normally accompanied by a philanthropic gesture, such as giving them food or firewood, and this derived

and Scotland, 1801–1846 (Oxford, 2001), pp 98, 103–4. **42** Whelan, *The Bible war*, pp 55–6, 62–3, 161. **43** *Report of the commissioners appointed to take the census of Ireland, for the year 1841*, p. 84, HC 1843 (504), xxiv, 196; *Report from her majesty's commissioners of inquiry into the state of the law and practice in respect to the occupation of land in Ireland*, pp 571–2, HC 1845 (605–6), xix, 633–4. **44** Hempton and Hill, *Evangelical Protestantism*, p. 87. **45** J.R.R. Wright, 'An evangelical estate *c*.1800–55: the influence of evangelicalism on the Manchester estate, Co. Armagh, with particular reference to the moral agencies of William Loftie and

from a paternalist and evangelical sense of duty to relieve poverty and suffering.[46] Some of the estate's geological and architectural features were inscribed with verses from holy scripture so that the tenantry were always exposed to the word of God (fig. 7.2). These examples of Roden's unique personal involvement in the Second Reformation are further evidence of his sense of Christian stewardship as a landlord.

A wave of conversions throughout Ireland in late 1826 and early 1827, totalling almost 2,000 people according to contemporary reports, reassured evangelicals that their efforts were bringing forth fruit and that the time was at hand when Protestantism would become the largest denomination on the island.[47] In March 1827, Roden publicly welcomed 'that glorious Reformation which is now working its rapid way through every part of the country'.[48] The Bible gentry's country houses, as the heart of their estates, became beacons of hope for the objectives of the Second Reformation and attracted several notable individuals who were excited by the perceived prospects of the gospel in Ireland.[49] Among those recorded as visiting Tollymore Park to enquire about local evangelism were the Irish Methodist preacher, Anne Lutton (1826), the champion of Irish Presbyterian orthodoxy, the Revd Henry Cooke (1826), the English aristocratic evangelical clergyman, the Revd Baptist Wriothesley Noel (1836) and the English writer, Charlotte Elizabeth (1837).[50] Perhaps most interesting were the visits of evangelicals connected to continental Protestantism. They included the Scottish activist in the European *Réveil*, Robert Haldane (1822), the Swiss Protestant clergyman, Pierre Méjanel (1822), another minister from Switzerland, César Malan (1826) and the Jewish convert from Bavaria, Joseph Wolff (1826). Observers noted that Malan and Wolff preached sermons to large crowds that had assembled on Roden's front lawn.[51]

Clearly, there was excitement about these events in Ireland, but the hope for the wholesale conversion of Catholics to Protestantism was short-lived. The number of new conversions decreased significantly from mid-1827, and this was chiefly due to the vehement Catholic opposition to the Second Reformation. The

---

Henry John Porter' (PhD, Ulster Polytechnic, 1982), pp 74–5.   **46** B.W. Noel, *Notes of a short tour through the midland counties of Ireland, in the summer of 1836, with observations on the condition of the peasantry* (London, 1837), pp 58–9; Elizabeth, *Letters from Ireland*, p. 230; C.R. Jocelyn, *Kilcoo parish church, Bryansford* (Newcastle, 1971), p. 16; Bradley, 'The call to seriousness', pp 119–20; David Roberts, *Paternalism in early Victorian England* (London, 1979), p. 5.   **47** Hempton and Hill, *Evangelical Protestantism*, p. 87.   **48** *Hansard's parliamentary debates*, new series, vol. 16, col. 1233 (16 Mar. 1827).   **49** Whelan, 'The Bible gentry', p. 67.   **50** *Memorials of a consecrated life compiled from the autobiography, letters and diaries of Anne Lutton of Moira Co. Down, Ireland, and of Cotham, Bristol*, ed. J.H.W. (London, 1882), pp 170–2; J.L. Porter, *The life and times of Henry Cooke, D.D., LL.D., president of Assembly's College, Belfast* (2nd ed., London, 1871), p. 112; Noel, *Notes of a short tour*, pp 53–66; Elizabeth, *Letters from Ireland*, pp 226–96.   **51** Alexander Haldane, *Memoirs of the lives of Robert Haldane of Airthrey, and of his brother, James Alexander Haldane* (New York, 1853), p. 429; *Memorials of a consecrated life*, p. 171; *Tipperary Free Press*, 11 Aug. 1827.

intensification of the movement from c.1820 led to open theological conflict with the Catholic church. Priest and parishioner united to defend their faith and found a common purpose in supporting Daniel O'Connell's campaign for Catholic democracy that would give Catholics full political rights without having to convert to the established church.[52] The advocates of the Second Reformation received a heavy blow when Catholic emancipation became law in 1829. By passing this act, the state acknowledged that the population in Ireland would remain overwhelmingly Catholic.[53] Some evangelicals expressed their disappointment by turning to biblical prophecy to explain worldly events, and three prophetic conferences were organized by the dowager Viscountess Powerscourt in Powerscourt House, Co. Wicklow, in the early 1830s.[54] However, the Second Reformation did not end and in many respects actually grew in intensity after emancipation. For example, several new evangelical societies were formed that were dedicated to missionary activism in the west of Ireland.[55] The movement's persistence was indicative of the evangelicals' genuine sense of religious responsibility to extend the gospel and lead the Irish population to salvation by faith in Christ, which was always their primary motivation for supporting the Second Reformation – not ambitions like moral improvement or political stability, though they believed these would be the natural result of conversions. That is why Roden continued to evangelize his tenantry and promote their spiritual welfare throughout his life using the same methods he began in the 1820s, including preaching, teaching, visiting tenants, distributing Bibles and supporting missionary agencies. As Charlotte Elizabeth noted during her visit to Tollymore in 1837, the 'presiding influence' of Roden's country house and estate was marked by 'a persevering proclamation of gospel truth'.[56]

This essay has highlighted the ways in which evangelicalism permeated every level of life in a specific number of Irish country houses and that these buildings were central to the development of networks between elite families with a shared religious outlook. The case study of Robert Jocelyn, 3rd earl of Roden, has demonstrated how the Irish country house provided a space for evangelicals to express their spirituality, often in a way that may not have been acceptable in the parish church. Yet, the evangelical elite remained committed to the Church of Ireland and demonstrated their commitment as supporters of the Second Reformation. The Bible gentry's country houses were the focal point of their missionary endeavours, and although they failed to achieve the wholescale conversion of Catholics to Protestantism, the country house continued to be at the centre of local evangelism for much of the nineteenth century.

[52] Brown, 'The New Reformation', pp 198, 204, 207–8; Whelan, *The Bible war*, pp 193, 203; Hempton and Hill, *Evangelical Protestantism*, p. 89; S.J. Brown, *Providence and empire: religion, politics, and society in the United Kingdom, 1815–1914* (Abingdon, 2013), pp 57–8. [53] Brown, *The national churches*, p. 146. [54] Whelan, 'The Bible gentry', p. 75; Grayson Carter, *Anglican evangelicals: Protestant secessions from the via media, c.1800–1850* (Oxford, 2001), pp 203–7. [55] Whelan, *The Bible war*, pp 237–54. [56] Elizabeth, *Letters from Ireland*, p. 227.

Irish country house libraries and social change, 1650–1750

RAYMOND GILLESPIE

In the summer and autumn of 1698, the London bookseller John Dunton arrived in Dublin with a cargo of freshly reprinted books that he hoped to sell in the city over three auctions. The range of works that he carried was eclectic: divinity, history, philosophy, law, physic, mathematics, horsemanship, merchandise, limning, military discipline, heraldry, music, fortification, fireworks, husbandry, gardening, romances, novels, poems, plays, bibles and schoolbooks.[1] His market was primarily the wholesale trade, selling to booksellers who would then retail the books to readers all over Ireland. Dunton had hit on a lucrative and expanding market, but, ever the salesman, he was not above offering reasons why consumers in a newly affluent market would buy books. 'Gentlemen,' he declared, 'books are the best furniture in a house', but they were also the key to learning and knowledge. Even though 'there be a daily complaint that the world seems oppressed with books, yet do we daily want them; if it were not so, what is the reason that many of great estates can hardly make their minds stretch to a geometrical measuring of their own lands?' In short, he claimed, 'there's nothing comparable to the purchase of knowledge'. Current events, he asserted, made this of central concern to the Irish gentry in their country houses. While Ireland had once been famous for its learning,

> I am afraid the case is much altered since. Slavery and popery have so long and universal possession of that country that the spirits of the native (or wild Irish at least) are much degenerated ... If your design may be any way subservient to restore learning among them you will have cause to value yourself upon it while you live.

The reform of Ireland was a bigger problem than its military conquest and moreover 'methinks I see a storm coming upon you'. Reform, according to Dunton, was impossible until learning was well established but, he noted, 'learning I do verily believe, runs low in Ireland generally speaking and no wonder it should when they have not books at moderate rates'. The solution was 'dispersing those books in Ireland that are fitted for their introduction and

---

1 For an account of his expedition, see John Dunton, *The Dublin scuffle*, ed. Andrew Carpenter (Dublin, 2000), pp 17–18.

diversion; profit and pleasure ought to go hand in hand'. The agent of all this was to be Dunton himself who would 'make good books common there at a moderate rate, for which others would exact upon their customers'.[2]

Dunton could hardly expect to achieve this social transformation in one visit, though his expedition had some modest success. He certainly annoyed the important Presbyterian bookseller in Dublin, Patrick Campbell, but he seems to have been more successful in cultivating others who frequented his auctions. Professional users of books – lawyers and clergy – also lurked around his auctions hoping to pick up a bargain. At least some of these, such as the Edgeworths, bought books relating to their profession as lawyers and administrators, but as they prospered and acquired country estates these professional works became part of their country house library.[3] Some gentry with country houses to furnish attended Dunton's auctions. Colonel Butler, probably Francis Butler, from Belturbet in Cavan, was Dunton's patron in Dublin; he was 'a great lover of books' and seems to have purchased books that helped him become 'a great patron of learning'.[4] Other MPs were duly acknowledged as purchasers and Henry Echlin, builder of the now lost Co. Down house of Echlinville, was praised as

> a person of great honour and of a greatness of soul beyond most that I heard of; he is such a universal lover of books that very few, if any, shall escape him whatever they cost: he has a very large and curious library, yet as inquisitive still after rarities as if he has none: he is a most noble encourager of the book-selling trade, and whenever he dies the stationers of England and Ireland will have a great loss, besides what the public will sustain thereby.[5]

There is little doubt that Dunton had identified a significant potential market for his wares. Ireland in the late seventeenth century became rich as trade expanded and diversified. The number of country houses was growing while older, defensive tower houses were being abandoned or substantially modified to meet modern standards of comfort and display. Such new structures needed to be decorated and furnished, but on the back of rising rentals, landowners could afford to indulge themselves in the marketplace with consumer items such as tobacco, silver, pictures and other non-essentials.[6] Dunton's argument that books were the best furniture in a house resonated with some. Moreover, books were

---

2 Ibid., pp 21–4.   **3** On the Edgeworths, see Toby Barnard, 'Libraries and collectors, 1700–1800' in Raymond Gillespie and Andrew Hadfield (eds), *The Oxford history of the Irish book: vol. iii, the Irish book in English, 1550–1800* (Oxford, 2006), pp 131–4.   **4** Dunton, *Dublin scuffle*, p. 100.   **5** Ibid., pp 100–1.   **6** T.C. Barnard, *Making the grand figure: lives and possessions in Ireland, 1641–1770* (London, 2004). For the economic context, Raymond Gillespie, 'Economic life, 1550–1730' in Jane Ohlmeyer (ed.), *The Cambridge history of*

becoming more plentiful and cheaper. The output of the Dublin presses expanded dramatically over the seventeenth century, and these were joined by provincial presses in Belfast and Cork by the end of the century although their contribution was relatively modest. This was supplemented by growing book imports, particularly from England.[7] For those who were interested, there was another development that might expand the contents of their shelves. The collapse of the learned orders of Gaelic Ireland had released a reservoir of manuscript material (annals, genealogies, poetry and legal tracts), heretofore kept within learned families, onto the market where they could be bought, sold or exchanged among collectors who usually did not differentiate between manuscripts and print in their libraries. Collectors who were the owners of country houses and who acquired those manuscripts may only have had the scantest knowledge of their contents, but they had curiosity value or local interest.

These trends fed the growth of country house libraries in the late seventeenth and eighteenth centuries. Libraries, in the sense of being collections of books, grew significantly. In the sixteenth century, the few book and manuscript collections that are known about are small. The earl of Kildare's collection of about sixty titles comprised mainly manuscripts but with a few modern printed works, notably by Thomas More, the author of *Utopia*.[8] Within Gaelic Ireland, there were some signs that the greater families, possibly as a result of exposure to outside influences, were beginning to build up libraries, mainly of manuscript material. The O'Donnells of Donegal in the early sixteenth century were commissioning copies of older manuscripts and generating new ones, and there is evidence in the layout and arrangement of their manuscripts that suggests they may have been influenced by the world of printed books.[9] By the early seventeenth century, libraries came to be dominated to a greater extent by print and in elite households were appreciably larger. The earl of Thomond listed 200 books in Bunratty Castle in 1639, while in Castleisland, Co. Kerry, one landlord recorded 100 'great and little books'. These were large libraries by contemporary standards and more typical were the twelve books in Geashill castle in 1628 or the fifty-seven in Dunluce Castle in the 1640s. In the late seventeenth century, country house library sizes expanded very significantly. At the top of the social tree the duke of Ormond had several thousand titles scattered across his various houses and in Dublin Castle. The scholarly William Molyneux claimed in 1694 to have a library of about 1,000 books, but even the less academically inclined Sir

---

Ireland: vol. ii, *1550–1730* (Cambridge, 2018), pp 547–50.   **7** Raymond Gillespie, *Reading Ireland: print, reading and social change in early modern Ireland* (Manchester, 2005), pp 76–93, 187–9; T.C. Barnard, *Brought to book: print in Ireland, 1680–1784* (Dublin, 2017), pp 18–19. **8** Gearóid Mac Niocaill (ed.), *Crown surveys of lands, 1540–1* (Dublin, 1992), pp 312–14, 355–6.   **9** Bernadette Cunningham and Raymond Gillespie, 'The Uí Dhomhnaill and their books in early sixteenth-century Ireland' in Seán Duffy (ed.), *Princes, prelates and poets in medieval Ireland* (Dublin, 2013), pp 481–502.

John Perceval of Burton Hall in Cork could stretch to almost 500 titles in his country house library when he died in 1686. The literary-inclined earl of Orrery had almost 200 according to a list of the 1670s, but this must be regarded as a minimum number since library lists were often incomplete.[10]

If the size of book collections increased, so too did the infrastructure for books. Libraries, or book rooms, became increasingly common over the seventeenth century and by the eighteenth century were well established features of country houses. Prior to this, books had been stored in boxes, chests, cupboards or even bags. From the 1680s shelves were more commonly used, with books arranged by size, and in the eighteenth century glazed bookcases became more popular.[11] Both bookcases and shelves offered themselves as vehicles for display and the rise of ornate presentation bindings was noticeable in the late seventeenth century. Some of the duke of Ormond's books were bound in this form by the 'devotional binder' who probably worked for the Dublin bookseller William Norman.[12]

All this is relatively easily observable and documentable. What is more problematic is to explain why from the middle of the seventeenth century and through the eighteenth century the country house library (both as a collection of books and a book room in which to store and display them) became such a feature of gentry life. The supply side issues mentioned above certainly contributed, but the demand side factors were probably more important in promoting libraries. Dunton, of course, has already identified some of these. On a very large scale, fashion for book ownership certainly played a part, though it is noticeable that the bookseller Dunton rarely talks about his customers reading books. Thus, he observed of his patron Colonel Butler: 'for the books he buys do by their number sufficiently declare his love to learning and by their value and intrinsic worth the vastness of his judgment'[13] – though there is no mention of opening any of these books to read them. At a micro level, the interests of individuals created particular collections to supply personal wants. The earl of Orrery's library was crammed with literary works, plays, verse and even a pornographic novel, as befits an early novelist and playwright, while his contemporary and near neighbour, Sir John Perceval, eschewed such fripperies in favour or more solid conventional political and religious works.[14] However, somewhere in between the large-scale generalization and the particularization of the individual there was another set of factors at work, a set of factors that are about attitudes and values: in short, the creation of country house libraries was

---

10 Gillespie, *Reading Ireland*, pp 68–9, 91.   11 Ibid., pp 16–17; T.C. Barnard, 'Libraries and glazed bookcases in eighteenth-century Ireland', *Eighteenth–Nineteenth Century Irish Fiction Newsletter*, 14 (Feb. 1999), [4].   12 Joseph McDonnell, *Five hundred years of the art of the book in Ireland* (Dublin, 1997), pp 127–30.   13 Dunton, *Dublin scuffle*, p. 248.   14 British Library, Add. MS 47,024, ff 81v–83 (a partial list). I am grateful to Toby Barnard for a copy of the Orrery list now at Petworth, formerly National Library of Ireland, MS 13,190.

the result of shifts in the intellectual or mental worlds of their owners. This is not an easy idea to deal with. It is much more straightforward to handle the contents of country house libraries than it is to rummage about in the heads of their owners. It may be that part of the answer lies in the books themselves but connecting ideas and actions (such as the purchase of a book) is a very problematic activity. How people read in the past can be very different from modern reading practices and how they understood the books they acquired might vary a great deal from one person to another. One might take the case of the late seventeenth-century library in Belfast Castle owned by the Donegalls. Sometime in the 1690s, Arthur Chichester, 4th earl of Donegall, purchased a copy of John Milton's political works in London. He subsequently brought it back to Belfast and lent it to the Presbyterian minister John McBride, who was later accused of possessing it as subversive literature. It is difficult to believe that the two men read the text in the same way or even in remotely similar ways, although they probably both held Milton's 1649 condemnation of 'the blockish presbyters of Belfast' in contempt. Nor does it seem likely that the high church vicar of Belfast, to whom Donegall also lent the book, would have read it in the same way as the other two readers.[15]

The matter is even more complex than that because ownership did not even presume reading. While one owned a library, one did not actually have to open any book. In eighteenth-century Ireland, as the idea of a public sphere developed, libraries were increasingly understood as public spaces for meeting and exchange of polite conversation rather than private places. The earl of Moira was even prepared to lend books from his extensive library outside Ballinahinch to 'any lady or gentleman who asked', and as early as 1739 Bishop Rundle had a room for conversation created within his library.[16] In this way in the eighteenth century, such country house libraries could act as clearing grounds for ideas as landlords fresh from the fashions of Dublin, or the political machinations of parliament, could act as brokers of new ideas into the world of the middling sort on their estates, though it must be admitted that this strategy had a rather restricted use.

For some families, the library became not just a book room but more a cabinet of curiosities. Dunton, for instance, when visiting Trinity College in Dublin, noted that on display in the library as part of its collections were medals, the thighbone of a giant and the skin of an executed Tory that had been stuffed with straw though his face was nibbled by mice, a disfigurement that had been rectified by stitching on the face of an executed Catholic priest. Mrs Delany in 1758 found the earl of Moira's library full not only of books, but 'to amuse the fancy as well as improve the mind', there were telescopes, microscopes and other

---

15 William Tisdall, *The conduct of the dissenters in Ireland* (Dublin, 1712), p. 67; James Kirkpatrick, *A historical essay upon the loyalty of the Presbyterians* ([Belfast], 1713), p. 526.
16 Patricia McCarthy, *Life in the country house in Georgian Ireland* (London, 2016), pp 164, 169.

types of scientific apparatus. 'Everyone chooses their employment, it is the land of liberty, yet of regularity'.[17] At its extreme, this practice of dumping covered all sorts of activities and could result in rather strange combinations of books and other items, the nuances of which were not necessarily appreciated by strangers.

One way of trying to bridge the gap between the macro world of generalization and the specifics might be to consider how country house libraries evolved on a regional basis and to link their appearance and development with the problems that the families that created those libraries were facing at that time. This is not entirely satisfactory, but as a working method it has some advantages. While it does not provide a direct insight into mental worlds, it does at least allow us to identify some common themes that might be worth pursuing. For this purpose, Ulster in the late seventeenth and early eighteenth century has many advantages, most importantly Mark Purcell's study of libraries in National Trust properties in Ulster.[18] Ulster was not exceptional in the pattern of establishing or expanding country house libraries in this period. A few of the landed families in the early seventeenth century had books, most exceptionally the large library of Edward Conway at Portmore in Co. Antrim, which extended to over 10,000 volumes.[19] It seems clear that this was not a working collection. Conway spent most of his time in London and made little use of the house at Portmore. It is more likely to have been regarded as a store for infrequently used books from his estate in Warwickshire. Other settlers had more modest collections. For example, British Library, MS Egerton 2648 (a fourteenth-century Middle English version of the Life of Christ), appears to have been brought from England by George Theaker, the agent of the Chichesters on the Belfast estate who was sovereign of Belfast in 1619–21. The religious manuscript may have been part of a larger library or simply a stray volume picked up by Theaker, but it does attest to some level of book ownership. On the evidence of books or booklists, a number of country house libraries had their origins at this stage. The Hamiltons, viscounts Clandeboy, for instance, seem to have had a small collection of books in the early seventeenth century, perhaps to be numbered in the tens rather than the hundreds. By the time the estate had passed to a great nephew, James Hamilton of Bangor who died in 1707, the collection had grown to rather over 300 books, most of late seventeenth-century origin (now at Castle Ward). That library was subsequently expanded by the Ward family who married Hamilton's daughter, Anne, and some 1,200 titles were added from Michael Ward's uncle, the bishop of Derry. Michael was also an indefatigable book buyer and acquirer of other libraries. It seems highly probable

---

[17] Dunton, *Dublin, scuffle*, pp 242–3; McCarthy, *Life in the country house*, p. 170. [18] Mark Purcell, *The big house library in Ireland: books in Ulster country houses* (Swindon, 2010). [19] For this library, see Brenda Collins, 'Family networks and social connections in the survival of a seventeenth-century library collection', *Library and Information History*, 33:2 (2017), pp 123–42.

that when Castle Ward was rebuilt, it would have included a library room.[20] In the north-west of the province, the Coyningham family also began to assemble a country house library at Springhill by the end of the seventeenth century.[21] As families modified their houses in the early eighteenth century a library room became de rigeur. When Hillsborough Castle in Co. Down was inventoried in 1746 there was no mention of a library though there was a study with some oak shelves for books. From 1760, the house was rebuilt and when it was inventoried again in 1777, there was 'my lord's library' complete with glazed bookcase, commode, chairs, a backgammon table, a writing table and a looking glass.[22]

Some of the best evidence for the interest of Ulster families in developing private libraries comes from the south-west of the province. In Tyrone, John Stearne, bishop of Clogher, was hard at work assembling one of the great country house libraries of the early eighteenth century. Estimated by one contemporary as between 6,000 and 7,000 volumes, most of which were located in the see house at Clogher, after his death it would be divided with his manuscripts going to Trinity College Dublin, and his books to Marsh's library.[23] Stearne had absorbed a number of other gentry libraries around Fermanagh. For instance he had acquired the substantial manuscript collection of John Madden of Manor Waterhouse in Fermanagh that related to events in Ireland and England but was primarily concerned with genealogy. After his death, his widow sold the collection to Stearne in 1703.[24] There is other evidence of country house libraries being formed. At Florence Court, for instance, there is evidence that the Cole family were book owners in the 1710s and by the 1730s, if not before, the house had acquired a formal book room.[25] Most fascinating of all are the libraries formed by those of a Gaelic Irish background who aspired to gentry status. In Leitrim, Tadhg Ó Rodaighe of Crossfield, who maintained a very tenuous connection with the medieval coarbs of Fenagh, collected Irish manuscripts, especially legal manuscripts, but he also had a number of ecclesiastical works in a select library of some thirty works.[26] Even more significant is Brian Maguire of Knockninny. Maguire was socially mobile upwards, and attempted to reinvent himself in the late seventeenth and early eighteenth century as a gentleman, although he had an estate of only twenty-four townlands on lease from the Balfour estate. Part of that reinvention was the creation of a library at his house at Knockninny that by the 1720s comprised probably half a dozen manuscripts though some of these are large – 2,000 pages in one case. In so far as it survives,

---

20 Purcell, *The big house library*, pp 21–36.   **21** Ibid., pp 56–8.   **22** *Great Irish households: inventories from the long eighteenth century* (Cambridge, 2022), pp 123–45.   **23** T.C. Barnard, 'Bishop Stearne's collection of books and manuscripts' in Muriel McCarthy and Ann Simmons (eds), *Marsh's library: a mirror on the world* (Dublin, 2009), pp 185–202. **24** William O'Sullivan, 'John Madden's manuscripts' in Vincent Kinane (ed.), *Essays on the history of Trinity College, Dublin library* (Dublin, 1999), pp 104–13.   **25** Purcell, *The big house library*, pp 75–7.   **26** William O'Sullivan, 'The book of Domhnall Ó Duibhdábhoireann: provenance and codicology', *Celtica*, 23 (1999), pp 278–81.

Maguire's library was composed entirely of manuscripts, although it is entirely possible that Brian also owned printed books that lacked the prestige of manuscripts and cannot be traced. This was not a large collection, nor was it old, although some of the texts were medieval in their origin but most were modern religious works. It was entirely composed of manuscripts in Irish written for Brian Maguire by a number of scribes and was clearly tailored to Brian's interests.[27] Collecting Gaelic books was not the exclusive prerogative of those with a native Irish background. From Armagh one New English landlord, Arthur Brownlow, had assembled a collection of Irish-language manuscripts as part of his library. Some of these, such as the Book of Armagh, were indeed old and Brownlow actively co-operated with others in discerning their meaning.[28]

There is one significant feature of those who were establishing country house libraries, whether of books or manuscripts or both, at this point: they were intellectually curious though not necessarily scholars or even academically inclined. Settlers showed an interest in discovering their new world. That process was encouraged by the formation of societies such as the Dublin Philosophical Society dedicated to using the potential of new scientific observation to understand and improve (both physically and morally) the world in which they lived. For the practitioners of this art there was no division between describing the natural world and recording its human past: all revealed something of a new world. Arthur Brownlow, for instance, not only collected books and manuscripts but experimented with fossilized wood in Lough Neagh, inserting holly stakes into the lake to see if it would petrify like the petrified wood that was dug from the Bann clays. He was, in the words of a contemporary, 'more curious than ordinary'.[29] While their intellectual curiosity was wide-ranging it tended to centre on history, and particularly family or local history since approaches to the present were through history as much as contemporary observations. The Hamiltons, for example, at the same time as they were building up their country house library were also engaged on a history of the family – 'The Hamilton manuscripts' – compiled, probably in the 1690s, by 'William the secretary', that told the history of the Irish family from its archives and explained a particularly complex dispute over the estate.[30] This was not an isolated event. The Montgomerys, the other major Co. Down family (whose book collecting activities we know nothing about), were also engaged in what we now call the 'Montgomery manuscripts', written in the 1690s and 1700s by William Montgomery. This is less of an integrated history than the Hamilton compilation

---

[27] Raymond Gillespie, 'Captain Brian Maguire and his books' in Raymond Gillespie and Brendan Scott (eds), *The books of Knockninny: manuscripts, culture and society in early eighteenth-century Fermanagh* (Cavan, 2019), pp 92–109.   [28] Bernadette Cunningham and Raymond Gillespie, 'An Ulster settler and his Irish manuscripts', *Éigse*, 21 (1986), pp 27–36.   [29] Peter Barry (ed.), 'The journeys of Samuel Molyneux in Ireland, 1708–1709', *Analecta Hibernica*, 46 (2015), p. 21.   [30] T.K. Lowry (ed.), *The Hamilton manuscripts* (Belfast, 1867).

and is really just a set of sketches of the various branches of the family. It was held together by the idea that this was a distinctive Irish family history rather than a branch of the Scottish family.[31] About the same time, William Montgomery also wrote a history of the Savage family, who were connected by marriage to the Montgomerys.[32] The earls of Antrim, the MacDonnells, also had a history of the Irish family written for them, and in 1704, the 4th earl of Antrim had an ornate genealogy created for him in both Irish and English.[33] The Coles of Florence Court had a very similar ornate genealogy produced circa 1630.[34] It is probably no accident that Madden's manuscript collection that made up his library in Fermanagh was also genealogical. Among those book and manuscript collectors of Gaelic background the same pattern applies. Tadhg Ó Rodaighe, for instance, wrote a description of Leitrim and its families, probably in 1684, for the new Church of Ireland bishop, William Sheridan. It is a general description of the county not dissimilar in format to those being drafted at the same time for Moses Pitt's abortive Irish atlas, with which the Dublin Philosophical Society was involved. It begins with general comments on the county before examining each barony in detail and, in particular, charting the main families, both Irish and English, and explaining how they had come to be in their present state. It is clear the local past was important to Ó Rodaighe.[35]

There was a connection between those who were building up their own libraries in the late seventeenth century and their interest in the history of their regions and families. Many of those who bought books and manuscripts or commissioned new works did so to explore those worlds. In 1718–19, a person whose initials were 'T.D.' compiled a history of Fermanagh and its families – including its settler families – in English. 'T.D.' can now be identified as Turlough Dolan. He clearly had access to a library of printed books and it seems likely that the manuscript he worked on was intended for publication. Dolan was one of Brian Maguire's main scribes who worked on creating his manuscript collection and it seems highly probable that Maguire was behind this. Maguire himself commissioned a largely imaginary history of his own family – The Maguires of Fermanagh – that constructed a genealogy for him that linked him to the main branch of Maguire lords and provide a noble origin legend for his socially ascendant family.[36]

It is fair to point out that this surge in interest in local history and genealogy in the late seventeenth and early eighteenth century was not a peculiarly Ulster, or even Irish, phenomenon.[37] A similar surge took place in England indicated by

31 Raymond Gillespie, 'The making of the Montgomery manuscripts', *Familia*, 2 (1986), pp 23–9. 32 Edited in G.F. Savage-Armstrong, *A genealogical history of the Savage family in Ulster* (London, 1906). 33 PRONI, D2977/5/1/4/3. 34 PRONI, D1702/7/5. 35 Royal Irish Academy, MS 12 W 22. For further discussion of this theme, see Raymond Gillespie, 'Shaping Leitrim: local history and the world of Leitrim' in Liam Kelly and Brendan Scott (eds), *Leitrim: history and society* (Dublin, 2019), pp 243–56. 36 Gillespie, 'Captain Brian Maguire', pp 95–9. 37 For the broader context, see Mark Purcell, *The country house library*

a growth in the study of the local past with works such as Plot's history of Oxfordshire, Dugdale on Warwickshire or John Aubrey's investigations into Wiltshire's past.[38] However, the developments in Ireland had a specific local context. By the end of the seventeenth century, the generation of landowners from the initial settlement of Ulster were dead and the wars of the 1640s had forced many settler families to decide in which theatre of war they wanted to fight. Many had chosen Ireland and had sold estates in England or Scotland, but others would return there. The generation after 1660 who went to the university of Glasgow described themselves not as 'anglicus' or 'scotus' at matriculation but 'Scoto-hibernicus' or 'Anglo-hibernicus'.[39] These people had to find a past that could be made to perform a function in the contemporary world. In Ulster, it seems that they turned to books and manuscripts as a way of doing that and in the process created country house libraries that were intended, a least initially, to explore the local past. The dilemma for the few Gaelic Irish who had not just survived but profited from the colonization process, such as Ó Rodaighe or Maguire, was much the same. They needed to find a useable past to underpin their new found positions and they too turned to books and manuscripts to do that. Brian Maguire's massive Book of Knockninny was not a harking back to the past – a rescue mission – but a relevant contemporary document that was to reflect the social role he wanted to fulfil.

In the final analysis, Dunton had got it right about the origin and early development of the country house library in Ireland. It was a mixture of fashion, practicality and scholarship all made possible by economic advance. Above all, the private library was born out of a need for Irish settlers to find a social and cultural place in a fast-changing world and they turned to books to help them do that. In particular, they embraced the doctrine of improvement that encouraged them to believe that Ireland could be shaped into a model of a modern society with not only economic advance but also moral improvement with the spread of Protestantism, civility and wealth.[40] Book ownership and display convinced visitors to the country house of the commitment on the part of the owner to modern ideas and learning. But, books did more than furnish a room; they furnished the minds of some as well.

(New Haven, CT, 2008), chs 4–5; James Raven, 'Country houses and the beginnings of bibliomania' in Matthew Dimmock, Andrew Hadfield and Margaret Healy (eds), *The intellectual culture of the English country house, 1500–1700* (Manchester, 2015), pp 163–77. **38** For a convenient survey, see John Beckett, *Writing local history* (Manchester, 2007), pp 15–26. **39** For a broader discussion of this, see Raymond Gillespie, *Seventeenth-century Ireland* (Dublin, 2006), pp 259–63, 300–3. **40** For the idea of improvement, see T.C. Barnard, *Improving Ireland? Projectors, prophets and profiteers, 1641–1786* (Dublin, 2008).

The Moore brothers and the library at Moore Hall: differing visions of its legacy in a new Ireland

ELIZABETH GRUBGELD

A consideration of the intellectual and artistic life within the Irish country house, and the interpretation of that legacy by those who built and resided there, requires that we examine their autobiographical and biographical writings not only as sources of historical evidence, but also as literary narratives that in their very structure and style offer a distinct and subjective reading of the family history. Autobiography has always pivoted between the material dimensions of history and the inventions of imagination. As the titles of the first two of Paul John Eakin's many books on life writing suggest, readers acknowledge the 'fictions in autobiography', while acknowledging that the text is simultaneously 'touching the world'.[1] The recollections of Colonel Maurice Moore (1854–1939) in his biography of his father, *An Irish gentleman* (1913), partake of 'fictions' only as all narratives of memory must: like all histories, his narrative is built on suppositions about the nature of reality, in this case Colonel Moore's unflinching belief in the value and potential of his family's contribution to the nation. In contrast, his older brother, the novelist George Augustus Moore (1852–1933) – who will be referred to as 'Moore', in order to distinguish him from the many Georges who make their appearances in the family chronicle – felt deeply pessimistic about the future of his class in modern Ireland and ready to discount his family's efforts to build a national culture as futile and quixotic. He saw himself as both the apex and the last inheritor of a rich legacy. Such pessimism works hand in hand with Moore's skeptical views of what constitutes an authoritative narrative, as he challenges the claims of facticity and treats evidence as a malleable raw material from which to invent. His writings interrogate the ways we tell histories, linking together by reverie his agile parodies of the genres of memory.

Throughout *Hail and farewell* – his memoir of the ten years in Dublin spent in pursuit of a distinctly Irish art form and published after his departure from the city to London in 1911 – Moore spins insinuations and unsubstantiated gossip that intertwine with verifiable facts and public secrets: evidence that conventions of manners prohibit from display, though proliferating among intimates (including writers and their readers).[2] In addition to gossip are outright

---

[1] P.J. Eakin, *Fictions in autobiography: studies in the art of self-invention* (Princeton, NJ, 1985); P.J. Eakin, *Touching the world: reference in autobiography* (Princeton, NJ, 1992). [2] George Moore, *Hail and farewell* (Gerrards Cross, 1976). (Hereafter cited as G.M., *Hail and farewell*).

fictionalizations, speculations and exaggerations that nonetheless fix upon some key truth, much in the manner of his contemporary, the popular caricaturist Max Beerbohm. Moore broadens a definition of evidence to comic proportions in order to highlight the subjectivity of historical narrative and the experience from which it derives, while simultaneously putting forward a paradoxically earnest assessment of reality as he saw it. The reader, thus, proceeds cautiously if looking for facts, but with pleasure if alert to the ways Moore builds serious comedy and absurd tragedy out of a family history that ends with himself, as he left no heirs but his books and the imaginary son he created in the 1914 autobiographical fantasy 'Euphorian in Texas', a boy growing up in the wilds of the American West with his mother Honor Woulfe (a real person who playfully indulged Moore this fantasy throughout their correspondence across the Atlantic).[3] The sheer impossibility of this imaginary child speaks to the finality with which Moore closed the door on the legacy of his family.

Their family legacy is a considerable one. The first George Moore (1729–99), the younger son of the Moores of Ashbrook, returned to the west of Ireland from Alicante in the early 1790s, having amassed a large fortune in the shipping of specialty goods to and from Spain. With this new wealth, he bought land throughout the region and constructed a large Georgian house on a hill overlooking Lake Carra in Co. Mayo. Originally an English Protestant family but now Catholic by marriage, the Moores retained control of their properties through the era of the penal laws, although George's oldest son, John, later became briefly involved with the United Irishmen revolt. After being proclaimed president of the republic of Connaught, he was immediately captured by British forces and died in captivity, leaving the estate to be inherited by his younger brother, George II, called by his descendants and by biographers, 'The Historian'. And that he was, in addition to being a philosopher and author of didactic fiction. As a young man, George II participated in a literary salon hosted at Holland House in London and which included among its participants Lord Byron, Thomas Macaulay and Sir Walter Scott. Leaving the running of the estate to his capable wife Louisa, George II avidly collected books during a period frequently deemed 'the age of bibliomania' and accrued an extensive library of travel writing and historical and philosophical works.[4] Like most gentlemen of his time, he favored non-fiction, but he also accumulated a large

---

See also E. Grubgeld, 'Gossip, art, and the public secret: George Moore on his contemporaries' in A. Heilmann and M. Llwellyn (eds), *George Moore: influence and collaboration* (Newark, 2014), pp 137–50.   3 George Moore, 'Euphorion in Texas' in *Memoirs of my dead life* (London, 1915), pp 286–311; A. Frazier, 'On his honour: George Moore and some women', *English Literature in Transition, 1880–1920*, 35:4 (1992), pp 423–45.   4 A. Hunt, 'Private libraries in the age of bibliomania' in G. Mandlebrote and K.A. Manley (eds), *The Cambridge history of libraries in Britain and Ireland*, 3 vols (Cambridge, 2006), ii, pp 438–58. See also M. Purcell, *The country house library* (New Haven, CT, 2017), esp. ch. 7 '*Bibliomania*: the book craze of the late eighteenth and early nineteenth centuries, and its

collection of eighteenth-century novels. His grandson, Moore the novelist, recalls how this fiction sparked his own imagination as a boy rummaging through the library shelves at Moore Hall, although, with characteristic humour, also calls into doubt the degree to which his youthful self ever read anything with attention. Queried about his knowledge of the novelist Tobias Smollet in *Avowals* (1919), Moore quips: 'To say that I have read him would be untrue, and to say that I have not read him would be nearly as untrue. My memory of him is gusto, and plenty of it, and an outlook on life in strict conformity with his style.'[5]

Moore contends that while his grandfather's library nurtured his imagination when growing up in the second half of the nineteenth century, it was very much a product of its own historical moment:

> the Georgian house created a demand for the drawing-room entertainment, and Fielding fell in with the humour of our first drawing-rooms accidentally. He was followed by Johnson and Goldsmith, who wrote stories, hoping, of course, that their stories would please somebody ... Smollett may have made a good deal of money by writing, but he wrote to please himself, I think – in the main, for literature had not yet become a trade.[6]

Although Moore was a hard bargainer with his publishers and understood precisely the financial aspects of publication, he nevertheless saw himself in his later years as an eighteenth-century man who stood apart from the literary marketplace, a notion whose foundation lies in the array of eighteenth-century texts purchased by his forebear. In addition to book collecting, his grandfather also wrote prolifically. He produced a history of the ascension of William and Mary to the English throne published by Longmans in 1817; a book of anti-Kantian philosophy entitled *A treatise on the art of reasoning*; biographies of three politicians of eighteenth-century Spain and Portugal issued in two editions; a novel, *Grassville Abbey*, which went through several printings and was translated into French; and four volumes illustrating the effects of different passions by means of fictional narratives. Moore's grandfather devoted his later years to a manuscript entitled *Historical memoirs of the French Revolution*, that remained unpublished and is assumed to have been lost in the arson attack that destroyed Moore Hall in February 1923. Thus, while the Historian may have been a recluse of sorts and an eccentric among his peers, he also accomplished a great deal of writing that reflects the depths of his learning. Maria Edgeworth so admired his book on the 1688 revolution that she sought him out as a guest in her home and became in time an intimate friend of the family.

This was, indeed, a household devoted to reading and writing. From Oscott, the Catholic school near Birmingham where he was dispatched as a boy to be

afterlife', pp 160–79.   **5** George Moore, *Avowals* (London, 1924), p. 24. Hereafter cited as G.M., *Avowals*.   **6** Ibid., p. 26.

educated, the Historian's son and heir, George Henry Moore (1810–70) regularly sent home letters brimming with detailed discussions of English, French and Latin poetry. The correspondence indicates that both parents would have understood and been interested in such details. With typical Moorian impudence, the boy also sent corrections of his father's Latin scansions. At Oscott, George Henry Moore was recognized as a brilliant student, and his juvenile poems and the selections from his letters excerpted by biographers, as well as his satire lambasting the inadequacy of the education provided for the poor, show astonishing wit and intelligence in a boy only in his teens. They also reveal a sense of class injustice that would be the focus of his later years in politics and, thereby, force an early end to that career, as many landlords were reluctant to vote for a champion of tenant rights thought to be sympathetic to Fenian rebels.

But despite his intellect, literary talent and excellent education, young George Henry Moore was energetic and restless, like many of his class infatuated with horses and, as a young man, attracted to gambling – although like all the Moores, he never drank to excess and confined his sexual adventures to married women of his own class. Concerned about his mounting gambling debts and infatuation with an older woman, his mother packed him off on an extended tour of Russia, Syria and the Middle East; his journals and letters from those years of travel, excerpts of which are reproduced in Maurice Moore's biography, indicate again his talent for expression and a profound interest in art, literature and history.[7] Additionally, George Henry Moore conducted scientific and archeological inquiries in the region and made a small but significant contribution to the geographical study of the Dead Sea.[8] Some years after he became master of Moore Hall in 1840, he expanded the library to include all the ground-floor guest rooms at the back of the house, and he updated its collection to include novels, not only by the likes of Fielding, Smollet and Sterne from the eighteenth-century, but also more contemporary writers like Benjamin Disraeli, George Eliot and Walter Scott (whose poetry Moore recalled his father reciting to their mother when the family would picnic on Castle Island), as well as examples of fashionable sensation fiction of the period. George Henry Moore's development and modernization of the Moore Hall library seems all the more remarkable given that the financial hardships of the Famine years were not long behind. For many reasons, ranging from absentee landlordism to agricultural and economic distress, many country house libraries languished during the nineteenth century.[9] Although he kept Moore Hall afloat through an advantageous marriage and unusually good luck at the racetrack, it was heavily encumbered by debt, and the

---

[7] Maurice Moore, *George Henry Moore, an Irish gentleman: his travels, his racing, his politics* (London, 1913) (hereafter cited as M.M., *GHM*). [8] H. Goren, 'Irish explorers of the Jordan Rift and the Euphrates Valley in the 1830s: science, adventure, and imperialism' in C. Montague and A. Frazier (eds), *George Moore: London, Paris, Hollywood* (Dublin, 2012), pp 28–38. [9] M.L. Legg, 'The Kilkenny Circulating Library Society and the growth of reading rooms in nineteenth-century Ireland' in B. Cunningham and M. Kennedy (eds), *The*

expenditure on such a large quantity of books, as well as modifying rooms to accommodate them, must have been a challenge.

Books, however, formed an essential part of the family's everyday practices and as much more than signs of an elite class status or merely decorative objects, although after the fashion of the time, their bindings were probably beautiful. They existed to be read and discussed: what a Moore read became a sign of his political, philosophical and moral identity. Visiting friends shortly after his father's death in 1870 and bringing with him a copy of Immanuel Kant's *The critique of reason* (most certainly drawn from the Moore Hall library, which under his grandfather's curation contained many works of philosophy) earned the youthful nascent writer the derisive moniker 'Kant Moore', but he was undoubtedly flattered rather than chastened by this new aspect of his evolving sense of self. Ever an iconoclast and a contrarian, he would claim in *Hail and farewell* (1911–13) that as a boy, he sought to provoke his teachers by bringing to school a volume of Shelley's poetry discovered in the Moore Hall library and querying whether Shelley's atheism could constitute a moral problem. The school authorities confiscated the book, but much to his disappointment, he was not expelled. Whether these anecdotes are factual or fictional, they nevertheless bespeak how through his choice of reading material, a Moore of any age could make a statement about who he was and who he would come to be.

Likewise, the two brothers interpreted the legacy of their parents and grandparents as to affirm their own sense of who they were and their place in the emergent nation. Despite the subtitle of Maurice Moore's biography of their father – *His travels, his racing, his politics* (1913) – the preface his elder brother wrote at his request laments that so much space had been devoted to their father's political career: 'Were it not for the politics,' he chides, 'there would not be a dull page in this biography.'[10] Comparing the stories of their father's travels in Russia and the Middle East to the prolonged discussion of his breeding and racing of horses that followed it, Moore regretfully muses: 'He was one man in the East and another in the West; in the East he drew and painted; in the West he hung over billiard-tables winning or losing hundreds of pounds, and when tired of billiards he went away to the shires with a great stud of hunters.'[11] To Moore, it appeared that a return to Ireland robbed his father of the drawing, painting and writing stimulated by his travels and replaced such pursuits with horse racing and, worse, politics. Thirteen of the book's twenty chapters are in fact devoted to their father's political career and the causes about which he cared. That is Maurice Moore's primary focus, with the discussion of his father's travel serving primarily to establish the intellect of a mind that then turned its attention to agricultural reform. Similarly, the colonel's discussion of their father's immersion in horse racing serves to establish a courage of character that

experience of reading: Irish historical perspectives (Dublin, 1999), pp 78–98.   10 M.M., *GHM*, p. xviii.   11 Ibid., p. xiv.

underlay his political pursuits, pursuits which in his case were less concerned with power, station or the possible financial benefits of politics and more with the causes he had championed since his adolescent satire on the inadequacy of the education provided for the working class. For Colonel Moore, the legacy of George Henry is less one of a striking prose style, a capacity for subtle observations of culture and an exceptional knowledge of poetics and languages than it is a mastery over the affairs of Ireland. The colonel's assessment of their father's life is echoed by Isaac Butt in the funeral oration he delivered and which is included in the final chapter of *An Irish gentleman*. Praising his knowledge of, and devotion to, the complex issues of land reform, Butt declared: 'The men who die thus from intellectual toil are martyrs in their country's cause, martyrs as truly as if they had died on the scaffold or on the battlefield ; and among those martyrs we may, with Thomas Davis, count George Henry Moore.'[12]

George Augustus Moore, on the other hand, finishes the preface to his brother's book with a preposterous fantasy that Colonel Moore felt obliged to address with an erratum slip inserted into the first printings. Their father had collapsed in the spring of 1870 with what was apparently a stroke after facing threats of rent refusals and warnings of upcoming violence by local Ribbonmen, but much to his brother's horror, Moore concludes,

> he died killed by his tenants, that is certain; he died of a broken heart. My brother gives a letter which, I should like to believe, points to suicide, for it would please me to think of my father dying like an old Roman. His valet told me that he was quite well the day before; when he came to call him in the morning he was breathing heavily, when he called again my father was dead; and this tragic death seems the legitimate end of a brave life, and in my brother's book he appears to me as wonderful as any character invented by Balzac or Turguenev.[13]

George Henry Moore most decidedly neither committed suicide nor died of a broken heart, although stress might have exacerbated some pre-existing condition. But, the tale underscores Moore's desire to see his father's death as precipitated by disillusionment with his countrymen rather than dedication to a future Moore could not envision as anything but hopeless. In the face of that sense of futility, Moore makes a gesture both facetious and serious in proclaiming his father's life to be the material of the novelists he most admired.

As the brothers evaluate their father's politics through their own views of Ireland, so Moore also interprets his father's reading and its influence on himself. That interpretation stays remarkably consistent throughout his long career, and yet consistently ambivalent and consistently complicated. Although Moore declares himself to 'have come into the world … with a nature like a

12 Ibid., p. 383.   13 Ibid., p. xx.

smooth sheet of wax, bearing no impress, but capable of receiving any',[14] one who could 'shake himself free from race and language, and ... recreate himself as it were in the womb of a new nationality, assuming its ideals, its morals, and its modes of thought', he nevertheless repeatedly cites as a wellspring of his life's vocation the conversations about books overheard as a young boy.[15] In the opening passage of his *Confessions of a young man,* first published in 1888, the autobiographical narrator recounts the moment when he first heard the call:

> Scene: A great family coach, drawn by two powerful country horses, lumbers along a narrow Irish road. The ever recurrent signs – long ranges of blue mountains, the streak of bog, the rotting cabin, the flock of plover rising from the desolate water. Inside the coach there are two children. They are smart, with new jackets and neckties; their faces are pale with sleep, and the rolling of the coach makes them feel a little sick. It is seven o'clock in the morning. Opposite the children are their parents, and they are talking of a novel the world is reading. Did Lady Audley murder her husband? Lady Audley! What a beautiful name; and she, who is a slender, pale, fairy-like woman, killed her husband. Such thoughts flash through the boy's mind; his imagination is stirred and quickened, and he begs for an explanation.[16]

His mind is 'quickened', a verb whose biblical resonances suggest bringing into life and an infusion of divine spirit. Returning home, he ransacks the large library of Romantic and Victorian literature added by his father to his own father's collection of classical and eighteenth-century works, reading Mary Braddon's *Lady Audley's secret*, its sequels and one novel after another, finally discovering Byron and Shelley. 'These poets,' he writes, 'were the ripening influence of years otherwise merely nervous and boisterous'.[17] In one of his final works of autobiographical non-fiction, he offers an 'imaginary conversation' with his good friend Edmund Gosse, in which he recalls with affectionate nostalgia the many books he read as a boy: Dickens, Thackeray, Eliot, the Brontes and especially Lord Lytton. 'I owe to *Pelham*,' he tells Gosse, 'a certain whimsicality of mind that the years have never rubbed away, and I believe the tone of the book to have influenced thousands.' To Gosse's complaint that Moore 'never cared for painting or music or literature, but used them as a means of self-development', he makes no retort except to claim that such is true for all.[18] Yet again, the library stands as an early site of self-creation, one that would later duplicate itself in Paris where he would rebirth himself through an immersion in French poetry and fiction.

After his father's death and upon attaining his majority, he inherited that library, as well as a massive estate and a yearly income of £4,000, allowing him to

---

14 George Moore, *Confessions of a young man* (Montreal, 1972), p. 49.   **15** Ibid., p. 129.
16 Ibid., pp 49–50.   **17** Ibid., p. 50.   **18** G.M., *Avowals*, pp 47, 48.

relocate first to Paris, then London and then Dublin, before finally returning to London again to repeatedly reinvent himself as a painter, as well as a novelist, essayist and the author of multiple autobiographies. The intellectual legacy of Moore Hall, he claims, thus consummates itself in the astonishing emergence of the cosmopolitan artist from the awkward, if audacious, red-haired boy once sent back to Mayo as an unteachable dunce. Despite its rough and tumble life, the world of Moore Hall bred readers. In addition to the colonel's achievement as a biographer and writer of a clear, efficient and sometimes eloquent prose, even their feckless younger brother Julian dabbled in playwriting, and their disreputable sibling Augustus managed a living as a librettist and tabloid journalist.[19] Of his grandfather, the Historian, Moore recalls in *Conversations in Ebury Street* (1924) his pleasure at being told as a boy how much he resembled the 'kindly, peaceful face' of the 'sad old gentleman in a white waistcoat [whose portrait hung] over the chimneypiece'. The impression, he continues, 'enticed me and led me into a love of the library in which he had lived, writing histories and reading'.[20] But, more than the history of the Glorious Revolution that impressed Maria Edgeworth, and certainly more than any didactic fiction or anti-Kantian theological tracts, it was the preface to his grandfather's unpublished manuscript of more than 500 pages that most touches the emotions of the recollective narrator of *Conversations in Ebury Street*. The preface is a confession of loneliness and failure that establishes the sort of rhetorical intimacy between writer and reader that Moore himself perfects in *Confessions of a young man*, *Hail and farewell* and other autobiographical works.

There is an appealing sense of failure central to Moore's interpretation of his family's legacy. His recollective prose revels not only in the 'nervous and boisterous' years of life at Moore Hall with its stables, its horse racing and its endlessly fascinating population of grooms, dairymaids and brewers, but also in the equally vibrant world of books that offered him a way to become more than a wastrel son and, eventually, more than the affected foppish would-be poet he so viciously satirizes in the portrait of 'Landlord M', which appeared in the book of sketches that in many ways constitutes his first autobiography, *Parnell and his island* (1887).[21]

Yet in all this deeply felt recollection there remains a conviction that achievements of his grandfather and his father, both learned, literary men – one a recluse, the other an activist – were nevertheless futile because their world was nearing extinction and their relevance declining rapidly. 'We have outlived our day, that is all,' he declares to his ever-hopeful brother, the colonel, 'and in thirty

---

19 Of his sister, Nina Moore Kilkelly, almost nothing is known regarding her education or any literary talents or ambitions she may have harboured. Little correspondence survives, and when Moore comments on Nina in his own letters, he directs most of his attention to what he saw as her excessive childbearing.   20 George Moore, *Conversations in Ebury Street* (London, 1936), p. 262.   21 George Moore, *Parnell and his island* (London, 1887).

years we shall be, as I have said, as extinct as the dodo.'[22] A decade later in *A story-teller's holiday* (1918), he wrote of Moore Hall as 'a relic, a ruin, a corpse. Its life ceased when we left it in 1870, and I am one that has no liking for corpses. The wise man never looks on the face of a corpse, knowing well that if he does it will come between him and the living face.'[23]

Although Moore had astutely recognized the belated and utterly justifiable demise of a world which had once allowed his family to build a grand Georgian house and fill its library with thousands of books, he nevertheless grieved over its violent demise, and in a letter to an old friend he admits that he could never return to Ireland: 'the burning of my house forbids. I should crumble into dust the moment I set foot on the shore'.[24] There are many explanations as to why Moore Hall was targeted by anti-Treaty forces, but there is little question that the arson was well-executed and planned. Biographer Adrian Frazier was told by local historians and a descendant of James Reilly, the steward who was at the time the sole caretaker of the house, that the fire was an hour in preparation, with nine cartloads of furniture and other objects looted before the flames began.[25] As Terence Dooley has carefully documented, before being destroyed, targeted estate houses were routinely stripped of valuable items such as silver plate, clocks and jewellery, as well as practical objects that could be sold or kept for personal use in homes or farms. In most cases, paintings and books were abandoned to the flames, although there exists what Dooley calls 'anecdotal evidence' of valuable paintings suspiciously appearing in the shops and catalogues of antique dealers.[26] Reilly himself wrote to Colonel Moore that he had attempted to enter the library to save some books, but that the heat from the fire was impenetrable. The fierce blaze, he reported, had 'left but the walls, not a vestige of glass, timber or even plaster from the ground floor up'; no one would have been able to ascertain whether objects had been burned or looted.[27] It has been rumored that books from Moore Hall can in fact be found in the homes of certain families in the area, and Moore himself might well appreciate a story ending with such gossip, as this particular piece of hearsay suggests that at least some local people thought books to be sufficiently important to rescue them from destruction. And it would not be unlike Moore to believe that perhaps, in truth, his father's legacy best belonged in both the ashes of the old world and in a new world in which he would have no part.

22 G.M., *Hail and farewell*, p. 636.   23 George Moore, *A story-teller's holiday* (New York, 1918), p. 352. Moore here exaggerates, as his mother and siblings continued to occupy the house at irregular intervals for decades after his father's death in 1870, and Maurice Moore resided there and ran the estate himself after his return from the Boer War, living there on occasion, even after he and George had irreconcilably quarrelled.   24 George Moore to Richard Best, 17 Oct. 1923, cited in A. Frazier, *George Moore, 1852–1933* (London, 2000), pp 434–5.   25 Frazier, *George Moore*, pp 433–4.   26 T. Dooley, *Burning the Big House: the story of the Irish country house in a time of war and revolution* (London, 2022), pp 200–1.   27 The full text of James Reilly's letter is given in J. Hone, *The Moores of Moore Hall* (London, 1939), pp 263–5.

An intergenerational chronicle: the library at Adare Manor, Co. Limerick

ANNA-MARIA HAJBA

INTRODUCTION

There is a popularly held belief that country house libraries were created purely for show by means of bulk purchases,[1] or that books were accumulated unselectively, either as gifts or inherited from earlier generations. In both instances, the implication is that books were rarely used, except perhaps to provide entertainment for house guests.[2] We may add a third variant: the activities of a book collector, but even in this instance the act of reading remains questionable. 'If a man buys a book for any other purpose than reading it,' suggests T.A. Birrell, 'he is a collector, not a reader'.[3]

What adds to the perception of country house libraries as unused spaces filled with haphazard accumulations of books is that in their contents, they share remarkable similarities: in virtually all of them can be found books on sport, history and natural history, devotional works, political tracts, practical guides to gardening, forestry and agriculture, county histories and countless editions of popular literature, often in French, German and Italian, as well as English.[4] It has even been suggested that few country house libraries reflect the interests or preoccupations of a particular generation or individual.[5] Is this truly the case, and if so, is there anything useful that these libraries can tell us about the families who created them?

---

1 See, for example, P.H. Reid, 'The decline and fall of the British country house library', *Libraries and Culture*, 36:2 (Spring 2001), p. 351. In recent years, this idea has been largely debunked (see, for example, Mark Purcell, who calls for the disposal of this 'depressing cliché' in 'The country house library reassessed: or, did the country house library ever really exist?', *Library History*, 18:3 (2002), p. 161). However, it cannot be dismissed in its entirety. We know, for example, that the earl of Caledon not only purchased the entire library of Thomas Percy, bishop of Dromore, but also commissioned John Nash to design a room in which to display it (Reid, 'Decline and fall', 350; M. Purcell, *The country house library* (London, 2017), p. 110). 2 J. Ciro, 'Country house libraries in the nineteenth century', *Library History*, 18:2 (2002), 90–1; A.N.L. Munby, 'The library' in Roy Strong et al., *The destruction of the country house, 1875–1975* (London, 1975), p. 107. 3 T.A. Birrell, 'Reading as pastime: the place of light literature in some gentlemen's libraries of the 17th century' in R. Myers and M. Harris (eds), *Property of a gentleman: the formation, organization and dispersal of the private library, 1620–1920* (Winchester, 1991), p. 113. 4 Purcell, *The country house library*, p. 194; Munby, 'The library', p. 107. 5 Purcell, *The country house library*, p. 161.

10.1 Catalogue of the sale of the library at Adare Manor in 1982. Courtesy of Special Collections and Archives, Glucksman Library, University of Limerick.

These questions are tested here by exploring the library that existed at Adare Manor, Co. Limerick, home of the Wyndham Quin family, earls of Dunraven. The bulk of the library, along with other contents of the house, was dispersed at a two-day Christie's auction in June 1982, following a decision by the 7th earl of Dunraven and his wife to sell Adare Manor. Although the library no longer survives, sources such as the auction catalogue (fig. 10.1), an earlier library catalogue prepared in 1975, and family diaries and correspondence, make it possible to reconstruct some of its original substance and to come to a close understanding of the reading habits of the family and the role that books played in their lives. To keep the study within reasonable limits, it has been narrowed to focus on three individuals: Windham Henry, the 2nd earl of Dunraven (1782–1850), his son Edwin, the 3rd earl (1812–71), and grandson Windham Thomas, the 4th earl (1841–1926), all of whom led very different lives and pursued different interests.

Sales catalogues are, of course, notoriously difficult sources, full of frustrating lacunae.[6] They are replete with unhelpful phrases such as 'contents of shelves', 'miscellaneous literature', 'stack lot' and 'odd volumes', making it impossible to

---

6 Myers and Harris (eds), *Property of a gentleman*, p. vii.

evaluate the exact number or composition of titles. Mention is rarely made of bookplates or signatures that would provide clues as to which family member possessed or acquired a particular volume, nor do they reveal whether the sale encompassed the entire contents of a library or only a portion, and, if the latter, what criteria were used to select books for sale. When examined in isolation, sales catalogues can lead to misinterpretation, which must be balanced by taking into account the family history and the background of the individuals who created the library. By way of example, of the 640 named titles in the 1982 sales catalogue, twenty-nine relate to religious subjects. From this, it would be easy to draw the conclusion that the Dunravens had no particular interest in theological contemplation. However, in light of the fact that the 3rd earl was a Roman Catholic convert, the scarcity of religious literature appears odd. Fortunately, the earlier and more substantial library catalogue of 1975, compiled in the course of a year by a retired school teacher Thomas Pierce, incorporates more than 3,100 titles, of which at least 600 can be categorized as religious or theological.[7] This, if a lightsome pun is permitted, speaks volumes of the importance of religion to at least one member of the family. Of course, it also opens up yet another lacuna: what became of the titles that did not make it to the auction? Were they retained by the family or dispersed before the auction by some other means?

It is argued here that the creation of a country house library was a more complex affair than heretofore understood, and that in some country houses, libraries played an essential role in the lives of their owners. Notwithstanding their elusive nature, book catalogues can provide illuminating glimpses into the minds and personal interests of their owners. To illustrate this in greater detail it is proposed to examine three members of the Dunraven family and explore what can be learnt of them by perusing the family bookshelves.

WINDHAM HENRY THE ARCHITECT

The 2nd earl (fig. 10.2) is perhaps best remembered as the builder of Adare Manor, an undertaking which consumed much of his life and the completion of which he did not live to see. Initially, he commissioned the Pain brothers to provide designs, but within a few years his relationship with James Pain began to falter. Not only did Pain's drawings contain a number of mistakes, but his long absences in London forced masons at Adare to stand idle for want of work, costing Windham both money and patience.[8] Much worse was his dissatisfaction with Pain's lack of architectural refinement. In July 1835, Windham complained

---

[7] 'The Dunraven library, Adare Manor, Adare, Co. Limerick, catalogued for Thady, seventh earl of Dunraven and his countess Geraldine by Thomas Pierce in the year of our Lord, 1975', 55 vols (University of Limerick, Dunraven papers (hereafter cited as ULDP), uncatalogued item).   [8] See, for example, 2nd earl of Dunraven to Viscount Adare, 7 Dec. 1833 (ULDP, uncatalogued item).

The library at Adare Manor, Co. Limerick

10.2 Windham Henry Wyndham Quin, 2nd earl of Dunraven, by George Orleans Delamotte, November 1820. Courtesy of the Dunraven family.

that 'Mr Pain with gentlemanly qualities, & skill in some things, has no knowledge of, & no taste whatever in *Tudor* architecture & makes a shocking mess of it'.[9] Five years later, James Pain was politely but firmly dismissed and replaced by Lewis Nockalls Cottingham.

Windham's evident frustration with Pain suggests a more than superficial knowledge of architecture, as does his election in 1841 to the Oxford Society for Promoting the Study of Gothic Architecture, founded to encourage the use of the Gothic style in church design.[10] The scholarly nature of his interest is equally in evidence in his library. The books he owned reflect the sea-change in architectural design preferences that characterized the early 1800s. For much of the eighteenth century, symmetrical and well-proportioned classicism dominated tastes. Isaac Ware's 1738 translation of Andrea Palladio's *I quattro libri dell'architettura* (1570) was a staple in many a country house library, including Adare. Here, it was accompanied by Leon Battista Alberti's *Della architettura* (1726) and Ottavio Bertotti Scamozzi's *Il forestiere istruito delle cose più rare di architettura e di alcune pitture della cittá di Vicenza* (1761), most likely picked up by Windham's father during his grand tour of Italy in 1773.

With the emergence of the Romantic movement towards the end of the eighteenth century and its admiration of the distant past, the many medieval ruins in Britain's landscape became the subject of vibrant study. In the process, Gothic architecture became strongly associated with patriotism. Until about 1850, continental Gothic was ignored and the notion that Gothic was invented in England and reached its finest expression there remained the accepted wisdom.[11] One of the pioneering promoters of Gothic Revival was Thomas Rickman (1776–1841). His classification of English medieval architecture into Norman, Early English, Decorated and Perpendicular phases, as explained in his work *An attempt to discriminate the styles of architecture in England from the conquest to the Reformation* (1817), continue in use to this day. An 1833 edition of Rickman's work was to be found in Adare, alongside William Gunn's *Inquiry into the origin and influence of Gothic architecture* (1819), and also J.S. Hawkins' *History of the origin and establishment of Gothic architecture* (1813), a book that the antiquary John Carter violently attacked at the time of its publication for deigning to suggest that the Gothic style originated in France.[12] Here, too, were an 1838 edition of Matthew Bloxam's enormously popular *The principles of Gothic ecclesiastical architecture* (originally published in 1829 as *The principles of Gothic architecture*); *Observations on the architecture of England during the reign of*

9 Second earl of Dunraven to Viscount Adare, 1 July 1835 (ULDP, uncatalogued item). 10 G. Brandwood, 'Members of the Cambridge Camden and Ecclesiological Societies, 1839–1868', https:// ecclsoc.org/wp-content/uploads/2021/02/Brandwood-Cambridge-Camden-membership-list.pdf, accessed 11 May 2023; *Report of the Oxford Society for promoting the study of Gothic architecture for Hilary, Easter and Trinity terms* (1841), p. 23.   11 S. Bradley, 'The Englishness of Gothic: theories and interpretations from William Gilpin to J.H. Parker', *Architectural History*, 45 (2002), p. 325.   12 See Carter's review of Hawkin's work in

Queen Elizabeth and King James I (1837), written by C.J. Richardson, one of the early architects to appreciate and utilize Tudor and Elizabethan styles; and J.S. Storer's ten-volume *Antiquarian and topographical cabinet* (1807–11), 'a pretty work, full of prints & descriptions of old buildings in England', as Windham enthused to his son.[13]

The 2nd earl's interest in Gothic architecture was also practical. His library contained a wealth of pattern books and other illustrated guides to Gothic ornamentation, evidently purchased to facilitate an active part in the design process of Adare Manor. His particular favourite among authors was A.C. Pugin, father of the architect A.W.N. Pugin, almost all of whose works Windham owned. These included the 1825 edition of the two-volume *Specimens of Gothic architecture selected from various ancient edifices in England*, which at the time of its publication in 1821–3 was the first British architectural pattern book to give accurate drawings of Gothic details and widely read.[14] Windham also possessed copies of Joseph Nash's popular *Mansions of England in the olden time* (1839); T.F. Hunt's *Exemplars of Tudor architecture adapted to modern habitation* (1830), which emphasized the importance of accurate historical detailing in design; and the 1834 edition of *Details of Elizabethan architecture* (first published in 1823) by the prolific author and illustrator Henry Shaw. Windham's love of heraldry, utilized by Gothic Revivalism as a popular artistic device, is also apparent from the publications he owned by the celebrated stained glass artist, Thomas Willement. It was not only Willement's books that found their way to Adare, but also his magnificent stained glass gallery windows, commissioned by the 2nd earl in 1837.

Not all of Windham's architectural knowledge was accumulated by reading books. Throughout the 1820s and 1830s he and his wife visited country houses, both old and new, for ideas and inspiration. Patterns they liked were copied into sketchbooks by drawing or by taking rubbings. As country house visits at this time were becoming an increasingly popular pastime among the genteel classes, guidebooks to these buildings were occasionally published and, when available, quickly picked up by Windham. Among these were William Gauci's *Views of Windsor Castle and its adjoining scenery* (1827) and Samuel Rayner's *History and antiquities of Haddon Hall* (1836), a copy of which Windham purchased following a visit in 1840 in order to share the beauty of the place with his wife.[15] Haddon Hall rapidly became one of his favourite buildings and had a strong design influence on Adare Manor; its staircase tower, for instance, is a direct copy of one of the towers at Haddon Hall. Another topical guidebook in Windham's library

---

Gentleman's Magazine, 83:2 (1813), pp 321–4. **13** The work does not appear in either catalogue, but its purchase is recorded in family correspondence; see 2nd earl of Dunraven to Viscount Adare, 28 June 1830 (ULDP, uncatalogued item). **14** R. Hill, *God's architect: Pugin & the building of romantic Britain* (2007), p. 52. **15** 2nd earl of Dunraven to Countess Caroline, 31 Mar. 1840 (ULDP, D3196/E/3/125).

was John Britton's *Graphic illustrations with historical and descriptive accounts of Toddington, Gloucestershire, the seat of Lord Dudley* (1840), a house he and his wife visited twice in the 1830s, and which in its architectural detailing bears a notable similarity to Adare Manor.

Wider continental influences also played an important role in the design of the new family seat. In 1836, the Dunravens spent six months touring Germany and the Low Countries. Among the books they purchased during this tour was Charles de Graimberg's compilation of lithographic views of the ruin of Heidelberg Castle (*Vues lithographiées de la ruine, de la ville et des environs de Heidelberg*, 1826). Windham's interest in continental Gothic is also evident in the copies he owed of Charles Wild's *Select examples of architectural grandeur in Belgium, Germany and France* (1837) and A. Lange's *Picturesque views of the most remarkable cathedrals, churches and monuments of Gothic architecture on the banks of the Main, Rhine and the Lahn* (1836). Some of the interior arrangements of Heidelberg Castle were later utilized in the great hall at Adare, illustrating Windham's broad learning of Gothic architecture beyond the borders of the British Isles.

EDWIN THE ARCHAEOLOGIST

At the time of Windham's death in 1850, Adare Manor remained unfinished and it fell to the 3rd earl (fig. 10.3) to complete the south front. His initial reaction was to turn to A.W.N. Pugin for assistance. The two men had befriended each other in 1845, and Edwin had been instrumental in bringing the architect to Adare Manor to provide interior designs. Pugin, a Roman Catholic convert, was a popular but controversial Gothic Revival architect who, in his polemical works, *Contrasts* (1836) and *True principles of pointed or Christian architecture* (1841), argued that only Gothic architecture served the functional and moral needs of the nation.[16] Edwin owned a copy of *Contrasts*, and Pugin's architectural doctrines had a strong influence on him. During the 3rd earl's visit to Munich in the autumn of 1847, he was disappointed to find that 'there is no true taste for gothic: they have only built one church in that style … It is quite a different effect & one which is at variance with true gothic principles.'[17] Regrettably Pugin, by now ill and close to death, was unable to comply with Edwin's request to finish the south front. Instead, it was P.C. Hardwick who took on the task.

What attracted Edwin to Hardwick was not only the latter's evident skill as an architect, but the interest the two men shared in the Oxford Movement. The movement had emerged in 1833 as a consequence of the passing of the Church Temporalities (Ireland) Act, which reduced the size of the established church in

16 C. Brooks, *The Gothic revival* (London, 1999), p. 233.   17 3rd earl of Dunraven to Caroline, countess of Dunraven, 17 Oct. 1847 (ULDP, D/3196/E/8/8).

10.3 Edwin Wyndham Quin, 3rd earl of Dunraven, by Camille Silvy, 3 July 1861.
© National Portrait Gallery, London.

Ireland from twenty-two dioceses to ten and abolished certain church rates. Supporters of the Oxford Movement denounced the government's interference in the affairs of the church and called for spiritual independence and the re-awakening of certain pre-Reformation traditions, such as a greater appreciation of the holy communion. The leaders of the movement promoted their views by publishing a series of ninety pamphlets under the collective title *Tracts for the times*, which gave the movement its additional name of Tractarianism. A full set of these pamphlets was to be found in Adare, together with numerous works by the movement's most prominent leaders. These included Edward Bouverie Pusey's *Eirenicon* (1865), which sought to justify the apostolicity and catholicity of the Anglican faith, and John Henry Newman's *History of my religious opinions* (1865), originally published as *Apologia pro vita sua* in 1864. Edwin also owned a copy of Newman's famous *Essay on the development of Christian doctrine*, published in 1845 just weeks after the author's controversial conversion to Roman Catholicism. Although the Oxford Movement only sought to position the Anglican church midway between austere Protestantism and ostentatious Roman Catholicism, many, like Newman, found the line too difficult to hold and came to the conclusion that the only way to assert the catholic character of the Church of England was to return to the Roman Catholic faith. Edwin was among these converts, and his extensive collection of religious and theological works, amounting to over 600 titles, reveals the profound importance of faith in his life and the intensity of the private struggle he underwent before his conversion. These books included both Protestant and Catholic versions of the Bible, an extensive collection of sermons and devotional works, biographies of popes and saints, critical interpretations of sacred texts and seminal works on the history of the early church, such as H.H. Milman's *History of Christianity* (1867). Closely tied with Edwin's religious views was his interest in education. He emerged as one of the country's leading liberal Roman Catholics to campaign for the safeguarding of religious education in Ireland and to voice opposition to mixed education. Almost forty volumes in his library were related to the subject, including Isaac Butt's *The liberty of teaching vindicated* (1865), James Godkin's *Education in Ireland* (1862) and J.W. Kavanagh's *Mixed education: the Catholic case stated* (1859).

Edwin's approach to matters of personal faith is just one indication of the academic nature of his interests, which manifested itself at an early age. He studied astronomy at Trinity College Dublin under W.R. Hamilton, and acquired for his library essays and lectures by the celebrated astronomer J.F. Herschel, several works on magnetism by Edward Sabine, and telescopic observations made by the earl of Rosse, all men whom Edwin knew personally. When telescopic work ruined his eyesight and prevented further study, Edwin found a new passion in archaeology. Elected a fellow of the Royal Irish Academy at the tender age of nineteen in 1831, he became one of the leading figures of this emerging new science in Ireland. He was a co-founder of the Irish Archaeological Society in 1840 and of the Celtic Society in 1845, and in 1852 joined the Brehon Law Commission to support the translation of the Brehon laws into English.[18] In 1849, Edwin was elected president of the Cambrian Archaeological Association in Wales, where he became a popular guide on archaeological excursions, not only because of his profound command of the subject, but also because 'he brought his knowledge to bear without the least assumption of superiority, and with a vast deal of fun and humour, and never a trace of harshness or ill-nature'.[19] The 400-odd titles he owned on archaeological topics include some fifty works on geology, such as Charles Lyell's *Principles of geology* (1830), which popularized the concept that the earth was shaped by continuing slow-moving forces and not by biblical events, and descriptions of significant archaeological excavations such as the discovery of the biblical city of Nineveh, on which subject alone Edwin owned half a dozen books.

It was in the field of Irish architectural archaeology that Edwin made his greatest contribution. His most intimate friends included the renowned Irish archaeologist George Petrie. When Petrie died in 1866, Edwin formed a committee to oversee the publication of his unfinished manuscripts. One manuscript in particular, on the subject of Irish ecclesiastical architecture, caught his interest to such an extent that he eventually decided to take personal responsibility for its completion. The project was to occupy four years of his life, as he travelled all across Ireland in search of ecclesiastical remains. The 4th earl observed of his father that 'with the exception of Tory Island in the County of Donegal, I don't think that there is a single island or barony in Ireland containing anything of architectural value which escaped his notice'.[20] Sadly, Edwin's failing health prevented him from completing his work. The results of his research were edited by the Irish antiquarian Margaret Stokes and published posthumously in two volumes of *Notes on Irish architecture* in 1875 and 1877.

Edwin's bibliophilism is reflected in the very fabric of Adare Manor. In the 1860s, he converted the large drawing room on the ground floor at Adare Manor into a library, while the original and much smaller library was demoted to a billiard room.[21] While the new library continued to be used as a drawing room, it served a double function as Edwin's study. He also kept various book lists, including a wish-list of 'books on Irish History &c. which I ought to have' and a record of his purchases between 1869 and 1871.[22] The quantity of these purchases – 146 titles in 1870 alone – is tantamount to bulk purchasing and indicative of a conscious effort to build a scholarly library on the subjects of religion, history,

18 'The late earl of Dunraven', *Archaeological Journal*, 29:1 (1872), p. 79. **19** Ibid., p. 82.
20 Dunraven, E. Wyndham Quin, earl of, *Notes on Irish architecture*, ed. Margaret Stokes, 2 vols (London, 1875–7), i, p. xiv. **21** See plan of Adare Manor, *Memorials of Adare Manor, by Caroline, countess of Dunraven: with historical notices of Adare by her son, the earl of Dunraven* (1865), Plate 10. **22** Assorted lists of books compiled by the 3rd earl, 1860s (ULDP,

natural history, natural sciences and biography. Indeed, we may go as far as to say that the library as sold in 1982 was primarily of Edwin's creation.

WINDHAM THOMAS THE ADVENTURER

The 4th earl (fig. 10.4) inherited from his father not only his title but his extensive library. Using books published after Edwin's death in 1871 as a yardstick, it is clear that the 4th earl did not share his father's interest in book collecting: in the forty-five years of Windham's earldom, the library in Adare grew by just 300 titles or about seven books per year. Moreover, this accumulation was dominated by fiction, biography and memoir with strongly feminine undertones, suggestive perhaps of the reading habits of the 4th earl's wife and four daughters rather than those of himself. This does not, however, mean that he had no interest in books. From the other additions made to the library between 1872 and 1926 it is evident that father and son shared an interest in history, archaeology and travel. With such an extensive library on these subjects at his disposal, there was little need for Windham to extend it. Here, we are also faced with one of the weaknesses of sales catalogues as research sources. In his autobiography, *Past times and pastimes*, the 4th earl mentions a number of books he had enjoyed – Lord Dufferin's *Yacht voyage* (1859), Major Heckstall Smith's *The complete yachtsman* (1912), Owen Wister's *The Virginian: a horseman on the plains* (1902) and Sir Edwin Arnold's *The light of Asia, or the great renunciation* (1879):[23] not one of these titles feature in the 1975 or the 1982 catalogues. It is likely that these works never made their way to Adare from the 4th earl's London residence, where he spent much of his time as MP.

Windham's literary interests also extended to writing. He began his career as a war correspondent for the *Daily Telegraph* and as his first assignment was sent to Africa to cover the Abyssinian War in 1868 at the age of twenty-six. He later came to own several works on the subject, including a copy of *A history of the Abyssinian expedition* (1869) written by Clements Markham, who served as geographer to the Abyssinian expeditionary force. His next writing venture, undertaken jointly with his father, was a book on spiritualism. Windham's childhood was dominated by the crisis caused by his father's conversion to the Roman Catholic faith and did much to contribute to his atheism. 'Consider the controversy that I was so early plunged into,' he recalled, '[t]old on the one hand that Roman Catholicism was the sure road to indescribable physical agony, and on the other that it offered the only certain means of escape! The inevitable consequence was indifference, hardening into disbelief in anything; and for the subsequent reaction spiritualism has something to say.'[24] His book, *Experiments*

D3196/L/8). **23** Dunraven, W.T. Wyndham Quin, earl of, *Past times and pastimes*, 2 vols (1922), i, pp 41, 58, 74, 183. **24** Ibid., i, pp 9–10.

10.4 Windham Thomas Wyndham Quin, 4th earl of Dunraven, by F.A. Swaine, *post* 1904.
© National Portrait Gallery, London.

in spiritualism, outlined his experiences with the celebrated Scottish medium Daniel Douglas Home, whom he had met while recovering from a rheumatic attack at a hydropathy clinic at Malvern in 1867.[25] Some seventy copies of the book were privately printed in 1869, but most were subsequently withdrawn, possibly as a consequence of his father's conversion and the dim view taken on the publication by the Roman Catholic church.[26]

The 4th earl was a progressive landlord with a distinguished political career, who found relief from his heavy professional duties in travel. The library in Adare contained more than 200 travel books, and although many of these were purchased by Edwin, there can be little doubt that their most enthusiastic consumer was his son. Here could be found Fridtjof Nansen's *Eskimo life* (1893), J.D. Hooker's *Himalayan journals* (1854) and several works by the intrepid explorer R.F. Burton. Windham had a particular fascination for North America, where he spent his honeymoon in 1869 and where he returned in 1874 to explore Yellowstone Park and the great geological divide of the Rocky Mountains. This later journey inspired him to write his own travel book, *The great divide* (1876), the title of which led to a degree of confusion among readers, as Windham recalled in his memoirs: 'Some clergy bought it supposing it to be a theological work expounding the separation of the sheep and the goats; but, if I remember right, the book did not rely much upon that, and had a pretty good sale.'[27] The positive response encouraged him to publish two further travel books, *Canadian nights* (1914) and *Hunting in the Yellowstone* (1917). Another consequence of the 4th earl's interest in America was his experimentation with tobacco-growing in Adare. The Adare Cigarette Company Ltd was established in 1911 and enjoyed modest success until a series of crop failures and marketing problems caused by a change of Commonwealth status for Irish products forced the winding up of the business in 1922.[28]

The 4th earl is perhaps best remembered as a yachtsman. Yachting and sailing were pastimes enjoyed by several generations of the family owing to the proximity of the Maigue River, which ran through the estate on its way to the Shannon just 18km away. The 2nd earl was elected president of the Royal Western Yacht Club in 1832,[29] and regattas formed an important part of the family's summer schedule. Windham's love affair with sailing began as a teenager with the purchase of his first yacht in 1856.[30] In the 1890s, he made two unsuccessful attempts to win the America's Cup, a match race held between the yacht club that currently holds the trophy and one from a challenging club. Windham's library contained copious bound sets of *Hunt's Yachting Magazine*

25 Ibid., p. 10. **26** J. Webb, 'Introduction' in Viscount Adare, *Experiences in spiritualism with Mr D.D. Home* (New York, 1976), [n.p.]. **27** Dunraven, *Past times*, i, p. 87. **28** E. Kennedy, 'Tobacco growing in Limerick' in D. Lee and D. Jacobs (eds), *Made in Limerick: a history of trades, industries and commerce vol. 2* (Limerick, 2006), pp 113–14. **29** *Tipperary Free Press*, 18 Mar. 1832. **30** Countess Caroline's journal, 7–8 Aug. 1856 (ULDP, uncatalogued item).

and several books on sailing and yacht building, to which was added his own yachting guide, *Self-instruction in the practice and theory of navigation*, in 1908.

CONCLUSIONS

Although the contents of the library at Adare Manor extended from the mid-sixteenth to the mid-twentieth century, in essence it was a nineteenth-century collection and, as such, served as a remarkable record of subjects that dominated the Victorian age: architectural revolution, the rise of science, religious conflict and diversity, and the increasing modernization of society. Moreover, it is evident that family members were generally and sometimes personally engaged with these topics.

Exploring the catalogues relating to this library brings to light a number of conclusions. First, while each generation contributed to its contents, it was essentially the creation of the 3rd earl of Dunraven and, as such, reflects the exceptionally broad spectrum of his interests. In so doing, it also reveals the great personal dilemmas of his life: religious conversion and subsequent attempts to find balance in the conflict between faith and science. Second, while its range of topics is common to many country house libraries, the reasons for the acquisition of certain books remain deeply individual. A sales catalogue can tell us *what* books were there but not *why* they were there. Although certain generalizations can be made, a full understanding of a collection is difficult without knowledge of family or individual history. The converse is also true: knowing the contents of a library can considerably enrich our understanding of the mind and interests of its owner. In the case of Adare, it allows us access to the mind of a dedicated scholar.

Lastly, it is accepted that country house libraries are difficult to categorize in terms of the way they were created. Bulk purchases, indiscriminate accumulation and active collecting can all play a role in a library that spans several generations, as was the case in Adare. An examination of the library at Adare Manor also tells us that books did not merely sit idle on their shelves. They entertained, educated, diverted and transported both physically and intellectually. In a word, they mattered to the family who owned them.

Photographers and antiquarians in Paris: Goddard Orpen and Eugène Atget

JEREMY HILL

In 1891, an exasperated Goddard Orpen (1852–1932) of Monksgrange believed his personal demand for high standards was not being met, exclaiming to his wife, Adela: 'I think I have finished with photography!' Fortunately for history and photography, he had a change of heart – evidenced by the surprising recent discovery of an accrual of 110 glass plate negatives of a visit to Paris in 1899. Accompanying him was his wife, Adela, and their two children; though not a photographer, Adela was a competent watercolourist, as was her husband.

Orpen was born in 1852, the third son of lawyer John Orpen who lived at 58 St Stephen's Green, Dublin. He had a privileged upbringing, which he honoured in a life of quiet achievement as an author and scholar in aspects of human society and culture. At the Abbey School in Tipperary town, winning a silver medal in history in his first term was a portend of his later distinction as a scholar of medieval history.[1] He was also a competitive games player. Orpen won an entrance exhibition to Trinity College Dublin in 1869, graduating with several first-class honours and a scholarship in classics. Destined for the Bar at the behest of his father, he then studied Roman law. Finding work at the Bar disagreeable, Orpen turned towards historical and antiquarian research. His ability as a translator resulted in a version in English of Emile Laveleye's *Le socialisme contemporain*,[2] but of more substance was his translation *The song of Dermot and the earl*.[3] The original French poem, from a thirteenth-century Carew manuscript at Lambeth Palace, was written in Old or Anglo-Norman French, and chronicled the arrival of Strongbow in Ireland in 1170 and the subsequent arrival of Henry II of England; it is a poetic history of the arrival of the Normans in Ireland's south-east. The Royal Society of Antiquaries of Ireland, of which Goddard was a member, and ultimately president, published numerous papers by him in its annual journals. Adela Orpen (1855–1927) spent her first decade in America, to where her father had emigrated in 1849. On the family's return to Ireland in 1866, her education continued with enrolment at schools in Paris and conservatoires in Leipzig and Siena, leading to her becoming a published author of novels, an autobiography and journal articles; she also became proficient at the piano and violin.

---

[1] G.H. Orpen, *Ireland under the Normans, 1169–1333*, 4 vols (Oxford, 1911–20). [2] Émile de Laveleye, *The socialism of today*, trans. G.H. Orpen (London, 1884).   [3] G.H. Orpen, G.H.,

11.1 Rue de l'Échaudé, watercolour, Adela Orpen, 1899, Monksgrange Archives.

Goddard's exact contemporary, French photographer Eugène Atget (1857–1927), was born in south-west France; he had ambitions for theatre work but became an important documentary photographer. A studio sign above his shop in the fifth arrondissement announced his business as '*Documents pour artistes*'. The sign declared his modest ambition of providing other artists with images to use as source material in their own work; his inventory included landscapes, animals, flowers, monuments, documents, foregrounds for painters, and reproductions of paintings. His feel for the past, awakened by his 'documents for artists', led him to describe himself as 'E. Atget, creator and purveyor of a collection of photographic views of old Paris'. His stock of thousands of photographs of 'vieux Paris' is considered a pioneering project of its time and a large selection is held by the Museum of Modern Art, New York, while further collections are in the Bibliothèque Nationale, the Bibliothèque Historique de la ville de Paris, the École des Beaux-Arts, the Musée Carnavalet and the Service Photographique des Monuments Historiques. Atget became the ultimate flâneur, a uniquely French characterization, referring to someone who was a close observer of the beauty, fashion, lifestyle and industrial transformation of Paris.

As the narrow streets and cobbled laneways of medieval Paris wound their random way through the city, they occasionally created attenuated interstices at which were built narrow, prow-shaped houses known as 'demeures à étraves'.[5] It is easy to fail to notice these buildings of little significant, historical interest, but, once spotted, their curious structure is compelling. Strolling up Rue de Seine one spring morning in 1899, Goddard and Adela were intrigued by the building before them at the intersection with Rue de l'Échaudé; each painted a simple watercolour of the scene. The sketches helped them to analyse the opportunities of the location in terms of composition and light with the ultimate objective of photographing the place (figs. 11.1 and 11.2).

The Orpens had brought their two children with them to Paris for a three-month visit; the intention was to advance Goddard's research into the medieval period and to open a cultural opportunity for the rest of the family. He was seeking an understanding of medieval life through the surviving buildings, as he considered the prospect of extended research into the history of Norman Ireland. Goddard's Paris photographs from early-1899 record buildings relevant to this growing interest. In the district of Saint-Germain-des-Prés, and close by, he photographed the Pantheon, the Church of St Étienne du Mont, the Luxembourg Gardens, the Sorbonne, Les Invalides, Pont Neuf and Hôtel de Cluny; each building had pre-revolution origins.

The song of Dermot and the earl (Oxford, 1892).   **5** This French description refers to the likeness to the prow of a ship.

11.2 Rue de l'Échaudé, watercolour, Goddard Orpen, 1899, Monksgrange Archives.

It had been thirty years since Adela (then Richards) had first encountered Paris, when she was enrolled as a pupil at the schools of Madames Nigault and Rouyère; her schooldays were influential and these memorable times were recalled through souvenirs such as the *cartes de visite* images of Napoleon III and Empress Eugénie she purchased in 1869.[6] She had visited the studios of photographer J. Vallette at 39 Rue de Seine and A.A.J. Le Jeune at 22 Rue Choisel. The latter address was formerly the location of American daguerreotypist Warren Thompson who was followed in 1859 by Sergei Levitsky, father of Russian empire photography and one of Europe's most important early photographic pioneers. Adela's enquiring mind, even at fifteen years old, is unlikely to have ignored the studio titles on her cards and, almost certainly, she learned later of their significance. She must have had, at the least, a comfortable feeling of familiarity, a frisson of homecoming on subsequent visits to 'la Ville Lumière'. Thus, her husband had an assistant acquainted with photography and familiar with art and the city.

Orpen's photograph of Rue de l'Échaudé is of such quality that its making requires consideration. His photography is informed by his knowledge of fine art as an intellectual discipline, where the rationality of a painting is fundamental. A collection of his drawings and watercolours demonstrates his skill and understanding of the theory and techniques of art which induced a considered approach to his photography. He did not take snaps.

After his marriage to Adela Richards in 1880, the newly-weds moved to London's Bedford Park and purchased a house in the early garden suburb inspired by the Aesthetic Movement of the 1870s. Neighbours included the Yeats family; Elizabeth (Lolly) Yeats, later to form the Dun Emer and Cuala Presses in Dublin, taught the Orpen children at primary school. The Orpens thrived in the stimulating, cultural atmosphere of political, artistic and literary conversation at The Club, a private recreation centre for Bedford Park residents. The egalitarian principles of The Club are seen in an engraving where the room is shared by men and women though the dominant compositional placing of a lady at the reading table over the male-attended billiard table suggests the superiority of mind over matter.

Embracing photography, Orpen's camera became an important tool in recording the Gaelic, medieval and contemporary worlds that were now a centre of interest. In 1894, he purchased wood carving tools, a primer titled *Hints on wood carving* and two oak panels. The artist in him was taking an interest in another branch of the visual arts: an exploration into the three dimensionality of sculpture, demonstrated in his creation of Celtic decorative motifs on the newly acquired panels. He attended Irish language lessons and in 1896 joined the Chancery Lane branch of the Gaelic League. Philip Bull has noted how

---

6 The three *cartes de visite* are in the collection of Monksgrange Archives, uncatalogued.

essential was his learning Irish in order to pursue his interests in medieval Ireland.[7]

Orpen's intellectual capacity encouraged an eclecticism that is evident in the body of his photography. Apart from his historical interest in the classics, he enjoyed the cultural experience of visiting ancient sites on his many European trips with family members. He stood by railway lines to photograph the power and might of the steam engine, the fastest thing on wheels at the end of the nineteenth century. He thrilled to the might of warships at the Spithead coronation naval review of 1902. He encountered the sublime in the Alps and the city of dreams in Florence, and photographed farm labourers in the fields of Italy, France and Ireland. Although not alone in these interests, Orpen's imagery conveys a developed sensibility, sensitivity and humanity towards his subjects. He was also a modernist, aware of the changing world.

In the sixty years since the invention of Louis Daguerre's photographic process, photography had attracted a burgeoning number of practitioners, both amateurs and professionals, although the equipment required – a large format camera, tripod and glass plate negatives – was bulky and heavy, requiring skill, organization and operational planning. Goddard's photographs would be personal aides-mémoire and his knowledge of aesthetics, composition and light as a practising painter carried into his photographic imagery. While the corpus of Orpen's camera work, held at Monksgrange Archives,[8] remains largely unexamined and little known, his four-volume history, *Ireland under the Normans*, is still regarded as a seminal work. Through his photography, a rapidly developing medium of documentation in the late nineteenth century, he recorded landscape, portraits, antiquity, architecture, archaeology, genre and industrial mechanization; a younger cousin was the distinguished portraitist and official war artist, Sir William Orpen. While not strictly a professional photographer, he sold prints to friends and family; his eye was for authenticity, not commerce.

Following Goddard's studied observation of the scene on Rue de Seine, he began organizing his equipment and camera position. The actual practice of taking a photograph in those days was cumbersome, with heavy cameras, tripods and glass plate negatives. The principle behind the operation of the camera was similar to the camera obscura used by artists such as Vermeer. A hole in the front of a box allowed light to pass through to the back surface and the operator could then outline the projected image and transfer it to his canvas. Inside the box camera, at the back, was another box which held the glass plate and which could be slid forward to adjust the image size, and tilted to reduce distortion. The removal of a lens cover for a guesswork period of seconds perhaps qualified the

---

7 P.J. Bull, *Monksgrange – portrait of an Irish house and family, 1769–1969* (Dublin, 2019), p. 176.   8 Monksgrange Archives, owned by the Edward Richards-Orpen Memorial Trust, is located at Monksgrange, Co. Wexford.

photographer as a manual labourer. There were no light meters, though books of tables were available. A shoot required patience and thought; exposure time, now calculated automatically by the camera or phone, was based on guesswork that improved with experience. It was necessary to take several exposures to insure against mistiming with the lens cap and this added to the cost of the eventually selected image. Movement of people or objects during the exposure more often than not spoiled the result; occasionally, perhaps by design, it lent an unexpected overall improvement. Examination of the body of Orpen's work suggests that his timing intuition was accurate and his artistic knowledge heightened the resulting quality of his camera work. To what extent the photographers were taking a message from the contemporary artists – the Impressionists liked immediacy – might be explored in Orpen's and Atget's work, since both men must surely have been aware of the new art in the galleries of Paris at the turn of the century.

Robert Rauschenberg, an early leader of the Pop Art movement in 1960s New York, was an enthusiastic photographer who disliked well composed images. 'One gets as much information as a witness of activity from a fleeting glance, like a quick look, sometimes in motion, as one does staring at the subject,' he has said, adding, 'because even if you remain stationary your mind wanders and it's that kind of activity that I would like to get into the photograph.'[9] How would he have considered the earlier images of these early protagonists? The compositions are clearly considered, but what of the fleeting glance given how the author's/artist's eye is involved in the lens cap operation? Rauschenberg's observation was made decades after Atget and Orpen created their early morning images of stillness (fig. 11.3).

Orpen selected his camera location about 10 degrees left of square to the front face of the prow of the building; this opened the view of the Rue de Seine side of the subject building, that had been closed off by Atget. The angle also opened up the far end of Rue de l'Échaudé, intensifying interest in what might be found in the hazy distance. The close positioning of the kerbside cart with its load of soda water forces a contrasting element between its seeming instability, accentuated by the tilt of the nearside wheel, which dips into the gutter, and the authoritative rigidity of the older building. The dynamic projected by the kerbs, as in the watercolours, pushes the eye up onto the feature of the image. Dynamic elements defeat the tonal difference between the street level's light and contrast and the building's hazy softness in the battle for attention from the two major sections of the composition's lower and upper halves.

At that time of day, the streets were populated; dawn had given way to morning sun, allowing the light to reveal the surface of the street as it spread from the left-hand pavement, through the gutter, over the curved ridge and on to the opposite gutter and pavement. The left-hand kerb and gutter are defined

---

9 P. Gefter, 'Transmuting forms, click by click', *New York Times*, 17 Oct. 2013.

11.3 Rue de l'Échaudé, photograph, Goddard Orpen, 1899. Monksgrange Archives, GOAP 0373.

by dark water, while across the street the definition is made by shadow. This subtle distinction was not played to advantage by Atget in his image. Another contrast between Atget and Orpen is with the two gentlemen in the mid foreground of Orpen's image, with one clearly defined and immobile on the pavement, whilst the other is blurred, striding with purpose across the traffic free square. Behind them are several more figures, the first seeming to hurry, others strolling or chatting. Rauschenberg's liking for the fleeting glance is satisfied in Goddard's image.

In Montparnasse, Eugène Atget rose one morning in 1905 and walked from his home to his chosen spot for the day's shoot. He generally favoured the soft quality of early morning light, but here, the sun was up and giving good tonal contrast on the walls of the prow. Again, a delivery cart was parked on Rue de Seine and a shopkeeper stood watching the unusual sight of a photographer. Atget had set his tripod on the awkward cobbled surface which sloped down towards the gutter but set up a good aspect towards the central subject. However, his camera position was too far back to invite the eye up Rue de l'Échaudé, which Goddard's camera position had enabled. Also of interest is the absence of soft, diffuse light that Atget customarily worked in, but Orpen has finely exploited it in his. Had Orpen's work not preceded Atget's by six years it might almost seem that Orpen had obtained an Atget 'document' and copied the composition (fig. 11.4).

Atget considered his 'documents for artists' merely as models for use in the way plaster casts were once used in art school drawing classes. There was no inherent need on the part of the user of his documents for quality compositional or structural devices so the subject in his documents was invariably in the centre. The narrow angle between the two sides of the demeure à étrave on Rue de Seine allows its central compositional position to defy consideration of the rule of thirds; in this case, the structural strength of the lines of the kerbs diverging into the distance complete the integrity of the image. Atget returned to this site in 1911 and 1924 and recorded images from several different camera positions; in making prints from his negatives, he varied the exposure to obtain differing tones. The fact that both men maximized the compositional potential in front of them in similar ways, but with different results in terms of quality, opens up an interesting comparative perspective on the work of these contemporaries.

A comparative analysis of the men's images, with the watercolours added as a further reference, pits an unknown individual against a well-known professional and, in this instance, quality trumps reputation. Goddard Orpen made his luck in creating an exceptional image by understanding just what it took to raise his image over the ordinary. Haussmann's wrecking ball may have buried old Paris beneath the new – now forever haunted by the haze-enveloped demeure à étrave wreathed in the mystery of light by a master craftsman.

11.4 Rue de l'Échaudé, photograph, Eugène Atget, 1905. Musée Carnavalet, PH7389.

In time, Atget would become widely regarded for his project and his images were collected by national institutions. His vision influenced the emergence of the Surrealist artists who found his pictures beguiling and suggestive. His work was brought to light by Berenice Abbott, an American photographer living in Paris, who was a studio assistant to Man Ray, moving within the circle of the Dadaists and Surrealists. Abbott's ownership of Atget's collection after his death resulted in its acquisition by New York's Museum of Modern Art (MOMA) in 1967. 'The Atget prints,' wrote Ansel Adams, an advisor to MOMA, 'are direct and emotionally clean records of a rare and subtle perception and represent perhaps the earliest expression of true photographic art'.[10] His earliest photographs date from 1888, some forty years before his death.

A phenomenon known as vignetting is a feature of many of Atget's photographs; a dark circular arc appears at the top corners and seen at top left in his 1905 image of Rue de Seine. It arises from the tilt-shift technique used to correct the distortion of converging verticals. A lens has an ellipsoid, biconvex shape. It is thicker in the middle than at the edge. Refraction of light passing through the lens increases as its point of entry/exit moves from centre to edge causing distortion to the projected image on the plate negative. The lens standard (the front face of a box camera) can be raised to leverage the covering power of the lens, the intention of which is to counter the physics which would otherwise compromise the vertical components. The balancing of covering power, focal length and width of lens angle are all part of the skill of the photographer. More of one can mean less of the others. But, the need to move the old camera standard has been made redundant in the digital age; image manipulation software can now correct distortions with the quick click of a mouse.

It appears that Atget may have used a wide-angle lens for his photographs of buildings, giving him a wider angle of view in tight spaces, but compromising the rise of the lens standard, which results in his 'signature' vignettes.[11] Orpen, on the other hand, seems to have used a longer focal length, also ideal for portraiture. He is most likely to have had at least two lenses, interchangeable in less than two minutes. There is no evidence in any of his plates that he had ever used the 'wrong' lens; this further indicates his overall technical awareness.

Orpen and Atget, though close in age, came from backgrounds poles apart. Goddard's father was a lawyer whose wife, Ellen Richards, descended from a family of knighted, landed gentry. Money, land and titles do not guarantee recognition and success; equally, neither did Atget's humble beginnings from birth in the town of Libourne in 1857 to orphandom at the age of five. The

---

10 A. Adams in *The Fortnightly* (San Francisco), 1:5 (5 Nov. 1931), 25, quoted in 'Eugène Atget French, 1857–1927', https://www.moma.org/artists/229, accessed 15 Jan. 2024.
11 R. Hirsch, 'Atget, Jean-Eugène-Auguste' in M.R. Peres (ed.), *Focal encyclopedia of photography: digital imaging, theory and applications, history, and science* (4th ed., Burlington,

town's three ancient buildings – a restored Gothic church with its 71-metre-high stone spire, a sixteenth-century town house in the square (and now a museum), and a machicolated clock-tower on the river quay, a survivor of the fourteenth-century town walls – all bear witness to its medieval origins that are likely to have imprinted themselves on the young Atget, and Jean-Claude Lemagny found Atget 'a man deeply rooted in the past'.[12]

However, these two very different people came together as equals behind the lens of the camera. Goddard's wide-ranging intellect encouraged an eclecticism in his photography. Apart from his historical interest in the classics, he enjoyed the cultural experience of visiting ancient sites on his many European trips. He engaged with a wide variety of people, one day lunching with Sir Frederick Leighton when art would have been a likely topic of conversation. Just like his contemporary, Eugène Atget, Goddard liked the ordinary and the unsophisticated.

In technique, both were notably advanced, even though they were self-taught. This, however, raises the question of whether Atget's knowledge of lenses was quite what it might have been, whereas we know Orpen had been experimenting in photography since 1880. Their common interest in the built heritage of Paris is likely to have been purely coincidental, yet their driving motivations differed. Orpen was essentially an amateur, while Atget was a professional photographer with a shop as an outlet. Orpen was seeking personal insight into medieval life as a necessary part of his research for his magnum opus. Atget needed an income, and his objective of commercial success was based on his intuited camera ability rather than learning. He intended his images to be photographic documents devoid of any hidden meaning or sentiment; they were to be objective records rather than artistic photographs. Orpen's knowledge, accumulated through education and upbringing, insisted on the insertion of artistic parameters to his work, a consideration absent in Atget though not necessarily to his detriment. It is the viewer who has determined the artistic and professional importance of Atget's work despite the artist's previously declared modest approach. Another notable difference between the two is that Atget singularly avoided portraiture; no image exists of his friends or acquaintances, few though they appear to have been.[13] Some of his images are populated but in a generic role rather than as portrait studies; his street traders series is more about the merchandise than the merchant. Devoid of people, Atget's 'documents' embody the Atget aesthetic – 'the uncanny feeling of being abandoned in a communal space.'[14] The acquisition by institutions of Atget's work, sparked by the initial interest of Man Ray, led essayists and academics to begin the process of critical assessment. This brought

MA, 2007), pp 241–2. 12 Lemagny was a photographic historian and conservator at the Bibliothèque Nationale. 13 J. Szarkowski and M.M. Hambourg, *The work of Atget. Volume 1: old France* (New York, 1981). 14 M. Kosloff, 'Abandoned and seductive: Atget's streets' in idem, *The privileged eye: essays on photography* (Albuquerque, 1987), p. 288.

about the metamorphosis of the humble 'document' into art, something Atget disdained though it might have allowed him to be seen as a historian of his own time.

The questions now arise as to whether these two men ever met and whether they were aware of each other's images. The probability is that they were not acquainted. Orpen came to Paris with a specific purpose in mind. If he had come across an Atget 'document', it is unlikely to have satisfied his personal aims; Orpen wanted the feeling of the places he photographed, not just their look. It is possible Atget might have heard that another photographer had been to 'his' sites but he had no reason to engage with him. Had they encountered one another, Orpen would likely have enjoyed a conversation with Atget, but it appears from what little is known about him that Frenchman might not have reciprocated the feeling, as he and his partner kept largely to themselves.

Pursuing similar interests both Orpen and Atget ventured to capture records of ancient buildings and palaces, working boats on the Seine, parks and gardens, memorial arches, churches and statuary. Occasionally losing sight of his topical quarry, Orpen found humour in the Versailles pelicans, leisure in a family cycle ride through the forest at Fontainebleau and diversion by a locomotive at Sceaux's station, rather than the charms of the duke of Trévise's Chateaux and its park designed by André le Notre. Atget was diverted by flowers, horse-drawn carriages, shop fronts, street merchants and women of the night. The task for Atget was inexorable, for Orpen it was transitory – always another time, another place.

Orpen's compositions were improved by the inclusion of people, whereas Atget was happy to leave them out or, at most, give them a subsidiary role. Atget was not altogether without feeling, he is known to have ventured into the 'Zone,' a narrow strip of clear ground at the foot of the protective fortifications of the city erected in 1844; this area soon became filled with the shacks and flimsy dwellings of the poor and unemployed, who had been forgotten by the social transformation of Haussmann's urban renewal. Visitors were few for fear of the reaction that might arise from their intrusion into a tight-knit community whose inhabitants were seen as social outcasts. Atget's reserve may also have prevented personal engagement with the Zoniers in their space, so he peered from the edges; nonetheless, he did produce compassionate images of these people and their plight.

There was no such reserve in Orpen. He was quite able to cast off the aloofness of many of his class and, thereby, gain the confidence of members of *an lucht siúil*, 'the walking people', also known as Travellers, a nomadic indigenous ethnic group in Ireland. His cycle of peasantry images comprises about twenty-five works made in Ireland, France and Italy. Orpen's images cover a period of some fifty years and include a range of subjects photographed in Ireland, Wales, England, France, Italy and Greece. The collection at

Monksgrange indicates how Orpen's interest ranged from everyday images of family to academic research into history and archaeology. While few records exist documenting the time, date, location or subject of his images, evidence from diaries, journals and letters are helping to furnish some information.

Eugène Atget had an ambition to be a painter, a skill he does not appear to have developed, though one unlocated painting has been attributed to him. His artistic talents were manifested in glass plates and acetate negatives rather than on canvas. Goddard Orpen could draw, paint, carve, and photograph, and these skills were in addition to his expert abilities as a researcher, scholar, historian, antiquarian and author. There is thus a polymathic quality to the intellectual world of Monksgrange, these complementary disciplines denoting a restless and inquisitive mind on the part of its owner.

From muniment room to online access: family and estate archives at Cowdray House, Knole and Ham House

ELIZABETH JAMIESON

Written thoughts, ideas and accounts are the vehicle by which we understand the country house. These, together with the buildings and their remaining contents, comprise the bedrock of our research. As our reliance on all things digital continues to grow exponentially, it is very easy to lose touch with, or to completely ignore, the materiality of the documents and papers that have been preserved in country house archives and, latterly, in county record offices and history centres. By looking at the history of the three archives that are the focus of this essay, we can consider how far their eventual survival has depended on careful management and how far on sheer happenstance.

From the seventeenth to the late twentieth century, country house archives were more commonly referred to as muniments. Strictly speaking, muniments is a collective term for the documents, such as charters and title-deeds, relating to a property and to the rights and privileges of a family which are kept as 'evidences' for defending the same. Early country house inventories often refer to a muniment or evidence room, which was the place where these papers were stored. Inevitably, once this type of information began to be retained, then maps and drawings, household accounts, bills, letters and inventories would be stored with them – the sorts of papers which are especially interesting to country house historians. In his 1661 dictionary *Glossographia*, Thomas Blount published perhaps the earliest definition of the term 'Muniment House' as follows: '… a house or little room of strength purposely made for keeping the Seal, Plate, Evidences, Charters etc … such Evidences being called in Law Muniments … from munio, to defend; because man's inheritance or possession is defended by them'.[1]

The importance of these muniments or evidences was that they were absolutely essential for establishing the 'rights' of the ruling elites to the land and property that they managed. It was necessary that this vital paperwork be stored in a special building or space, ideally fireproof and protected from excess heat, damp and prying eyes. Such a place was usually locked or otherwise sealed by

---

[1] Thomas Blount, *Glossographia: or A dictionarie interpreting hard words* (London, 1661), quoted in G.H. Fowler, *The care of county muniments* (London, 1928), p. v.

12.1 The muniment room of Magdalen College, University of Oxford © Magdalen College.

heavy, sometimes iron-clad doors to increase security. The rooms themselves often shared many of the same characteristics: stone walls and rooves, tiled floors, high, often barred, windows, and walls lined with wooden shelves or drawers. There might also be wooden or metal trunks on the floor. The advantage, of course, of trunks was that they could be easily moved, which was convenient for families who had multiple houses or who led peripatetic lives, as many did.

There are a surprising number of surviving muniment rooms in England. The earliest of these chambers were not in country houses, but in abbeys, cathedrals and university colleges. The muniment room at Westminster Abbey, for example, was built in the thirteenth century and still has its tiled floors and ancient wooden chests. The adjacent library is housed in the former Benedictine monks' dormitory. Another early example is the late fifteenth-century muniment room at Magdalen College, Oxford, whose walls are lined with cupboards containing wooden boxes, some of which still have their medieval labels attached[2] (fig. 12.1).

Perhaps one of the first and most beautiful, dedicated country house muniment rooms is the evidence house at Hardwick Hall in Derbyshire. The space comprises two adjoining rooms, the inner of which is lined floor-to-ceiling with exquisitely crafted oak drawers of varying sizes, together with iron-clad trunks and boxes. The evidence house was built in around 1603 and contained all the important documents relating to the household and estate. Hardwick Hall was the administrative centre for the Cavendish family's northern land holdings throughout the seventeenth century, and although it ceased to hold that position in later centuries, the contents of the drawers remained in situ at Hardwick as late as 1989, when they were eventually transferred to join the rest of the Hardwick archive at Chatsworth House in Derbyshire.[3] Other surviving country house muniment rooms include the charter room at Hopetoun House near South Queensferry, built in 1706, and fitted with wooden shelves on which are stored small tin trunks, and the muniment room situated in one of the corner pavilions at Badminton House, Gloucestershire, completed in 1758 to an earlier design by James Gibbs.

The free-standing furniture used to store muniments advanced as time went on. Steane makes the distinction between chests that were suitable for travelling (round topped coffers, whose lids were more rain resistant) versus those designed to stay in one place (larger and flat-lidded, sometimes with feet).[4] Of the latter type, at St Mary's Church in Bruton, a thirteenth-century muniment chest from the north tower now stands at the entrance to the nave (fig. 12.2). Lady Margaret Beaufort's travelling chest covered in red painted leather and with twenty compartments inside was designed for travel; it belongs to the National Archives and is the pair to one in Westminster Abbey.[5] Interestingly, the National Archives (UK) owns one of the most important collections of medieval muniment chests dating from 1255 to 1600, which belonged to the Exchequer Treasury of Receipt and was formerly kept in the chapter room of Westminster Abbey. In 1859, the Public Record Office was established in Chancery Lane as a safer place for royal and state papers, and the chests which contained them were transferred at the same time.[6] Among country house collections is an extraordinary large wooden

---

2 For a fascinating account of early church and college muniment rooms and their associated furnishings, see J. Steane, 'Medieval muniment rooms, their furniture, fittings and information retrieval systems', *Transactions of the Ancient Monuments Society*, 54 (2010), pp 35–50.   3 D. Adshead and D. Taylor (eds), *Hardwick Hall: a great old castle of romance* (New Haven, CT, 2016), p. 330.   4 Steane, 'Medieval muniment rooms', p. 44.   5 TNA, E27/6, illustrated in C. Jenning, *Early chests in wood and iron*, PRO Museum Pamphlets no. 7, (HMSO, London, 1974), p. 8. Unfortunately, the chest was lost in 1985, possibly when it was moved from Chancery Lane to Kew.   6 Exchequer: Treasury of the Receipt, chests I–XI (TNA, E27). In 1859, the Chapter House's archival holdings were transferred to the Public Record Office in Chancery Lane. The chests that contained them were kept on display at the

12.2 Thirteenth-century chest at St Mary's Church, Bruton. Author's image.

chest, covered in sealskin, evidently made from a hollowed-out tree trunk, that sits beside one of the upstairs bedrooms at Chastleton House in Oxfordshire.[7] As time went on, and papers no longer needed to be transported so frequently, lockable cupboards, presses and chests of drawers were also used for the storage of important documents. At Shavington Hall in Shropshire, the family and estate records were kept in a 'large standing cupboard with numerous pigeon holes, and in a huge chest' before being moved to a dedicated muniment room. The reason for the move was that the records had 'overflowed their proper receptacles and were piled indiscriminately on the floor', as noted by Henry D. Harrod F.S.A., who produced an elaborately printed and bound catalogue of the collection in 1891.[8] Perhaps, one of the most attractive examples of this later type of storage facility is the set of four large muniment cases at Nostell Priory in

onsite museum until the late 1970s.   7 National Trust, item #1430182.   8 H.D. Harrod, *The muniments of Shavington* (Shrewsbury, 1891), p. 1.

West Yorkshire, designed by Robert Adam for Sir Rowland Winn and his wife Sabine d'Hervart, circa 1776.[9]

Some large collections of family and estate papers were completely separated from the house to which they were related. Rather than being loaned or given to the local record office for preservation, they were sold. Perhaps the most significant collection of British country house archives to leave in this way was the Stowe Archive, comprising nearly 3,500 items relating to the Grenville, Temple, Newton and Brydges families which were sold by Baroness Kinloss at the famous Stowe Sale of 1921. Happily, they were acquired by Henry E. Huntington from a London bookseller shortly afterwards and they have, since then, found a safe home in the Huntington Library in San Marino, California, where they can still be consulted by researchers today.[10]

THE COWDRAY HOUSE FIRE OF 1793

The first collection of papers to be examined in detail is that belonging to Cowdray House in West Sussex. The house exists today as a romantic ruin, following a catastrophic fire in 1793; it belongs to the 4th Viscount Cowdray and is occasionally open to the public. Our knowledge of the archives that were kept at Cowdray largely depends on two very detailed accounts. The first account was published in the 1880s and deals with the fire and its aftermath.[11] The second account was written when the bulk of the archive was acquired by the West Sussex Record Office from Viscount Cowdray in 1954, and at the point when the papers were properly catalogued for the first time (fig. 12.3).

The story of what happened makes disturbing reading. The fire of 1793 began in the north-west tower on the night of 24 September. At that time, the house was being refurbished. It is an all-too-familiar tale: several carpenters were working in a makeshift workshop up in the tower, they made themselves a fire to keep warm and some of the sawdust, which was lying around on the floor, caught alight. The fire spread so quickly that by the next morning, practically the whole house was burnt down. Numerous things went wrong: the key to the separate building that housed the fire hose and buckets could not be found and valuable time was lost trying to drag the door off its hinges.

Luckily, the muniment room was located high up in the kitchen tower at the south end of the building and managed to survive the fire largely intact. However, Elizabeth Browne who had only just inherited the house and its estate from her brother, the 8th Lord Montague, following his tragic death abroad, appears to have been so traumatized by the double disaster of losing her brother

---

9 National Trust, items NT 959803 and NT 959804. The cases are fitted with drawers and pigeonholes in the centre and adjustable shelves to either side.   10 https://oac.cdlib.org/findaid ark:/13030/c8ht2qq9/entire_text/, accessed 2 June 2023.   11 C. Roundell, *Cowdray: the history of a great English house* (London, 1884).

12.3 West view of the ruins of Cowdray House, Sussex, John Buckler, 1825.
Yale Centre for British Art, Paul Mellon Collection.

and her home that she deserted the house and moved to a lodge on the estate instead. Thereafter, no members of the family attempted to repair Cowdray, nor to salvage any of the contents that remained in the house. Roundell records that there 'seems to have been an entire absence of interest in saving what was left of the contents of the house and the whole neighbourhood was allowed to roam through the ruins, carrying away anything that could be moved'.[12] In 1834, a fifteen-year-old boy named Howard Dudley wrote and then subsequently printed and self-published the following account of his visit to the ruins:

> On the South end, is a massive tower of large dimensions, braced with iron, which escaped the fury of the flames; the kitchen occupies the ground floor, and is nearly filled with rubbish: by a winding stair-case, you reach another room, of equal dimensions with the kitchen; the floor is covered with ancient deeds, valuable MSS., and private letters, which are suffered to lie about in wild confusion, submitted to the inspection of every visitor.[13]

12 Ibid., p. 130.   13 H. Dudley, *Juvenile researches, or, A description of some of the principal*

Two years later, a member of the British Archaeological Association noted that one of their members had visited the room which 'having become ruinous and unsafe and many of the papers having been carried away by persons who chanced to visit the ruins, the remainder had been thrown in the closets which surrounded the room, which were then nailed up and the papers left to decay'.[14] When the estate was eventually sold to the 6th earl of Egmont in 1843, a new house was built on the site of the lodge, while the ruin was left untouched.[15] Almost unbelievably – and even with new owners – no attempt was made to save the documents which, for half a century by then, had been left in their scattered and disorganized state in the kitchen tower. A decade later, the Scottish antiquarian, Sir Sibbald Scott, asked to be allowed to visit the ruin, which was by then locked to visitors. He reported that:

> The floor was strewn with parchments and papers; some had been thrust by handfuls into the cupboards, and many were gathered into little heaps in corners where gusts of wind had probably driven them, and where the damp had caused them to adhere in masses, rendering many of them illegible ... more ruthless had been the spoiling hands of casual visitors before the door had been closed to the public. The worst of these – as far as the deeds and court rolls were concerned were the collectors of autographs and seals who had in frequent cases torn off these appendages ... and then flung them down on the floor as valueless.[16]

So, things remained, and despite protests by the local archaeological society, still nothing was done. It was not until the beginning of the twentieth century that what was left of the papers began to appear in scattered locations, as recorded by A.A. Dibben, senior assistant archivist at the West Sussex Record Office in 1960.[17] Three hundred deeds of the estate were presented to the Sussex Archaeological Society in 1934 by their honorary curator, the Revd W. Budgen; one volume, *Title-deeds of Viscount Montagu*, was purchased by the British Museum from a Mrs L. Danby in 1882; fifty documents relating to Sussex, which clearly came from the Cowdray estate records, are now among Lord Spencer's muniments at Althorp House in Northamptonshire. The bulk of the papers though found their way to the West Sussex Record Office in the late 1950s where they remain to this day and where they can be freely consulted.

---

towns in the west of Sussex and the borders of Hants (2nd ed., Eastbourne, 1835), pp 56–7. **14** Roundell, *Cowdray*, p. 137. **15** The house is now called Cowdray Park, as distinct from Cowdray House. **16** Roundell, *Cowdray*, p. 138. **17** A.A. Dibben and A.J. Browne, *The Cowdray archives*, vol. *1* (Chichester, 1960). I am grateful to Diane Ladlow of the West Sussex Record Office for this reference.

NATHANIEL WRAXALL'S INTERVENTIONS AT KNOLE

The second example is from Knole in Kent, a former archbishop's palace situated in a deer park, which has been the home of the Sackville family from the beginning of the seventeenth century. While researching the gatehouse tower, prior to its opening in 2016, it became clear that as well as being the early twentieth-century retreat of Eddie Sackville West, it had also housed the evidence or muniment room for well over 100 years.[18] Vita Sackville-West described it as 'a gate-house flanked by two square grey towers, placed between two wings which provide only a monotony of windows and gables'.[19] This was an ideal space to store valuable papers, since it was high up and relatively inaccessible, owing to its being guarded by the porter who controlled who visited the rooms directly above and surrounding his lodge. The gatehouse tower accessed via a porter or warden's lodgings had long been the preferred location for Oxford College muniment rooms such as those at All Souls, Lincoln and Exeter Colleges.[20]

The 1730 inventory records the following for the evidence room: 'Press wth Writings./ Table leave & fram/Table – 3 old Stools – old Trunk.'[21] A few years later, listed in the evidence room in the 1765 inventory are 'Five old Trunks and two old Boxes with old Writings', together with 'a great deal of lumber' and various old pieces of furniture, and in the inner room a 'Great many Old Writings in bags and Hampers'.[22] Thus, we know that by this date there is an inner and an outer room (as at Hardwick Hall) and that there are a large quantity of papers, some of which are not organized, stored with timber and disused furniture in the gatehouse.

In 1797, John Frederick, 3rd duke of Dorset, appointed the author and politician Sir Nathaniel Wraxall[23] to catalogue and edit the Sackville papers. Wraxall had recently lost his seat as an MP and found a new patron in the duke, who he had been cultivating for some months, presumably in the hope of being offered a position at Knole as his personal librarian. He suggested to the duke that he would be able to arrange and publish the more important papers in the collection, but his involvement in the archive proved disastrous. Having gathered the papers together in one place, Wraxall settled himself at Knole and started trying to arrange them in a way that suited his purpose. In doing this, he wrote notes in ink on all the papers he examined. This not only spoiled the papers, but his comments were often repetitive and unhelpful. His favourite comment seems

---

18 This section draws on an unpublished research report commissioned by the National Trust: see E. Jamieson, 'A survey of the documentary and visual evidence relating to the former appearance and use of the West Range and Gatehouse Tower at Knole' (Sept. 2012). 19 V. Sackville-West, *Knole and the Sackvilles* (London, 1922), p. 3. 20 Steane, 'Medieval muniment rooms', p. 41. 21 From a transcription – the original has been mislaid. 22 Inventory, 1765 (Kent History and Library Centre (KHLC), U269 E4). 23 Sir Nathaniel William Wraxall, first Baronet (1751–1831).

144 *Elizabeth Jamieson*

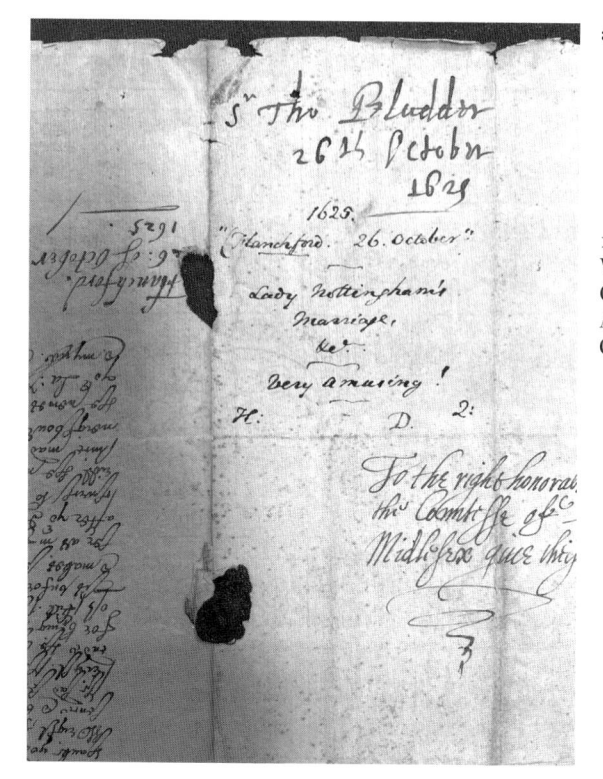

12.4a & 12.4b. Sir Nathaniel Wraxall's notes: U269/1 CP144 & CP 147. © Kent Archive Service, Kent County Council.

to be '<u>Curious</u>!', followed closely by 'Mysterious & Unintelligible' or 'Of no use!' or, finally, a simple cross to show that the contents were of no interest to him. Today, this would be seen as vandalism, especially the instances where he wrote long historical explanations, which he later scribbled out. However, this was not the worst thing he did, as noted by the Historic Manuscripts Commission: 'Many of the letters of the seventeenth century had beautiful seals. When these took his fancy, Wraxall cut them out with a sharp pen knife regardless of the damage that he did to the papers, which he sometimes thus made unreadable'[24] (figs 12.4a and 12.4b).

After Wraxall had been working for a couple of years in this manner, the duke of Dorset suddenly became unwell and died in July 1799. At this point, Wraxall moved out of Knole and took much of the archive to his house in Frant in Sussex. A year later, Arabella Diana, the widow of the 3rd duke, asked Wraxall to stop what he was doing and to return everything he had taken, which he refused to do unless he was allowed to finish his work according to his arrangement with the late duke. The duchess engaged her lawyers to get Wraxall to return them, the case went to arbitration and, following a lengthy process, they were eventually returned in 1802 upon payment of an effective ransom of £700.[25]

The papers having returned safely 'home' were consulted by a new generation of researchers. George Scharf, founder of the National Portrait Gallery and expert on British portraiture, was invited to Knole in order to identify the sitters in the portraits and to advise on their hanging. In the late 1870s and early 1880s, he stayed as a guest on several occasions and investigated the archives, as well as drawing sketches of the exteriors at Knole. On 13 June 1878, he recorded that he was 'In the Muniment Room with Lord Sackville looking through Patents etc. Made a list of them. Sketching in the chapel room.' The following day, he returned: 'In the Muniment Room looking over patents of nobility and appointments and documents.'[26]

By the time of the 1911 inventory, the papers sound as if they have been returned to much better order. In the entry for the muniment room, there is mention of a '4ft 6 mahogany portfolio Stand', '7 wood racks for papers', 'An oak cupboard fitted deal drawers', and '13 jap'd Deed boxes'; in Lord Sackville's office next door, there were '2 grained presses fitted pigeon holes enclosed by paneled doors', together with 'a grained office desk'.[27]

When Vita Sackville-West was compiling her book *Knole and the Sackvilles*, she noted the now empty old 'nail studded trunks' in the attics and which were

---

24 *Calendar of the manuscripts of Major-general Lord Sackville K.B.E., C.B., C.M.G., preserved at Knole, Sevenoaks, Kent. Volume I: Cranfield papers 1551–1612*, ed. A.P. Newton (HMC, London, 1940), p. viii. The Knole archive was fully catalogued between 1951 and 1961 by Elizabeth Melling under U269/1. I am grateful to Dr Mark Ballard (KHLC) for this information. **25** Bond by Diana, duchess of Dorset (KHLC, U269/1/ZZ2). **26** Scharf personal diary for June 1878 (National Portrait Gallery, NPG7/3/1/35). **27** Inventory for Knole, 1911 (property of Sir Robert Sackville West).

kept 'carelessly stacked: on one of them was stabbed the date in big nails, 1623: and there were others curved to fit the roof of a barouche; of later date these, but all intimate and palpitating to a very ignorant child'.[28] She also records the time she spent in the muniment room and is generous about Wraxall's interventions, which she mentions as 'neat, ejaculatory notes which I find on the reverse side of many of the papers'.[29]

HAM HOUSE AND THE WARTIME BOMBING OF THE CHANCERY LANE SAFE DEPOSIT

The final example is that of the Ham House archive. The house itself was built in the seventeenth century on the banks of the River Thames. It is filled with an outstanding collection of furniture, paintings and objects, so much so that the paperwork was pretty much overlooked until the house was donated to the National Trust in 1948 and its documentary history began to be studied more carefully.[30] In 1844, the author and topographer Edward Wedlake Brayley noted that the family papers and muniments were stored in 'cabinets and lockers' throughout the house, rather than in a dedicated muniments room as one might have expected.[31]

At the outbreak of the Second World War, the contents of Ham House were felt to be vulnerable. At this point the furniture was removed into storage and the estate and family papers were taken to the Chancery Lane Safe Deposit, at 61–2 Chancery Lane, now the site of the London Silver Vaults. The Safe Deposit was a place where strong rooms and safes could be rented in order to secure valuables from fire and burglars, and where 'each renter has a separate safe and he is possessed of the only key of it in existence, so that he alone has the means of access thereto'.[32] As well as the strong rooms, there were also writing, waiting and telephone rooms, and even a separate room for ladies. The Safe Deposit had opened in 1876 with 5,750 safes and was extended in 1890 with the addition of 250 new strong-rooms and two large strongholds for deposits 'designed principally to meet the requirements of solicitors and trustees who have the responsibility of valuable deeds and other documents'.[33] By the early twentieth century, it had gained the reputation of being able to withstand fire and burglary intact. Among other things, it housed the coins and antiquities from Tharros in Sardinia, as well as the Halliwell Phillips collection of Shakespearian manuscripts (fig. 12.5).

28 Sackville-West, *Knole and the Sackvilles*, p. 83.   29 Ibid., p. 193.   30 For a fuller explanation of how the archive found its way to Buckminster Park from Ham House, see E. Jamieson, 'A history of the Ham archive' in C. Rowell (ed.), *Ham House: 400 years of collecting and patronage* (London, 2013), pp 430–1.   31 E.W. Brayley, *History of Surrey*, 5 vols (London, 1844), iii, pt. i, p. 216.   32 *Illustrated London News*, 12 Mar. 1887, vol. 90, p. 295. 33 Ibid., May 1890.

12.5 Chancery Lane Safe Deposit, *Illustrated London News*, 12 March 1887, vol. 90, p. 295.

Unfortunately, being fire and burglar resistant was of no help when the deposit suffered a direct hit during a German air raid on 25 September 1940. The building above the vaults was almost totally destroyed and the place where the Ham archive was stored was flooded with water by the firefighters. *The People* newspaper described the scene rather imaginatively two months afterwards:

> In the heart of commercial London, sunk deep in the earth beneath a fifty-foot-high pile of masonry, twisted iron and clay, is a treasure store richer and more romantic than the legendary caves of Cocos Island or the Inca Mountains.[34]

Once workmen had managed to open the safes and get access to their contents, the majority of the Ham archive was removed to Buckminster Park, the Leicestershire home of the Tollemache family. The papers which had been badly water damaged were put in the stables at Ham House where they remained until 1973, when they were given by Sir Humphrey Tollemache to the Surrey Record Office (now Surrey History Centre), then based in nearby Kingston. Thus, the separation of the papers had nothing to do with the information contained within them, but it was all to do with their physical state.

CONCLUSIONS

These three examples illustrate the fact that country house archives are essentially vulnerable. They are more ephemeral than the buildings, furniture and paintings to which they are connected. As we have also seen, before the twentieth century, the estate and family records of the British landed elites were largely uncatalogued and inaccessible, and subject to fire, theft and damage. All this despite the efforts made over the years to keep them safe and protected. However, just as the destruction of historic buildings during the Second World War marked a turning point in the value we placed on our built heritage, so too did it bring about a wider understanding of the importance of these documents as part of our shared history. In 1945, the Historical Manuscripts Commission founded a central index of archival holdings called the National Register of Archives which was based in Quality Court just off Chancery Lane (ironically near the Chancery Lane Safe Deposit). By the time of the 1951 Festival of Britain, county record offices had started to spring up, but they were still in their infancy. *Country Life* published a short piece about the flagship Lancashire County Record Office which was at Preston:

---

34 *The People*, 22 Dec. 1940.

> Here at Preston, in specially designed fire-proof strong rooms, are stored not only public records but many thousands of historical documents which have been handed over on permanent loan by famous county families. Students from all over the world come here and visitors can inspect the treasures on application to the county archivist.[35]

County record offices started indexing and cataloguing collections and sending this information back to the National Register of Archives to be added to the central register. Even as late as the 1990s, if one wanted to discover where the documents relating to a house were kept, it was necessary to visit Quality Court to consult the register.

Now, in England at least, there is the extensive resources of the National Archives, a virtual, as well as a literal, repository of material. Furthermore, the wide availability of online search tools and digital scanning has significantly improved our ability to discover new archival records. As a result, it is much easier for researchers to retrieve papers even if they are scattered in different locations. So easy really, that perhaps we stop thinking about where they actually are or indeed where they once were. Those first county archivists who put together the catalogue level descriptions of collections of papers did so much to set out the context and interest of the papers in their care. Now we rely on more targeted searching, so much so, that we often miss the hidden histories that the papers themselves contain.

Our exploration of these archives also raises the question as to how we should go about caring for more recent types of research material such as sound recordings and digital outputs, be they visual or textual. Most of what we find nowadays is via specialist electronic management systems and unless we are careful, it may become impossible to access some information that is stored in outdated software. In some ways this could be seen as a modern equivalent to the fire and neglect that has been explored in this paper. Overall, though, the ancient documents, valuable manuscripts and private letters described earlier are so much better protected now than they were before. They are also more accessible, thanks to the advances in and transformation of electronic record retrieval systems.

Every country house archive is, by its very nature, a partial survival that exists because certain individuals took the trouble to protect and care for it. These documents and papers have a history of their own as objects, a history that reveals – if we only take the trouble to look – why they are where they are and what has happened to them over the years.

---

35 V. Cable, 'Records of a royal country', *Country Life*, 23 Feb. 1951, 562–3.

Reading the eighteenth-century print room

KATE RETFORD

The life of prints in the eighteenth century was rich and diverse, supported and promoted by a rapidly expanding European trade and market. As the numbers of printmakers, publishers and sellers grew, new techniques, such as stipple, emerged, and innovative sales strategies, including subscription, were developed. 'Furniture prints', intended for glazing and framing, were increasingly popular. Purchasers might store acquired material loose in portfolios, often kept in library cabinets, or they might paste their prints onto the pages of albums, which could sit on the shelves there, alongside the books.[1] However, the close relationship between prints and books was still more intimate than this, not least because illustrative material was typically issued separately, to be bound with related letterpress. Publications would often be advertised with an additional sum quoted for binding, but one might well choose to oversee that job oneself, arranging for loose or stitched folded sheets to be fixed into leatherbound volumes, to match a larger collection.[2] While guidance would often be provided as to where to position illustrations in relation to the text, a consumer might instead choose to bind plates separately or perhaps group them together at one end of the volume or the other. More choice still came with the fashion for extra-illustration, in which prints would be freely selected from among the thousands on the market for pasting onto the margins of, or interleaving with, the pages of a book. More dedicated extra-illustrators would mount individual pages of text into larger sheets able to support additional visual material, sometimes enlarging and 'thickening' the codex to an extraordinary degree. Robert Bowyer's Bible, now in Bolton Central Library, for example, runs to a grand total of forty-five volumes.[3] The fact that print and book collections are typically maintained and catalogued separately today belies both their intimate relationship, and the fact that many loose plates will have come from bound volumes, dismantled by booksellers and dealers to maximize their value.

In this essay, it is intended to focus on one aspect of the interwoven histories of prints and books, within a longer and wider tradition of creative engagement with these objects. Since the sixteenth century, people had been cutting up prints

---

[1] For two excellent surveys, see A. Griffiths, *The print before photography: an introduction to European printmaking, 1550–1820* (London, 2016) and T. Clayton, *The English print, 1688–1802* (London, 1997). [2] The Multigraph Collective, *Interacting with print: elements of reading in the era of print saturation* (Chicago, 2018), pp 49–51. [3] L. Peltz, *Facing the text: extra-illustration, print culture and society in Britain, 1769–1840* (San Marino, CA, 2017).

for decorative purposes, glueing them onto items of furniture, for example, or into wooden wall panels.[4] In the 1750s, this practice was amplified and systematized in the form of the print room, which became highly fashionable in British and Irish country houses.[5] Reproductive prints would be trimmed, embellished with paper borders, and then pasted around the walls to create a *trompe l'oeil* gallery. One of the first signs of this emergent tradition is to be found in the correspondence of Mary Delany, while she was living at Delville, just outside Dublin. In 1750, Delany described 'making frames for prints' with the Veseys at nearby Lucan House, and the following year she thanked her brother for sending her 'six dozen borders': 'They are for framing prints, I think them much prettier than any other sort of frame for that purpose, and where I have not pictures, I must have prints; otherwise I think prints best in books.'[6] As this trend became established, printmakers, such as Thomas Major and François Vivares in London, began increasingly to market and develop material expressly for such schemes, offering printed bows and rings from which to 'suspend' prints; engraved floral swags and festoons with which to adorn displays; and paper brackets which could 'support' sculptural prints of busts and urns.

Prints could, thus, end up within the covers of a portfolio, on the bound pages of a book or album, or be glued around the walls of a room. Indeed, they might move between these contexts, as extant library collections were mined for the making of a print room, and print rooms were subsequently dismantled, the battered impressions then returned to portfolios and cabinets. The mutability of this material is particularly striking in the case of print series, often issued for binding with letterpress or for the illustration of a substantial text, but also well suited for inclusion in a pasted display. The acquisition of such a set would provide a substantial number of images for a print room in one fell swoop. The plates would be of matching dimensions, thematically related in some way, and so invaluable in helping to structure what were typically tightly organized and symmetrical schemes. Thus, images conceived to sit alongside descriptions or to illustrate broader discussions could be extracted from larger publication projects in order to operate solely as pictures. However, they did not, thereby, fully pass from the textual realm to the visual, but rather carried information, ideas and associations with them, heavily loaded with significance from their original contexts.

4 For examples, see S.K. Schmidt, *Altered and adorned: using Renaissance prints in daily life* (Chicago, 2011) and P. Elliott et al., *Cut and paste: 400 years of collage* (Edinburgh, 2019).
5 This article is part of a book project on print rooms: see Kate Retford, 'Cutting and pasting: the print room at Woodhall Park', *British Art Studies*, 24 (2023): https://doi.org/10.17658/issn.2058-5462/issue-24/kretford. For recent work on other examples, see E. Chadwick, 'Patterned with paper pictures: the print room at Petworth house', *Art and the country house*, Paul Mellon Centre, 2020: https://doi.org/10.17658/ACH/PTE531; K. Heard, 'The print room at Queen Charlotte's cottage', *British Art Journal*, 13:3 (2012/13), pp 53–60; R. Johnstone, 'Lady Louisa Conolly's print room at Castletown House' in E. Mayes (ed.), *Castletown: decorative arts* (Trim, 2011), pp 67–77. **6** Mary Delany to Ann Dewes, 30 June

THE CLASSICAL CANON

To unpack the relationship between books and print rooms further, I will here focus on a number of those publications concerned with classical architecture and sculpture, predominantly Roman, which formed the cornerstone of virtually every elite eighteenth-century library. A browse through almost any country house library catalogue or inventory will turn up ubiquitous titles such as Bernard de Montfaucon's *L'Antiquité expliquée*, published in Paris from 1719 onwards, and key works issued in Rome, including the volumes produced by Pietro Santi Bartoli and Pietro Bellori, intended both to preserve the legacy of the 'eternal city' and to provide models for artists.[7] These tomes were the cornerstones of gentlemanly education, working in tandem with both classical schooling and the experience of the Grand Tour. As Roger de Piles opined:

> every thing that has been engraved belonging to sacred or profane history, the fable, the antique basso relievo, the Trajan and Antonine pillars, the books of medals and stones engraved ... may help [the curious in history and antiquity] in the knowledge of those things they would know, or to keep those they know already in their memories.[8]

Roman architectural remains and sculpture were featured in paintings, such as *capricci* created by the likes of Giovanni Paolo Pannini, and they were reproduced and disseminated through reduced-scale plaster copies. However, the medium of print was undoubtedly the most critical in spreading this classical knowledge across Europe. As Viccy Coltman has noted, 'the library was the prime site for the reception, preservation, and display of antiquity'.[9] Engravings and etchings were especially critical in providing a lexicon for country house décor, as famous reliefs and statues were remediated into sculpted, moulded or painted ornament, to elicit approving nods of recognition from others of the same social class.

The *Collection of Etruscan, Greek and Roman antiquities*, edited by Pierre d'Hancarville, is an excellent case in point. In this series of folios, published from

1750, in Lady Llanover (ed.), *The autobiography and correspondence of Mary Granville, Mrs Delany*, 3 vols (London, 1861), ii, p. 563; Mary Delany to Bernard Granville, 11 Apr. 1751, in ibid., iii, pp 34–5.   **7** See Adriano Aymonino's extensive work in this area, including 'Playing with the canon: West Wycombe Park's iconography and the principle of citation', *Art and the country house*, Paul Mellon Centre, 2020: https://doi.org/10.17658/ACH/WWE519 and his new, revised and updated edition of Francis Haskell and Nicolas Penny's seminal *Taste and the antique: the lure of classical sculpture, 1500–1900*, co-edited with Eloisa Dodero, 3 vols (forthcoming, Turnhout, 2024). See also S. Cree, 'Translating stone into paper: sixteenth- and seventeenth-century prints after antique sculpture' in R. Zorach and E. Rodini (eds), *Paper museums: the reproductive print in Europe, 1500–1800* (Chicago, 2005), pp 75–88.   **8** R. de Piles, *The art of painting, with the lives and characters ... of the most eminent painters*, 3rd ed. (London, 1754), p. 54.   **9** V. Coltman, *Fabricating the antique: neoclassicism in Britain 1760–*

13.1 Clongowes Wood College. Photo courtesy David Skinner.

1766 onwards, Sir William Hamilton's famed collection of antique vases was described, analysed and reproduced, but it was also reworked in various plates, the better to negotiate translation into two dimensions.[10] Copies were eagerly acquired for libraries. In 1767, for example, William, marquis of Kildare, wrote to his mother from Naples, suggesting that both his father and his aunt, Lady Louisa Conolly, might like to subscribe to a publication sure to be a 'very good ornament to the library and a pleasant book to dip in'.[11] But, as d'Hancarville had emphasized, the 'very pretty figures' which the marquis admired could also lend themselves to the adornment of 'well understood Collections of Prints and Designs, or [furnishing] in a manner not only agreeable, but usefull and instructive, the Cabinet of a Man of Taste and Letters'.[12]

1800 (Chicago, 2006), p. 196. **10** Sir W. Hamilton and P. d'Hancarville, *Collection of Etruscan, Greek, and Roman antiquities from the cabinet of the Honble. Wm. Hamilton*, 4 vols (Naples, 1766); V. Coltman, 'Sir William Hamilton's vase publications (1766–1776): a case study in the reproduction and dissemination of antiquity', *Journal of Design History*, 14:1 (2001), pp 2–3. **11** William, marquis of Kildare, to Emily, duchess of Leinster from Naples, 24 Feb. 1767, in B. Fitzgerald (ed.), *Correspondence of Emily, duchess of Leinster*, 3 vols (Dublin, 1949–57), iii, p. 459. **12** Hamilton, *Antiquities*, i, pp 168–70.

That last option was promoted when the German artist Wilhelm Tischbein (responsible for the publication of Hamilton's 'second collection' of vases) used a number of the plates to decorate a 'cabinet' for an ambassador in Naples in the early 1790s.[13] The precise nature of this lost scheme is unclear, but Charles Heathcote Tatham described the prints and borders as 'used in the way of our modern paper hangings', and praised the effect as a 'new & tasty method of fitting up rooms'.[14] Furthermore, around the same time, Thomas Wogan Browne had a number of the prints from Hamilton's *Antiquities* pasted onto the walls of the new library he had created, in an extension at Castle Browne near Dublin (now Clongowes Wood College) (fig. 13.1). In the mid-twentieth century, when a bookcase was moved, eight prints from this publication were discovered pasted between the windows. They had been arranged in two groups, enhanced with additional paper frames, and connected in broadly cruciform arrangements with wide decorative strips.[15] Rather than being contained in bound volumes on the shelves in that space, the prints were here used to adorn the walls, both creating a pleasing pattern and presenting their iconography to open view.

Coltman has unpacked the influence of the plates from Hamilton's *Antiquities* across the eighteenth century in full, variously reproduced in marquetry, silver and ceramic, most famously by Josiah Wedgwood, the images 'cropped, shaped and made to fit according to the specifications of the patron and the practices of the manufacturer'.[16] They also underpinned the vogue for 'Etruscan rooms', distinguished by ornately bounded painted images linked by tendrils and swags, all in those striking hues of black and terracotta featured at Clongowes.[17] But, in Wogan Browne's library, these prints did not merely provide models and inspiration for decoration: they became the decoration.

This same process can be traced through active engagement with the second work to be considered: the *Raccolta di statue Antiche e Moderne*, published by Domenico de' Rossi in Rome in 1704, another mainstay of elite book collections. This was a deluxe publication, documenting both works from antiquity and more recent pieces by sculptors such as Bernini and Michelangelo. De' Rossi had hired a number of the most skilled engravers then in Rome to work on the plates and commissioned the antiquarian, Paolo Alessandro Maffei, to write an accompanying text.[18] Again, these prints were often translated into decorative

---

13 W. Tischbein, *Collection of engravings from ancient vases*, 3 vols (Naples, 1791–5). **14** Quoted in Coltman, 'Sir William Hamilton's vase publications', p. 6.   **15** B. Cullen, *A short history of Clongowes Wood College* (Clongowes Wood, 2019). On these prints, see A. Longfield, 'Print-rooms', *Kildare Archaeological Society*, 14 (1970), pp 572–4, and D. Skinner, *Wallpaper in Ireland, 1700–1900* (Tralee, 2014), pp 117–20. Thanks to Conor Lucey and Margaret Doyle for their help in this research.   **16** Coltman, 'Sir William Hamilton's vase publications', p. 11.   **17** J. Wilton-Ely, 'Pompeian and Etruscan tastes in the neo-classical country-house interior' in G. Jackson-Stops et al. (eds), *The fashioning and functioning of the British country house* (Washington, DC, 1989), pp 51–73.   **18** F. Haskell and N. Penny, *Taste and the antique: the lure of classical sculpture, 1500–1900* (New Haven, CT, 1982), p. 23.

Reading the eighteenth-century print room 155

13.2 Petworth, West Sussex: the print closet – west wall. Paul Mellon Centre for Studies in British Art

schemes, as Adriano Aymonino has recently explored in his work on Robert Adam's interiors at Syon House, Middlesex. Adam's patron, the 1st duke of Northumberland, had a copy of de' Rossi's volume in the library there, and its plates provided the basis for plaster bas-reliefs and painted grisailles throughout the décor, as well as the cast figures positioned above the entablature in the ante-room.[19] However, again, the prints from the *Raccolta* could also be used as decoration in their own right. In the mid 1750s, no fewer than eighty-five of these sculptural prints were pasted around the walls of a print room at Petworth, Sussex, for the 2nd earl of Egremont (fig. 13.2). Together with other sculptural prints published by de' Rossi, after the triumphal arches of ancient Rome, they

19 A. Aymonino, *Enlightened eclecticism: the grand design of the 1st duke and duchess of Northumberland* (London, 2021), pp 166–7.

there provided a meticulously organized framework for a display of reproduced paintings.[20]

This print room has close ties with the contents of the original library at Petworth, only a short distance away on the first floor, as revealed by a 1780 catalogue. Four plates from a series illustrating Paul Scarron's *Roman Comique* (1651–9) are included in the print room; the novel itself was in the library. Topographical prints of British buildings from the extended series published by Samuel and Nathaniel Buck from the 1720s to 1740s were neatly fitted into upper sections of the panelling in the print room: a folio of other 'Buck's Views some loose with other Prints' was stored in the library along the corridor. But, most significantly, as Esther Chadwick has noted, a copy of the *Raccolta* recorded in the library catalogue is described as having the 'letterpress only'.[21] It was, thus, most likely the source of the plates utilized in the pasted display. In this case, a single publication was split between the text in the book collection and the engravings in the print room.[22]

In bound volumes of the *Raccolta*, the reproduced statues sit within ruled borders, fixed by plate numbers into a set running order structured around key collections, such as the Borghese and the Medici. Inscriptions name, briefly describe, and identify the location of each piece, but the reader can also look to Maffei's much longer discursive accounts for further information and analysis. These were sometimes bound in before the plates; sometimes after; sometimes interleaved. But, taken out of the library and out of the codex, the prints are transformed at Petworth. Every statue has been excised, carefully trimmed around and within its contours, removing the shadows which root each piece on the page. They have become freestanding elements in a display which retains thematic threads, but which ultimately privileges the formal and the business of pattern making. While some pairings do relate to shared ownership, or subject matter, they are predominantly reliant on shape; on whether the figures stand, sit, recline or are mounted.

Although the Petworth print room is the only surviving example of such deployment of the *Raccolta* prints, an album documenting three lost print rooms at Wricklemarsh, in Blackheath, now at the Yale Center for British Art, reveals parallel use.[23] In both the 'Print Dressing Room' and 'Print Closet' detailed in these elevation drawings and catalogue lists, a large number of the same sculptural prints are to be found pasted along the dado rails and above the doors, 'placed' on these architectural features rather than free-floating on the walls. At Petworth, Claude Randon's prints of the recumbent statues of the Rivers Tiber

---

20 G.P. Bellori, *Veteres arcus augustorum triumphis insignes* (Rome, 1690). **21** Chadwick, 'Patterned with paper pictures'. **22** West Sussex Record Office, PHA 5379. I am most grateful to Andy Loukes for his help with my research into Petworth. **23** YCBA, B1975.2.779. For the property, see J. Brushe, 'Wricklemarsh and the Collections of Sir Gregory Page', *Apollo*, 122 (Nov. 1985), pp 364–71.

and Nile, found in the Baths of Constantine and subsequently displayed in front of the Palazzo Senatorio, are suspended in the centre of the west wall. At Wricklemarsh, those same figures once reclined above one of the door frames in the dressing room, either side of an engraved vase. While the diagrams in this album are not explicit, the fact that the identified *Raccolta* prints are numbered, rather than given defined, demarcated shapes, like most of the others, indicates that they were likely again cut out around the outlines of the figures, engaging with the popular scrapbook practice of silhouetting.[24]

STON EASTON PARK, SOMERSET

The surviving print room at Ston Easton Park provides a particularly valuable case study for unpacking this intimate relationship between the library and the print room, and the ways in which images, and connected ideas and allusions, travelled between books and these paper galleries.[25] This scheme was likely created by Richard Hippisley-Cox in the 1770s, in one of the wings which he added to the house in that period.[26] At Petworth, the print room was only a few rooms away from the library. At Ston Easton Park, the two are fully adjacent and clearly explicitly conceived as cognate spaces.

Hippisley-Cox appears to have undertaken the requisite gentlemanly travels on the Continent between completing his schooling at Westminster in 1763 and inheriting the estate in 1769. His epitaph in the local church declares him to have been 'matured by all the advantages of refined education and foreign travel'.[27] This 'refined education' was underpinned and evidenced by the family's established library, stocked with publications concerned with the history, mythology and art of antiquity, including familiar titles, such as Montfaucon's *L'Antiquité expliquée* and Hamilton's *Antiquities*. Although that book collection is now long dispersed, the cases which housed it have survived the property's difficult and chequered history.[28] A *capriccio* of Roman ruins, complementing

24 For silhouetting, see J. Zelen, *Blinded by curiosity: the collector-dealer Hadriaan Beverland (1650–1716) and his radical approach to the printed image* (Lieden, 2022), ch. 5. 25 For Ston Easton Park, see A. Woodward, 'Ston Easton Park, Somerset', *Country Life*, 191:46 (13 Nov. 1997), pp 62–7. See also Bryan Little's earlier series of three articles on the house in: (i) *Country Life*, 97:2514 (23 Mar. 1945); (ii) ibid., 97:2515 (30 Mar. 1945); and (iii) ibid., 97:2516 (6 Apr. 1945). 26 I am in agreement here with C. Archer, 'Festoons of flowers for fitting up print rooms', *Apollo*, 130 (Dec. 1989), pp 386–91, 437. Richard owned the house between inheriting in 1769, and being declared insane in 1784, at which point it was taken over by his brother Henry. Henry, however, seems to have concentrated on making improvements to the grounds. For the family, see I.F. Jones (ed.), *Some notes on the Hippisley family, collected by Alfred E. Hippisley* (Taunton, 1952), pp 117ff. Thanks to Kat Bowhay and Aerolene Stephenson for supporting my research at the property. 27 St Mary's Church, Ston Easton. 28 'An Inventory of the Household Goods, Linnen and China of the late John Hippisley Coxe Esq[r] ... June 1769' (Somerset Heritage Centre (hereafter SHC), DD\HI/A/328). The library collection was sold in the Sotheby's sale of 27–30 Nov. 1956: see SHC, DD\BRC/28.

13.3 Ston Easton Park, Somerset: library.

13.4 Ston Easton Park, Somerset: print room.

such texts, also survives, still contained within the library overmantel. Unattributed, it is broadly of the type associated with Pannini (fig.13.3).[29]

Moving through the connecting door, one enters a print room created in the heyday of the fashion (fig. 13.4). Much of the material has deteriorated and is now discoloured, some has been lost, and there is unfortunately no record of restoration work undertaken. However, the evidence that does survive indicates that much of the scheme is original. A total of twenty-seven prints after French, British and Italian paintings remain pasted around the room today, framed with a range of paper borders. Between these, a number of floral garlands and festoons add further embellishment and structure, representative of the decorative material devised expressly for print rooms in this period.[30] The *trompe l'oeil* conceit in the 'hanging' of these elements is underscored and developed by the 'placing' of a number of sculptural prints of urns and vases along the dado rail, as if their two-dimensional forms are supported by this three-dimensional feature, echoing the use of the *Raccolta* prints at Wricklemarsh.[31]

Eleven plates from Domenico Cunego's series of *Views of antique buildings and famous ruins*, after Charles Louis Clerisseau, dominate the upper portions of the walls, continuing the theme of the overmantel next door. Cunego's *Views* were billed as providing meticulously accurate vistas 'of the most remarkable Antiquities in Italy ... exactly historical, no Circumstance added or altered ... precise Portraits of what [travellers] have seen abroad'. They were thus framed as visual counterparts to those texts which described the same fabric, housed in the library. One might acquire Cunego's prints as a complete set or perhaps just purchase the selected six which were widely advertised in the London papers in 1767 as appropriate for display: 'Being highly finished, they are extremely proper to frame and glaze for decorating of Apartments.'[32] At Ston Easton Park, however, that suggested mode of presentation was foregone in favour of inclusion of the *Views* in a pasted scheme.

Some prints used in the print room here were probably already in the collection.[33] The Italian material could have been purchased in London, but was more likely acquired on Richard's travels in the 1760s. Cunego was a very popular printmaker in Rome, and Hippisley-Cox could well have picked up the

---

[29] For the library and print room, see Little, 'Ston Easton Park' [part iii], p. 596. [30] For surviving impressions of a festoon by François Vivares, published in March 1758, used in the room, see Victoria & Albert Museum, E.24199–3 and E27933–2. For an impression of a festoon by Peter Mazell, published by Thomas Major in the 1750s, see V&A, 16318. [31] These urns would have chimed with the 'vase mania' of the later eighteenth century. One of the vases, by Peter Benazech after Charles Eisen, 1760, is in the V&A, 29778:17. A couple are also included in a scrapbook owned by the Chippendale Society, now at Temple Newsam: C1981/1. [32] *Public Advertiser*, 2 Jan. 1767. The six prints were available for £1 16s.: see M. Hopkinson, 'Cunego's engravings after Gavin Hamilton', *Print Quarterly*, 26:4 (2009), p. 365. [33] Perhaps included in the 'Three Large Port Folio's of Prints' listed in the inventory made on the death of Richard's father: SHC, DD\HI/A/328.

Views directly from the producer. He also probably acquired the first volume of Paolo Fidanza's series of prints after Raphael, *Teste scelte di personaggi illustri* (1757), on that trip, from which the four striking heads in the scheme have been taken.[34] However, the publication used most prominently in the room was definitely acquired in England: Thomas Worlidge's *Select collection of drawings from curious antique gems*. In 1766, Worlidge had produced a specimen publication of five etchings, with an introduction addressed 'To the Publick', some 'General Observations on the Art of Engraving on Gems' by John Wickstead, and details of the subscription.[35] Following his unexpected death later that same year, the work was completed by his pupils, and his widow was able to make the full publication available in 1768, for the substantial sum of 18 guineas (unbound).[36] Both specimen and complete publications include 'Mr Cox' among the listed subscribers.[37]

While most of the purchasers bound their copies of Worlidge's *Gems*, deciding whether to have the letterpress positioned before or after the plates, or whether to intersperse the two, 'Mr Cox' took a different approach. More than 100 plates from the publication were pasted to the lower register of the print room walls in groups, linked by tiny paper chains, illusionistically suspended from paper rings and bows. Again, a pronounced emphasis on pattern making is apparent, with clusters of between four and seven prints arranged in diaper formations.[38] The diminutive individual components of each group contribute to a visually effective and dramatic range of scale in the display, contrasting with the more substantial engravings higher on the walls. However, the groupings also create larger entities, more complementary in their dimensions.[39] Furthermore, in their hanging forms, they echo those floral festoons produced by Vivares and Peter Mazell.

Thus, once again, we find material most commonly bound and stored on library shelves fragmented, transmuted into pictures to display as part of a paper gallery. However, the relationship with the codex here is particularly interesting for two reasons. First, with only a couple of exceptions, Worlidge's full plates have been used, complete with their inscriptions. In his 'trailer' publication,

---

34 These heads are not from the much better known *Recueil de têtes choisies de personnages illustres*, published in 1785. The inscriptions make it clear that they are from this earlier set of impressions. See https://cicognara.org/catalog/324, accessed 1 July 2023.   **35** T. Worlidge, *A specimen of a select collection of drawings, from the most curious antique gems* (London, 1766). See S. Sloman's *ODNB* entry on Worlidge: https://doi-org.ezproxy.lib.bbk.ac.uk/10.1093/ref:odnb/29976. See also Neil Jeffares on Worlidge in the *Dictionary of pastellists*: www.pastellists.com/Articles/WORLIDGE.pdf, accessed 1 July 2023.   **36** Thomas Worlidge, *A select collection of drawings from curious antique gems* (London, 1768).   **37** There are two entries for a 'Mr Cox' in the 1768 publication. The other might be either Richard's father, John, or his brother, Henry.   **38** Similar clusters of small prints, linked by chains, can be seen in the surviving print room at Woodhall Park, Hertfordshire, and in the Wricklemarsh album, described as 'strings'.   **39** These are likely the impressions published by Robert Strange after he had acquired Dorigny's original plates: *Catalogue of Mr Strange's prints* (London, n.d. [c.1761]).

Worlidge had emphasized that each of his plates would not only reproduce a gem, but also detail its size, subject and the name of the collection in which it was housed. As in the case of the *Raccolta*, provenance was key. While all the other prints in the display were trimmed (as was conventional), the letterpress removed, transformed from intermedial objects into pictures, the text on the Worlidge gem plates was retained. The visitor is, thus, invited to read, as well as to look. Here, one has a clear sense of the pages of a book laid out across the walls, even though the longer discussion of each gem produced by Worlidge for the full publication is unavailable.

However, Worlidge's sequence has also, significantly, been broken up, with key decisions made as to which gems to select and which to cluster together. At times, the groups are tightly organized by subject: one cluster, for example, consists of gems showing Roman empresses (fig. 13.5). Material from across the publication was, thus, arranged so as to facilitate comparison. In another group, the viewer is able to see how Hercules appears on 15 different gems: young and old; alone, with Iole, or accompanied by Cerberus. One can similarly compare the head of Medusa as represented on various gems owned at the time by Thomas Hope, the earl of Carlisle, and Thomas Dundas in Britain, and by the Strozzi family in Rome. The curated display enables the immediacy of a synchronous viewing of related material that

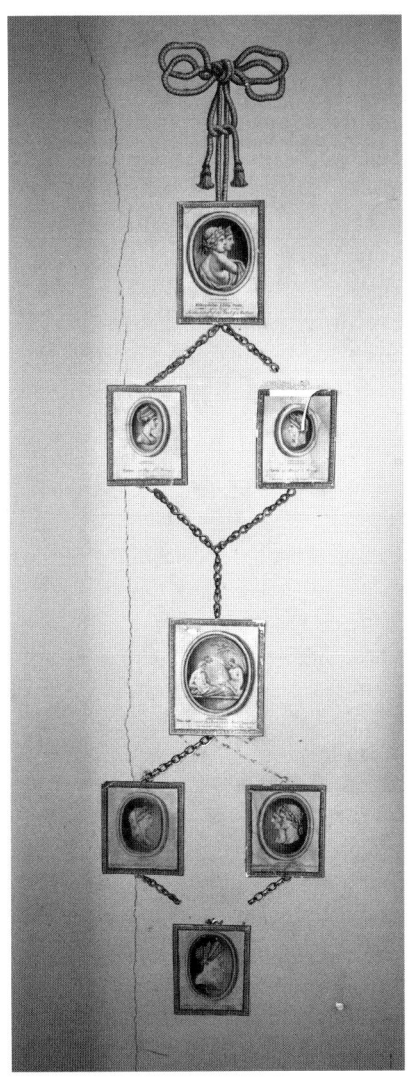

13.5 Ston Easton Park, Somerset: print room – detail of prints of gems from Thomas Worlidge, *A select collection of drawings from curious antique gems*, London, 1768, showing Roman emperesses.

could never be seen at the same moment in a bound book, with its sequential limitations. The book would be leafed through, fingers inserted in pages to mark comparable items, as the reader moved back and forth. The Ston Easton print room, thus, shows the kind of personal engagement with, and manipulation of, images and knowledge so richly evident in the cognate practice of extra-illustration. Indeed, extra-illustrative practices sometimes made use of remarkably similar formal devices to create connections. Printed paper chains can also be seen in Richard Bull's personalized volumes of James Granger's *Biographical history* (1769), there creating relationships between portrait prints laid out across the pages.[40]

One final aspect to the reciprocal relationship between the books and the prints – the contents of the library shelves and cabinets and the walls of the adjacent room – is critical here. The Ston Easton Park print room is dominated by two, large shallow cabinets built into the north and west walls. Filled with grooves for narrowly spaced shelves, it seems probable that these once housed a collection of seals, gems, cameos and/or medals.[41] If that is indeed the case, then the spread out pages of Worlidge's publication would have functioned as valuable reference material, while actual examples of the illustrated items were being studied. Richard Hippisley-Cox's own collection would, thus, also have been flatteringly connected with those built up by considerably more illustrious connoisseurs across Britain and Italy. And three-dimensional material objects and their two-dimensional representations would have been engaged with in tandem, handling of the gems (whether original or – more likely – paste reproduction) enhanced by the comparative examples pasted around the walls.[42] Those engraved images of gems, meanwhile, would have been conversely enhanced by the ability to appreciate the colour, size, weight and shape of the adjacent three-dimensional objects, together with the quality of their relief and intaglio lines.

CONCLUSION

Serried ranks of gilt tooled books on the shelves of a country house library are a decorative feature in their own right, as well as housing the stories, information and ideas that underpinned learning and fuelled polite conversation. These volumes contained plates as well as text, and, in the case of that extensive canon of literature concerned with preserving and disseminating the heritage of Rome, those illustrations underpinned decorative schemes and furnishings throughout the surrounding interiors. Plaster statues in hall niches; arabesque designs in Etruscan rooms; inset paintings by the likes of Biagio Rebecca; plasterwork

---

[40] See Peltz, *Facing the text*, p. 71. [41] This view is also expressed in M. Jourdain, 'Print rooms', *Country Life*, 104:2695 (10 Sept. 1948), p. 525; D. Guinness 'The revival of the print room', *Antique Collector*, 49:6 (June 1978), p. 89; S. Calloway, 'Engraving schemes', *Country Life*, 185:16 (18 Apr. 1991), p.103; Little, 'Ston Easton Park' [part iii], p. 597. [42] I am grateful to Alison FitzGerald for conversation on this point. See https://armaghrobinsonlibrary.co.uk/collections/past-exhibitions-and-displays/gems-and-gem-literature/, accessed 1 July 2023.

detailing by craftsmen such as Joseph Rose: all drew on an established, recognized and approved classical lexicon. But, in the print rooms here explored – at Clongowes, Petworth, Wricklemarsh and Ston Easton Park – that illustrative material joined other etchings and engravings to become decoration in a strikingly unmediated way. A volume might be set open on a library stand, but the distribution of the plates from the unbound publication on the walls of a print room laid them out fully, transmuting them into pictures, creating patterns, but always evoking the attendant knowledge and understanding embedded in the accompanying text. Randon's prints of the statues of the Tiber and Nile, isolated in the Petworth and Wricklemarsh print rooms, would still bring Maffei's learned paragraphs on the 'Tevere' and 'Nilo' to the mind of the informed viewer.[43] Together, these texts, pictures and objects in the country house interior embodied the classical learning which underpinned elite education, taste and status.

[43] *Raccolta di Statue*, vi and vii, pp 7–10.

The house of ideas

CHRISTOPHER RIDGWAY

Country houses are masterpieces of material culture: they are triumphs of architecture, fine and decorative art, and landscape design, but they are also about the history and transmission of ideas. In varying degrees, their occupants (above and below stairs, indoors and outdoors) thought, conversed, read and responded to their milieu through books and newspapers, as well as other media and forms of knowledge. In recent years, country house libraries and archives have steadily revealed more evidence for how people in country houses fashioned themselves and their views of the world.

Thus, the intellectual background to the country house is of enormous importance, not just in terms of the wider cultural or political zeitgeist at a given moment, but within the walls of the building itself. What was the meaning of all those volumes in bookcases? Did they do more than just decorate a room? How were books acquired, read and put to use? By what means did elite society exchange ideas, absorb new trends and engage in wider debate, especially when at home in the country, and away from the sociability of the metropolis? To what degree was this knowledge valued and displayed in terms of stylish library design, and how did houses preserve their books and other records? In what ways did members of a household entertain or better themselves, and what was popular to read with whom – men, women, and children? The classics, natural history, literature, genealogy, fiction and other subjects feature in many country house libraries, and very often, a battered, plain copy of a publication might reveal more than the most pristine edition in a lavish ornamental binding.[1]

Much of the research into books and reading has focused on learned or metropolitan elites, close to centres of learning and the book trade.[2] By contrast, the term 'the mental world' of the country house might occasion amusement among those sceptical of its intellectual value, and credentials for sanity. But,

---

[1] M. Purcell, *The country house library* (London, 2019); idem, *The Big House library in Ireland: books in Ulster country houses* (Swindon, 2011); idem, 'The country house library in Scotland' in E. Boran (ed.), *Book collecting in Ireland and Britain, 1650–1850* (Dublin, 2018), pp 206–22. See also essays by J. Raven, S. West and H. DeGroff in M. Dimmock et al. (eds), *The intellectual culture of the English country house, 1500–1700* (Manchester, 2015). [2] See, for example, J. Raven et al. (eds), *The practice and representation of reading in England* (Cambridge, 1996), esp. the essays by N. Tadmore, J. Raven and J. Fergus; S. Colclough, *Consuming texts, readers and reading communities, 1695–1870* (Basingstoke, 2007); W. St Clair, *The reading nation in the Romantic period* (Cambridge, 2004); M. Towsey, *Reading the Scottish enlightenment: books and their readers in provincial Scotland, 1750–1829* (Leiden, 2010); I. Jackson, 'Approaches to

questions as to the management of a household and the running of an estate, as well as wider cultural, aesthetic or intellectual forms of debate, have begun to open up some sense of the life of the mind in the country house. The endeavour is to understand how a place functioned as well as fathoming the workings of the minds of owners and other occupants, from below-stairs staff, to agents, foresters, farm managers, and neighbours. Such lines of enquiry frequently bring one back to a central question: did books furnish minds as well as interiors?[3]

The traditional elements that so define country houses have governed a great deal of scholarship: the architecture, the landscape, the fine and decorative art collections – the stuff that households would surround themselves with, and which conventionally have been defined as the trappings of power, status and wealth. Nobody would gainsay the importance of these elements: they are visible, tangible, and enduring, and they are the bedrock of the perception of these places as treasure houses.

The challenge here is to explore those aspects of country house culture that lie beyond the customary assembly of material culture. This means a focus on the immaterial in this most material of worlds: to look beyond physical manifestations of culture, and to trace patterns of thinking, the generation of ideas or the consequences of reflection. Country houses are not just about the history of places, people, and objects; they are about the history of ideas and in a world of things, it is important to pay heed to ideas.

This is a point that quickly strays into the world of philosophy: what, after all, is an idea? And, if one can agree on a definition, how can one evaluate such? Ideas can be evanescent: they evolve, they can be singular or plural, and they can remain fixed too. One of the challenges is how to follow through an idea, to trace the experience of thinking, to open up the mental world as process. How was this manifested, how can it be comprehended? Are we able to pursue ideation from the intangible and unseen to the concrete and visible?

In many cases, the instances of material culture represent the fruits of prior thinking. Information as to the origins of things – a building, a portrait, a landscape, a decorative object – can be traced through letters, journals, memoranda, plans and accounts (which helpfully materialize expenditure). The archival trail supplies a narrative, a critical hinterland beyond the physical presence of things. This can be a straightforward process, inferring backwards from the presence of something material, which can be proven to be the conclusion of some previous process. For this to work successfully, there has to be a reliance on the written word, the evidentiary trail, and country houses that

---

the history of readers and reading in eighteenth-century Britain', *Historical Journal*, 47:4 (2004), pp 1041–54. 3 M. Girouard, *Life in the English country house* (London, 1978), pp 164–71; P. McCarthy, *Life in the country house in Georgian Ireland* (London, 2016), pp 169–73. There are numerous mentions of books in households in T. Barnard, *Making the grand figure: lives and possessions in Ireland, 1641–1770* (London, 2004).

14.1 Allan Ramsay, Emily, duchess of Leinster, 1765. Courtesy of Conor Mallaghan.

retain their archives are well equipped to support this form of enquiry, opening up an understanding of how people acquired and consumed knowledge, and how they put this to use. As a result, one can begin to comprehend libraries and muniment rooms not just as repositories filled with written material, but as functioning intellectual spaces.[4]

However, this focus is two-way: one need not start with an outcome – building, portrait, artistic commission, acquisition or whatever. One can begin with the paper trail itself, which marks a moment of inception, intent, decision: 'I will this or that to happen' – every action is preceded by thought. The archival trail can chronicle the thinking process, the deliberation over choice, as well as influences, and decisions relating to taste, cost and so on. This might be said to exemplify the maxim 'I read therefore I do', and in turn, this can open up a path to a mental QED. The documentary trail illuminates an intellectual thread present in written material: reading, reflecting and writing forming an evidential core.

In this most visual of worlds, it also pays to scrutinize the images that depict the country house and its inhabitants, to see if they can reveal intimations of an inner life. Portraits that capture the act of reading are a strong visual prompt to such enquiry. Allan Ramsay's luminous depiction of Emily, countess of Kildare, painted in 1765, is as good an example as any[5] (fig. 14.1). In this portrait, the sitter adopts an informal pose, arms folded, resting on the open pages of a book; her head is bowed, the eyes are lowered and she appears lost in concentration (no matter that any book conservator would shiver at the sight of the open spine bent backwards as it rests on another volume beneath). But what is she reading? There is no clue as to the title of the book, but we can infer from its folio format that it likely contains illustrations and is a work of some scholarship. Conjecture has it that she might be reading Voltaire, a favourite author of hers, although the first folio edition of Voltaire did not appear until three years after the portrait; possibly she was reading the great *Dictionnaire*, something that would chime with her educational interests.[6] We can be confident that this representation was significant for her. It was not an arbitrary one. She could have easily chosen a

---

[4] For libraries as interiors, see C. Hussey, 'The country house library', *Country Life Annual* (1958), pp 40–3; G. Jackson-Stops, 'Most learned decoration', *Country Life*, 182 (24 Mar. 1982), pp 120–3; C. Wainwright, 'The library as living room' in R. Myers and M. Harris (eds), *Property of a gentleman: the formation, organization and dispersal of the private library, 1620–1920* (Winchester, 1991), pp 15–24; S. West, 'Life in the library' in G. Perry and K. Retford (eds), *Placing faces: the portrait and the English country house in the long eighteenth century* (Manchester, 2013), pp 63–95. [5] The version in the national Museums & Galleries on Merseyside, Walker Art Gallery, was commissioned by Emily's sister, Caroline, Lady Holland, 1765; a slightly smaller copy of uncertain date is in a private collection; A. Smart, *Allan Ramsay: a complete catalogue of paintings* (London, 1999), p. 147, fig. 574. [6] *Collection complete des oeuvres de Mr. de Voltaire*, 30 vols (Geneva, 1768–77); Emily's correspondence is peppered with references to Voltaire and his works: B. Fitzgerald (ed.), *Correspondence of Emily duchess of Leinster*, 3 vols (Dublin, 1949–57), i, pp 91, 287, 343, 420, 424, 471, 507, 511, 532.

14.2 George Howard, Pencil Portrait of Sir David Dundas, c.1870–5.
The Castle Howard Collection.

different setting and pose; clearly, erudition mattered and was a reflection of her many interests. We cannot tell from this portrait what she is reading, even less do we know what she is thinking – is the sense of studious concentration real even? The details of Emily's life suggest a cultured and educated woman who derived pleasure from reading, but her time and energy for intellectual pursuits must have been limited given that she gave birth to an incredible twenty-one children over a period of thirty years.

Ramsay's representation is a passive one: the reader is absorbed by a text and immersed in thought. A century later, George Howard, 9th earl of Carlisle, chose to depict a family friend not in the act of reading but while writing. This pencil portrait of the Scottish lawyer, politician, agricultural improver, and bibliophile, Sir David Dundas, dates from the early 1870s[7] (fig. 14.2). The sitter is shown at

[7] For Dundas, see G. Goodwin, rev. H.C.G. Matthew, 'Dundas, Sir David (1799–1877)' in

14.3 Arthur Devis, Lord and Lady Kildare in the grounds at Carton House, 1753, Malcolm Park. Alamy stock photo.

his desk, his hands are outlined and unfinished, yet convey a physical sense of writing with what looks like a quill pen. However, the exact focus of his concentration is unclear. Is he composing a legal judgement, drafting a political speech or writing a letter? We cannot tell. Unlike Emily Kildare, Dundas is not so much reading as transmitting his thinking to paper, possibly intended for a wider readership; but like the Ramsay portrait, any information the viewer might glean is limited.

More promising is Arthur Devis' 1753 portrait of Emily and her husband James, 20th earl of Kildare (fig. 14.3). Typically for Devis, the elements combine to articulate one of his carefully posed snapshot moments. Kildare engages the

Oxford dictionary of national biography, https://doi.org/10.1093/ref:odnb/8248, accessed 18 Jan. 2024.

14.4 Augustus Charles Pugin, interior of the library at Cassiobury Park, Hertfordshire 1816, watercolour and graphite on paper. The Cooper-Hewitt, Smithsonian Design Museum.

viewer while holding his stick, his hat resting on the table surface; Emily is inspecting the architect's plans in front of her for a new bridge in the park at Carton, but without the same degree of introspection as in the later Ramsay portrait. The image encapsulates a moment, but it also hints at mental activity, and not just any generic example – the couple are deliberating upon a specific architectural proposal in an appropriate outdoor setting. It may be that Kildare is not looking at the viewer but staring into the park as Emily reads out details from the plan. As an example of the genre known as a 'Conversation Piece', there is the suggestion of a focused dialogue between the sitters as they engage with the material they are contemplating; in turn, this stimulates a sense of enquiry on the part of the viewer.[8]

These examples, as would many others, raise numerous questions but fewer definitive answers as to the workings of the sitters' minds. At the very least, the

8 Sale of Old Master Paintings, Bonhams, London, 4 July 2018, lot 26. For the context of this portrait, see F. O'Kane, *Landscape design in eighteenth-century Ireland: mixing foreign trees with the natives* (Cork, 2004), pp 102–3; on Devis and this genre of painting, see K. Retford, *The conversation piece: making modern art in eighteenth-century Britain* (London, 2017).

individuals in these portraits valued their engagement with reading and writing; they chose to be depicted as intellectually alert. Another kind of illustration that hints at the mental word of the country house can be found with interior views, especially of libraries, of which there are many. Typical is Augustus Charles Pugin's 1816 watercolour of the library at Cassiobury Park, Hertfordshire, home to the Capel family, which reveals a furnished and decorative space containing bookcases, portraits and furniture (fig. 14.4).

There are hints of activity faintly visible with a seated figure on the right in the act of writing or possibly drawing, and with a second shadowy presence on the left at the far end inspecting a volume on a table. (These occupants of the room would be more clearly delineated in a later coloured version of 1837.) No matter how contrived this composition may have been, it has been designed to show off a grand interior, but also to represent some measure of engagement with the life of the mind, whether acquiring, recording or transmitting knowledge. The furniture is also subordinate to intellectual pursuits: the folio stand on the left, the cradle for prints and drawings on the right, as well as an architect's table. The functional nature of these pieces denotes mental activity.[9]

For visitors to country houses, libraries occupy a curious space. Countless properties reveal interiors arranged to display and order knowledge and information. These rooms are often located in the core apartments, distinguished by, and presented in terms of, their decor and furnishings. Generally, the books are subsumed within the totality of the interior, and for the visiting public little attempt is made to individualize these volumes. Occasionally a book or two may be placed on a table, but there is no real insight into what these kinds of titles might have meant to the occupants.

Hence, the common response to libraries in country houses, 'Have these books been read?' It is a pertinent enquiry that goes to the heart of that central question, 'Do books furnish a room or do they furnish a mind?' Neither answer is mutually exclusive. It is apparent that in many cases, rare editions and fine bindings were prized as expensive, even luxury, artefacts; their contents of secondary importance. But there is ample evidence that books in country houses were read, with tastes encompassing the high-, middle- and low-brow. Bernard de Montfaucon's *L'Antiquité expliquée* (1719) could co-exist with Agatha Christie's *The mysterious affair at Styles* (1920), the first case for Belgian detective Hercule Poirot; the novel is something of a country house meta-fiction, for the text includes floorplans of the Inglethorp family residence where the murder has taken place – sadly, however, not in a library.

---

9 The Capel family sold Cassiobury in 1922 and five years later, the house was demolished: G. Worsley, *England's lost houses, from the archives of* Country Life (London, 2002), pp 53–4. For the demise of libraries see, P.H. Reid, 'The decline and fall of the British country house library', *Libraries & Culture*, 36:2 (spring 2001), pp 345–66. For library furniture, see Purcell, *Country house library*, pp 135–7.

Just as country houses are not empty spaces, so the aristocracy, contrary to stereotype, was populated by brainy minds and not simply vacuous heads. For example, Robert Gascoigne Cecil, 3rd marquess of Salisbury, was not only a consummate nineteenth-century politician, leader of the Conservative party and three-times prime minister; he also supervised the family estates totalling 20,000 acres, was a prolific journalist and an amateur scientist with his own laboratory at Hatfield House. He was also an avaricious reader. For Salisbury, the world of ideas, whether scientific, religious, cultural, geographical or political, was very real and something he engaged with on a daily basis. His reading and writing would translate into political action, foreign policy, experimental truth or empirical knowledge, and in 1894, he published his Sheldonian address on evolution.[10]

Fellow scientists included the 3rd earl of Rosse, who constructed the leviathan telescope at Birr Castle in 1845. His credentials included astronomer, naturalist, engineer and president of the Royal Society, as well as landlord and MP. Among his contributions to learning was the identification and naming of the crab nebula.[11] A century earlier at Burton Constable in East Yorkshire William Constable assembled a fine library in the Long Gallery, which also doubled as a laboratory filled with scientific instruments (fig. 14.5). He created a cabinet of curiosities in an adjacent room filled with natural history specimens, fossils, coins and gems. His had an omnivorous appetite for knowledge, and such was his spirit of scientific enquiry that one experiment resulted in a spectacular indoors explosion in 1757.[12] It would not be hard to find numerous other individuals who were intellectually active as scientists, antiquarians, novelists, poets, theologians, philosophers or in other branches of learning.

Science, politics, economics and religion still remain under-investigated topics in country houses when compared to the wealth of scholarship on art, architecture and landscapes. This imbalance is conditioned in part by an erroneous belief that the public are not interested in such histories or that they are too difficult to tell, especially since they revolve around the life of the mind. This is both timid and unimaginative, and undervalues the significance of the written testament, which is the key to the intellectual core of a house.

---

10 P. Smith (ed.), *Lord Salisbury on politics* (Cambridge, 1972), pp 3–9, 19–20; A. Roberts, *Salisbury, Victorian titan* (London, 1999), pp 35, 52, 109–12, 242, 593–6.   11 The earl of Rosse, 'William Parsons, third earl of Rosse', *Hermathena*, 108 (autumn 1968), pp 5–13; *The scientific papers of William Parsons, third earl of Rosse, 1800–1867*, ed. C. Parsons (London, 1926); P. Moore, *The astronomy of Birr Castle* (London, 1971); more generally, see A. Chapman, *The Victorian amateur astronomer: independent astronomical research in Britain, 1820–1920* (Chichester, 1998); D.L. Opitz, 'Aristocrats and professionals: country house science in late Victorian Britain' (PhD, University of Minnesota, 2004).   12 B. James, 'An explosion in a country house' in G. Mulcahy (ed.), *A view of the hall: discovering the houses of the East Riding* (Burton Constable, 2005), pp 41–5; I. and E. Hall, *Burton Constable Hall: a century of patronage* (Hull, 1991), chs 3–7, 11.

14.5 William Constable's cabinet of curiosities at Burton Constable.
Photograph courtesy of Burton Constable.

14.6 One of the library door hinges at Tyntesfield, with the motto *Litera scripta manet* – the written word remains. The National Trust.

Trawling through country house archives, it clear that many occupants wrote as well as read: there are countless draft essays (begun if not finished) on subjects as diverse as politics, religion, history, genealogy, geology, agriculture and what we would call today anthropology; as well as literary endeavours – novels, poems and plays – not to mention personal reflections in diaries and journals. More locally, there are memoranda and correspondence with agents and other deputies detailing the workings of house and estate, and which reveal minds grappling with land, finances and neighbourhood affairs. The wider epistolary world too was central to the exchange of ideas and news, as well as the obligations of sociability. The book trade, subscription libraries, and the rise of provincial and national newspapers also enlarged the country house universe, in ways that laptop and internet connection do today. And there was always verbal exchange. Conversation did not have to be about manners and society gossip; for many, it was an essential means for social and intellectual interaction.[13]

In recent years, scholarship on the history of reading, letter-writing, book-buying and knowledge networks has boomed. Nevertheless, the evidential trail

---

13 See, for example, C. Brant, *Eighteenth-century letters and British culture* (Basingstoke, 2006); A. Kempton, *The epistolary muse: women of letters in England and France, 1652–1802* (Lausanne, 2017); C.J. Ferdinand, 'Newspapers and the sale of books in the provinces' in M.F. Suarez and M.L. Turner (eds), *The Cambridge history of the book in Britain*, vol. 5, *1695–1830* (Cambridge, 2008), pp 434–47; on conversation, see L.E. Klein, *Shaftesbury and the culture of politeness: moral discourse and cultural politics in early eighteenth-century England* (Cambridge, 1994), pp 9–10, 96–100; Retford, *Conversation piece*, pp 63–91.

for understanding the individual experience of reading remains problematic, given the largely silent and private nature of this activity.[14] Having said that, communal reading aloud was not uncommon in households; for example, the 7th earl of Carlisle would read to his mother and sisters in the evenings, either religious texts such as the sermons of Thomas Arnold or the latest instalments of a Dickens novel.[15] On the other hand, while staying at Cobham Hall, Kent, in 1837, Prince Puckler Muskau commented on a pleasurable two hours spent in the library after dinner among a group of nine guests, each silently reading their own book.[16] When conversation did take place, no trace would remain unless it was recorded by someone: little wonder then that the Gothic door hinges on the library door at Tyntesfield contain two inscriptions – *Verba locuta volant* ('spoken words fly away') and, more pertinently, for the space inside, *Litera scripta manet* ('the written word remains')[17] (fig. 14.6).

The topic of marginalia has also received attention of late, but marked copies of books do not always yield much insight. Horace Walpole, who claimed to 'love nothing so much as writing notes in my books', littered his volumes with crosses, asterisks, exclamation points and dashes; the earl of Bristol also marked his books at Ickworth with pencil lines.[18] In themselves, such hieroglyphics do not always betray a meaningful dialogue between reader and text, unlike the more substantial commentaries found in volumes once owned by John Stuart Mill, William Gladstone and Sir Joshua Reynolds; these examples reveal a critical intelligence taking issue with the page.[19] Elsewhere, diaries might reveal reading habits; thus, the 15th earl of Derby's journals are filled with references to books and reading; commonplace books were another level of textual engagement, whether commenting on books and ideas, or simply copying out passages worthy of note, as discussed by David Allen in his recent study of the practice in Georgian England.[20] These examples gainsay any idea that books went to sleep in country house libraries.[21]

We can never fully comprehend the processes of a mind with its reflective energies and abeyances unless these experiences are recorded in writing. An

---

14 On the sociability and privacy of reading, see A. Williams, *The social life of books: reading together in the eighteenth-century home* (London, 2017), ch. 3; C. Lupton, *Reading and the making of time in the eighteenth century* (Baltimore, MD, 2018); E. Jajdelska, *Silent reading and the birth of the narrator* (Toronto, 2007). **15** Diary of the 7th earl of Carlisle, 13 Oct. 1843 (Castle Howard Archives (hereafter CHA), J19/8/1); ibid., 15 Nov. 1843, 17 Jan., 12, 27, 29 Feb., 10 Mar., 6 May, 7 Oct. 1844. **16** Prince H. von Puckler-Muskau, *Letters of a dead man*, ed. Linda B. Marshall (Dumbarton Oaks, Washington DC, 2016), p. 368, 4 July 1837. **17** J. Miller and F. Fortune, *The story of Tyntesfield* (Swindon, 2003), pp 68–70. **18** Horace Walpole to Revd William Mason, 3 Apr. 1775, in W.S. Lewis et al. (eds), *The Yale edition of Horace Walpole's correspondence*, 48 vols (1937–83), xxviii, p. 187; M. Purcell and J. Fishwick, 'The library at Ickworth', *Book Collector*, 61, National Trust Libraries 6 (Sept. 2012), p. 377. **19** J. Powell, 'Small marks and instinctual responses: a study in Gladstone's marginalia', *Nineteenth-Century Prose*, 19:3 (1992), pp 1–17; H.J. Jackson, *Marginalia, readers writing in books* (New Haven, CT, 2001), ch. 4. **20** Purcell, *Country house library*, p. 198; D. Allen, *Commonplace books and reading in Georgian England* (Cambridge, 2014). **21** Ibid., p. 28.

especially clear example is found in the diary of Rosalind Howard, 9th countess of Carlisle, whose breathless entry in 1869 signals how reading John Stuart Mill's *On the subjection of women* was a defining moment in her life:

> I go <u>with</u> him in every word he says throughout. He is a wonderful champion for women's cause[s] … It has roused me to care more about women's liberty. I have always had liberty myself & so can well appreciate what value it would be to the mass of womankind.

This is an unusually explicit articulation, and in Rosalind's case this epiphany resulted in a lifetime working for women's suffrage.[22] On the other hand, a more indirect, but no less revealing, instance of intellectual cause-and-effect might be found with the library of the earl of Burlington and the manuscript catalogue of books at his villa in Chiswick, where, appropriately given his status as an arbiter of Palladian taste, a good proportion of the titles listed are on architecture and antiquities.[23]

Very often, however, historians are forced to fill in the gaps. The bare coordinates of the mental journey – a book in a library, a written sentence, a passing comment – are pointers; they do not chronicle the full mental process from beginning to end. They may lead to action of some kind, a resultant effect – an acquisition, a life of political activism, a sharpened intellect – but frequently, the iterative chain has to be inferred from incomplete evidence. One case study will demonstrate these challenges with adjudication between implicit and explicit evidence, certainty and conjecture; this example also firmly shifts one's understanding of a house away from conventional material culture.

In 1801, the marriage of Georgiana Cavendish, eldest daughter of the famous Georgiana, 5th duchess of Devonshire, to George Howard, future 6th earl of Carlisle, united the great houses of Chatsworth and Castle Howard. Among her copious papers, there are numerous items that begin to unlock her character; one of the earliest is her schoolbook, dating from when she was aged 15, which itemized her daily educational routine. In it, her reading is recorded, including plays by Shakespeare and newspapers, as well as her music practice, and letters sent and received. She made notes about her daily conversation, recording in one instance 'no conversation worth marking'. Her exercise routine, as well as her bedtime hours, were also entered; and there was a space for 'Extra Observations', which included at one moment a comment on her sister's illness (fig. 14.7). This is an invaluable account of the growth of her mind, as she passed from childhood to adulthood, but it also prepared her as an acute observer of herself and others – a pattern that would last her lifetime.[24]

22 Diary of Rosalind Howard, 8 Sept. 1869 (CHA, J23/102/15). For her extensive papers on women's suffrage, see J23/302–456.   23 P. Ayres, 'Burlington's library at Chiswick', *Studies in Bibliography*, 45 (1992), pp 113–27; J. Harris, *The Palladian revival: Lord Burlington, his villa and garden at Chiswick*, exh. cat. (London, 1994), pp 268–71.   24 Georgiana Cavendish

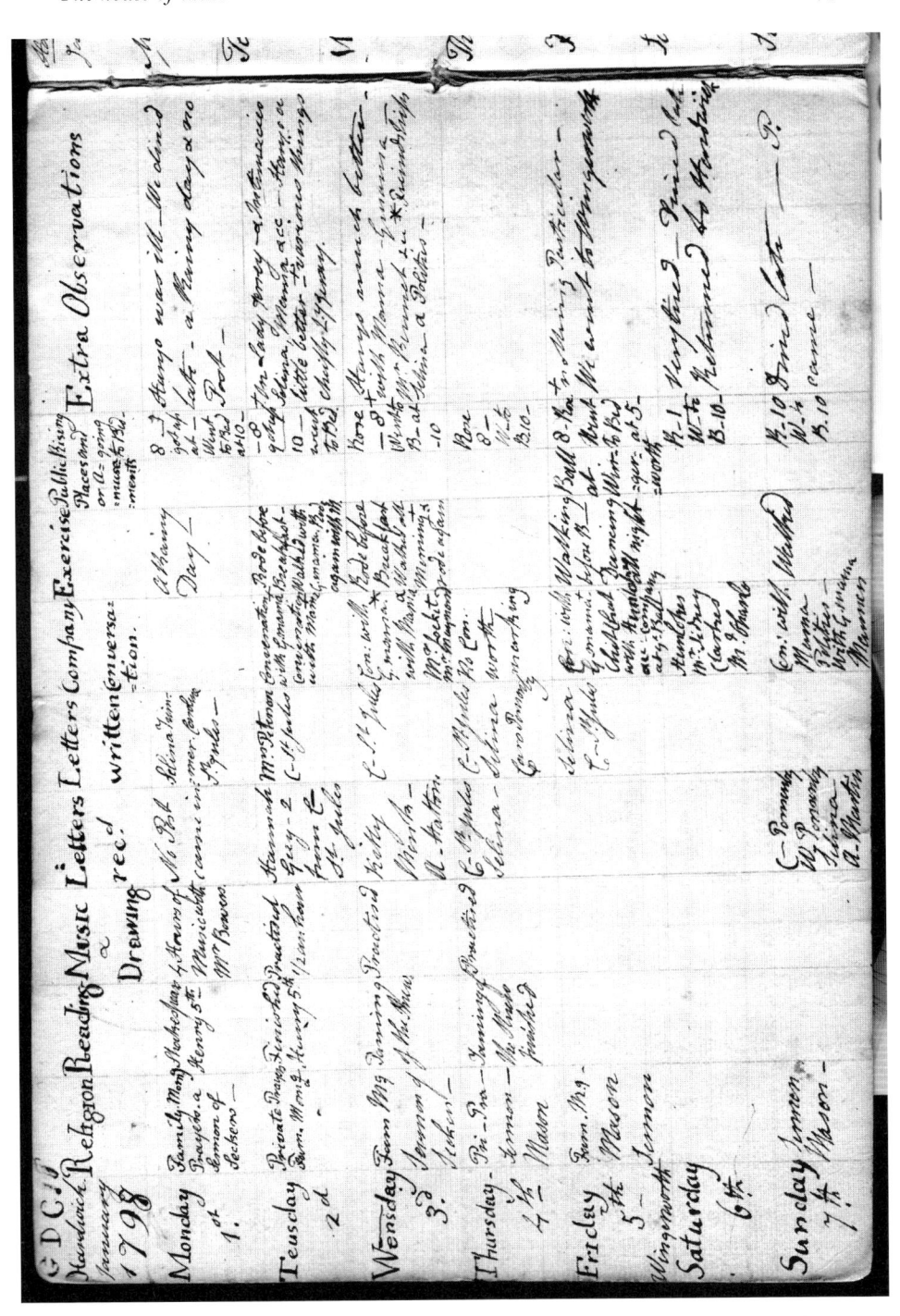

14.7 Page from Georgiana Cavendish's schoolbook, 1798. The Castle Howard Collection.

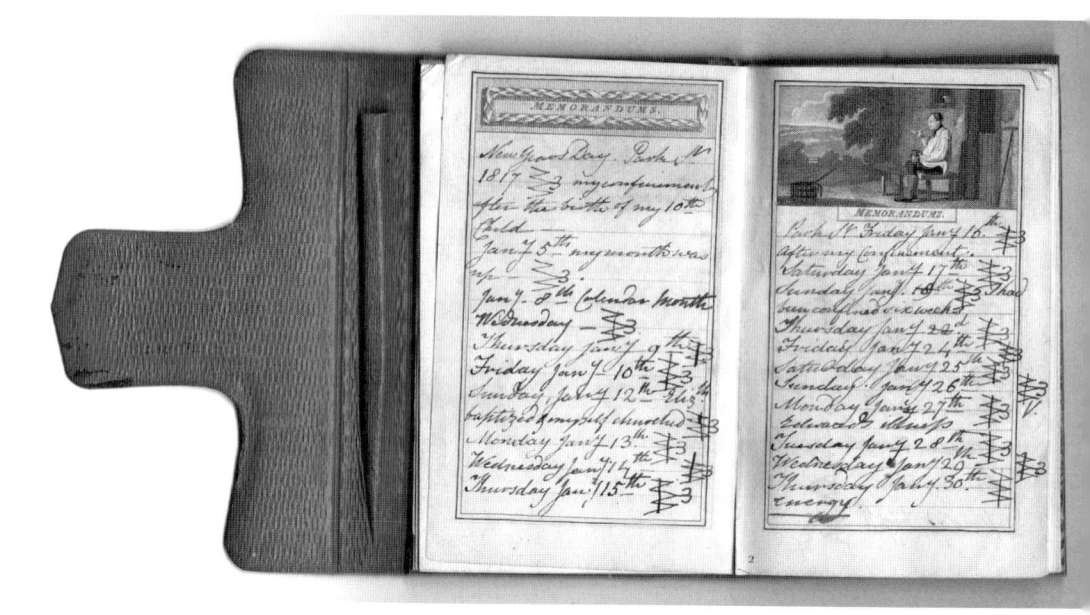

14.8 A page from the 6th countess of Carlisle's manuscript notebook on her health. The Castle Howard Collection.

Between 1802 and 1823, Georgiana gave birth to twelve children; thus, for the best part of two decades she was pregnant on average every eighteen months, not unlike Emily Kildare half a century earlier. She was afflicted by depression for much of her life, and part of her struggle against melancholy was likely related to repeated pregnancies. The clergyman, wit and near neighbour, Sydney Smith, who visited regularly to borrow books from the Castle Howard library, described Georgiana as 'very little calculated to bear up against the storms of life, she has lived all her days in the greenhouse of prosperity, and shrinks from the open air'.[25] But, her troubled state owed less to a delicate aristocratic constitution and more to real mental health issues, a topic that by its very nature is private and often fiercely protected. To combat this, Georgiana composed prayers, and undertook various exercise and dietary regimes in an attempt to improve her spiritual well-being. Throughout her life, she wrote a series of memoranda on her own health. Some of these were summaries of her life to date, others took the form of resolutions and regimens.[26]

'Schoolbook register for 1798' (CHA, J18/62/2); R.M. Larsen, 'Dynastic domesticity: the role of elite women in the Yorkshire country house, 1685–1858' (PhD, University of York, 2003), pp 101–4. For Georgiana's famous mother, see A. Foreman, *Georgiana, duchess of Devonshire* (London, 1999). **25** C. Ridgway, 'Sydney Smith and Castle Howard', *Sydney Smith Newsletter*, 14 (Apr. 2009), pp 8–18. **26** Georgiana, 6th countess of Carlisle, journals and pocketbooks (CHA, J18/62); memoranda about her health (ibid., J18/63); writings on religious topics (ibid., J18/74). See also Larsen, 'Dynastic domesticity', pp 221–6.

The most revealing examples of her extensive self-scrutiny are found in a series of tiny diaries-cum-notebooks, of which only a few survive. A series of zig-zag-hieroglyphs marked the pages, perhaps relating to dosages of medicine, while other entries recorded her adherence to William Cadogan's system of improvement (as prescribed in his popular 1771 publication on gout and chronic diseases); but solace was also found in devotion to her husband and in strict religious observance (fig. 14.8). Georgiana needed to regulate her life, to adhere to disciplines that would provide stability, structure and purpose, and these intimate documents begin to reveal a troubled inner self, as well as strategies for counselling 'occupation' and 'fortitude'.

She participated in society and assisted her husband in his political career, but she was never the flamboyant celebrity that her famous mother had been. She found greatest solace in her duties as mistress of Castle Howard and in her devotion to her family. Ultimately, it was this self-effacing quality, this immersion in service to others, that enabled her to conquer her melancholy. This inner life would be entirely invisible if we were to rely on the several painted likenesses for gauging her personality. One portrait by Yorkshire artist John Jackson of *c*.1808 depicts her with two of her children; only a few years later she confided in her book, 'my confinement after the birth of my 10th child', a statement that is squeezed between coded marks about her own state of mind. Together, the portrait and the written text offer a poignant illustration of her outer and inner life.[27]

Georgiana's arrival at Castle Howard in 1801 coincided with a burst of activity on the part of her father-in-law, the 5th earl of Carlisle. After a colourful and extravagant earlier life, which had included a Grand Tour, prodigious expenditure on art treasures and building works at Castle Howard, a political career in America and in Ireland, as well as a near brush with bankruptcy, at some point in the 1790s Carlisle woke up to the virtues and pleasures of farming. The evidence for this is found first and foremost with his library. He was a regular purchaser of books, with titles on literature, art, architecture, law, the classics and history, as would be expected in an aristocratic household. Among these books are several relating to agriculture: for example, a run of the *Communications of the Board of Agriculture* between 1797 and 1806; a copy of R.W. Dickson's *Practical agriculture* of 1805; and an 1807 edition of the two-volume manual *The complete farmer*. These titles were distinguished by illustrations of the latest machinery, modern building designs, new breeds, and were written in an authoritative and scientific manner.[28]

27 Volume for 1816 (CHA, J18/62/3–8); for Cadogan, see J. Rendle-Short, 'William Cadogan, eighteenth-century physician', *Medical History*, 4:4 (Oct. 1960), pp 288–309.
28 The literature of improvement is extensive, but see J.D. Fisher, *The enclosure of knowledge: books, power, and agrarian capitalism in Britain, 1660–1800* (Cambridge, 2022); also N. Goddard, 'The development and influence of agricultural periodicals and newspapers, 1780–1880', *Agricultural History Review*, 31:2 (1983), pp 116–31.

Christopher Ridgway

14.9 Title-page to Erasmus Darwin's *Phytologia, or the Philosophy of Agriculture and Gardening*, 1800. The Castle Howard Collection.

14.10 Page from the 5th earl of Carlisle's manuscript notebook, 'Manures'. The Castle Howard Collection.

The house of ideas 181

In themselves, they perhaps tell us nothing unusual. Here was a nobleman with an interest in agriculture – hardly surprising when he owned estates across the north of England totalling more than 80,000 acres. But, this cluster of titles suggests a concentrated period of interest in the literature of improvement, dating from the late 1790s into the first decade of the nineteenth century. The estate papers for this period reveal how Carlisle built a model farm in 1796, which was surveyed in the same year; each field was named after a branch of the Howard family, and the buildings were refurbished and enlarged.[29]

He was interested in improving his livestock, and by 1825 Castle Howard could boast its own famous breed of oxen. Special forms were printed to standardize weekly farm reports, and by 1815 the income from his estates had grown substantially; crop yields were good, and the fruit harvest promising.[30] Moreover, his desire to improve his estates extended to direct involvement in enhancing the fertility of his lands and nourishing the soil. Other titles in his library corroborate this interest: for example, a first edition of Erasmus Darwin's famous treatise on botany, *Phytologia, or, The philosophy of agriculture and gardening*, published in 1800 (fig. 14.9).

While not as famous as his grandson Charles, Erasmus Darwin was an eminent physician, inventor and natural philosopher. In 1765 he was a founder member of the Lunar Society, based in Birmingham, whose members debated science, industry and philosophy. For some there was a whiff of dangerous radicalism about this group, especially during the 1790s.[31] But, it is clear that Carlisle's own interest in botanical science was real and first-hand, and was probably in part stimulated by Darwin's own abiding interest in the topic. Carlisle also possessed an illustrated edition of Darwin's heroic poem *The botanic garden*, published in 1791; this was partly an attempt to versify the table of botanical knowledge and partly a celebration of contemporary industrial progress.[32] Evidently, Carlisle prized this volume, for he had it bound in a green morocco, armorial binding. These connections could be dismissed as no more than an interest in contemporary matters on his part, but there is a deeper link between Carlisle and Darwin that goes to the heart of improvement. Among Carlisle's miscellaneous papers is a small notebook, written in his hand, containing notes on 'Manures'; these detail the composition and chemical make-up of manure[33] (fig. 14.10).

Darwin's *Phytologia* is now credited as one of first treatises to recognize the importance of nitrogen in improving agricultural productivity. Manure was a

---

29 'Plan of the Earl of Carlisle's Farm at Castle Howard, Survey'd in the year 1796 by F. White of York' (CHA, P3/32–33).   **30** Dairy book (CHA, F/27/4); farm reports (CHA, F4/25).
31 J. Uglow, *The lunar men: the friends who made the future* (London, 2002).   **32** P. Elliott, *Erasmus Darwin's gardens: medicine, agriculture and the enlightenment sciences* (Martlesham Suffolk, 2021).   **33** 'Manures' (CHA, J14/76); see also F.A.L. James, '"Agricultural chymistry is at present in its infancy": the Board of Agriculture, the Royal Institution and Humphry Davy', *Ambix*, 62:4 (2015), pp 363–85.

lively topic, and all of the published agricultural volumes in Carlisle's library contained sections on the subject. It is unclear if Carlisle's notes were the result of his own trials, or whether they were copied out of published manuals, but they stress the importance of the decomposition of organic matter and the breakdown of chemical elements into the soil.

The manuscript likely dates from the first years of the nineteenth century. At precisely this time, Carlisle, like most of England, was anxious about the state of war with France. This conflict led him in 1798 to raise a local militia, the Castle Howard Riflemen, but he was perfectly able to ponder the topic of manure at the same time as organizing home defence.[34] So far, the QED is relatively straightforward to follow: the elements in this sequence – land, reading, improvement, experimentation and written record – connect to establish a particular intellectual pathway. The published titles in the library and the manuscript notes also present a startling contrast between the flamboyant aristocrat in Sir Joshua Reynolds' celebrated swagger portrait and Carlisle the farmer experimenting with soil. Here is a distinctly rustic example of materiality.

However, the connections with Darwin extend further still from agricultural improvement to self-improvement. In the archives there exists a letter from Darwin to Carlisle's son, Lord Morpeth, dated 1800. In it he replied in his capacity as a renowned physician to a medical enquiry and identified the malaise in question as a 'Tic douloureux', a form of facial neuralgia that causes sharp pains and uncontrollable twitching. He went on to say that this malady was covered 'in a new edition of my work on Zoonomia in octavo'.[35] Unsurprisingly, the library contains the third edition of *Zoonomia*, issued in 1801, and this medical portal opens up a route back to Georgiana's notebooks and her own health.

With this particular clutch of documents, ideas about moral, physical, and environmental well-being begin to coalesce, stretching across two generations, and encompassing contemporary thinking on education, religion, medicine, philosophy and agriculture. Intellectual curiosity, as well as medical concern, reveal a moment when books and other authorities were consulted in a very real quest for knowledge and answers. The irony is that these two generations of the Howard family were greatly responsible for the material opulence of Castle Howard – building, decorating, commissioning, and purchasing extensively; their physical stamp remains today throughout the house. These are accomplishments that are important, enduring and concrete; they declare themselves unequivocally and immediately, unlike the shadowy traces of thought. However, it could be argued that the achievements of material culture do not open up the life of the mind to the same degree as written material does.

---

[34] He was appointed captain of the Northern District of the North Riding of the Yorkshire Volunteer Riflemen on 10 May 1798 (CHA, J14/42/7). [35] Darwin to Lord Morpeth, 13 Nov. 1800 (CHA, J17/1/53).

Nevertheless it is important not to exaggerate the distinction between ideas and the concrete, after all these two spheres can be profoundly complementary. It would not be hard to find similar intellectual trajectories across numerous other country houses in many different fields of thought, albeit with varying degrees of connectedness according to the evidence available.

Because country houses were – and still are, in many instances – microcosms, they represent the most fertile ground for interdisciplinary enquiry. There is always more than one mental thread in this particular multiverse of ideas, and books and manuscripts are much more than just textual midwifes for material accomplishment. Their value is intrinsic *and* applied; the written word reveals insight, nuance and complexity, as well as gaps and questions. They provide a robust foundation for any house of ideas.

The library at Annes Grove

AILEEN SPITERE

Libraries tell us much about the history of a country house and those who lived there. The collections held in libraries often reflect haphazard acquisition on the part of different generations and highlight what was popular at different times. Sometimes, the contents show what really mattered to the owners. Horticulture and gardening were important to the Grove Annesley family, and their library at Annes Grove, near Castletownroche in Co. Cork, reflected those interests. Situated on the first floor of a mostly eighteenth-century house, it has views over the front and rear of the gardens, which were so important to the owners. It was a place to linger and relax, and by the early twentieth century, somewhere to consult a small but specialized collection of botanical and horticultural books and journals.[1]

Annes Grove is a 192-acre estate with thirty acres of gardens. The Groves purchased lands in north Cork and in Limerick, including the townland of Ballyhimmock (now Annes Grove) in the early seventeenth century. The lands passed to the Grove Annesleys came through the marriage settlement of Mary Grove and Francis Charles Annesley, 1st earl Annesley, in 1766. The Annes Grove estate grew substantially throughout the eighteenth and nineteenth centuries under Arthur Grove Annesley and his son, Richard Grove Annesley who died in 1892. His son, Richard Arthur Grove Annesley, inherited the then 1,800-acre estate while he was still a minor, gaining full control when he was twenty-six in 1905. The estate house is Georgian and most likely dates from the early eighteenth century. Subsequent generations of the Grove Annesley family added to and altered its shape and size throughout the nineteenth and twentieth centuries. The Grove Annesley family gifted the estate to the Irish state in December 2015. Following several years' work to restore the gardens, the site was opened to the public in April 2022. The Office of Public Works (OPW) is at present in its second year of sensitively restoring the gardens.

The thirty acres of gardens at Annes Grove are renowned and well known in the horticultural world. While they are mostly the twentieth-century creation of Richard Arthur Grove Annesley, who devoted more than sixty passionate years creating them, earlier occupants had set out some elements of the gardens. In the late eighteenth and early nineteenth centuries, Annes Grove was let to tenants,

---

[1] With thanks to Mary Heffernan, Colm O'Shea (OPW), Neil Porteous and the Grove Annesley family particularly Patrick Grove Annesley for generously sharing his knowledge of the family, gardens and library.

15.1 Hilda's Gate, walled garden, Annes Grove. Annes Grove Archive.

15.2 Richard Grove Annesley, *c.*1940s. Annes Grove Archive.

including the Aldworths. It was Mrs Ann Aldworth's gardens that were admired by Arthur Young in 1776, who observed she had 'ornamented a beautiful glen which winds behind the house in a manner that does honour to her taste. She has traced her paths as to command all the beauties of rock, wood and a sweet river which glides beneath both. It is a most agreeable scenery.'[2] This is the earliest known mention of gardens at Annes Grove. When Lieutenant-General Arthur Annesley took possession of the estate in 1820s, he made many improvements to the house and gardens, in particular altering the walled garden and the course of the River Awbeg. In 1837, Samuel Lewis was suitably impressed and commented how the grounds were 'laid out with great taste and surrounded by thriving plantations'.[3] These alterations were to prove influential on Richard Arthur Grove Annesley when he created the new parts of his garden.

Richard Arthur Grove Annesley (Richard), born in 1879, built on the tradition when he inherited fully in 1905. He most certainly was influenced by his cousins' gardens in Castlewellan, Co. Down. From the early 1900s until his death in 1966, Richard developed gardens that became world renowned. Influenced and informed by the great gardens and gardeners of the time, he became a source of inspiration and information for those interested in exotic plants and how to incorporate them into their planting schemes. He was a patron of the plant hunters, those botanists and horticulturalists who explored the world in order to find exotic plants to bring home, often at considerable personal risk. With his friends and acquaintances in many of the large estates in Ireland and in Britain, he was part of an informal seed-sharing network. Furthermore, as is clear from his library, he took it upon himself to learn and stay abreast of current horticultural developments in order to create, expand and maintain his paradise gardens. His was no ordinary interest or hobby.

He was a generalist in his interests, always researching new findings, although rhododendrons and primulas remained a passion. Ultimately, he had a vision for his gardens, and where he thought a particular species could add to the overall landscape, he was relentlessly curious and always prepared to push out the boundaries. Some parts of the garden were planted and remained relatively unchanged from the 1920s and 1930s, while other areas continued to change up until the 1960s. The many photo albums within the Annes Grove archive document, from 1908 onwards, the unfolding gardens, including some of the experiments that did not last; they are a crucial supplement to the written records that remain. For example, lillies, a staple in the early walled garden, were planted in various locations, but were supplanted in favour of other herbaceous plants. A well-stocked and regularly updated horticultural library informed his choices.

2 A. Young, *A tour in Ireland, 1776–1779* (London, 1897), p. 302.   3 S. Lewis, *A topographical dictionary of Ireland*, 2 vols (London, 1837), ii, pp 311–12.

In 1955, he was appointed president of the Royal Horticultural Society of Ireland and re-elected the following year in recognition of his efforts in the preceding years and also the extent of his achievements. Richard created a number of different areas or rooms in the gardens, the oldest of which are the walled gardens. They were originally laid out as orchards and are now filled with herbaceous borders, specimen trees and plants, an almost secret water garden and a small summer house. The woodland garden contains some of the earliest rhododendrons introduced to Ireland, as well as acers, hoheria, embothrium, camellias and magnolias. A subtropical riverside garden, complete with islands and footbridges, was created to allow bamboo, primula, gunnera and an assortment of trees to flourish and to create a breathtaking landscape that was visible from the house.

There are more than 700 books and journals together with an eclectic collection of correspondence in the library at Annes Grove. They are a mixture of the great novels of the day, as well as dictionaries, encyclopaedias, books on hunting and fishing, and a significant number of Bibles. The collection, while not extraordinary, gives an insight into the reading habits of the inhabitants of this country house estate over a period of 200 years. Side by side with Shakespeare, Charles Dickens, Jane Austen, Maria Edgeworth and Sir Walter Scott are histories of the Roman and British empires. Queen Victoria's letters share space with James Grove White's *Historical and topographical notes* (1905). There are fourteen volumes of the *Six Penny Magazine* from 1867 and six volumes of *Macmillan's Magazine* from 1864. The library is a mix of fiction and non-fiction, including history and encyclopedias. Old schoolbooks and Latin grammar books are a reminder of the educational aspect of private libraries at a time when many occupants, particularly women, were educated at home. Favourite books were handed down from earlier generations and were incorporated into what was mostly an eclectic collection. There was something for everyone in this library and it is easy to imagine the many pleasant hours spent browsing in such a peaceful place.

This library takes on a different character when it relates to gardening and all things horticultural, reflecting a more specialized interest. These books were part of Richard's working library and, from the evidence of the well-thumbed pages, were used and consulted regularly. It is this library which provides insights into what Richard Grove Annesley was doing in his garden and how he kept up to date on the developments in horticulture. Richard signed and dated many of his books, which helps to give a good idea of not only what he was reading but also when.

The earliest gardening book in this collection is *Every man his own gardener, being a new and much more complete gardener's kalendar and general director than anyone hitherto published* (1793), primarily written by John Abercrombie, but assisted by Thomas Mawe, gardener to the duke of Leeds, who was credited as a co-author. John Abercrombie was a Scottish horticulturalist and one of the most

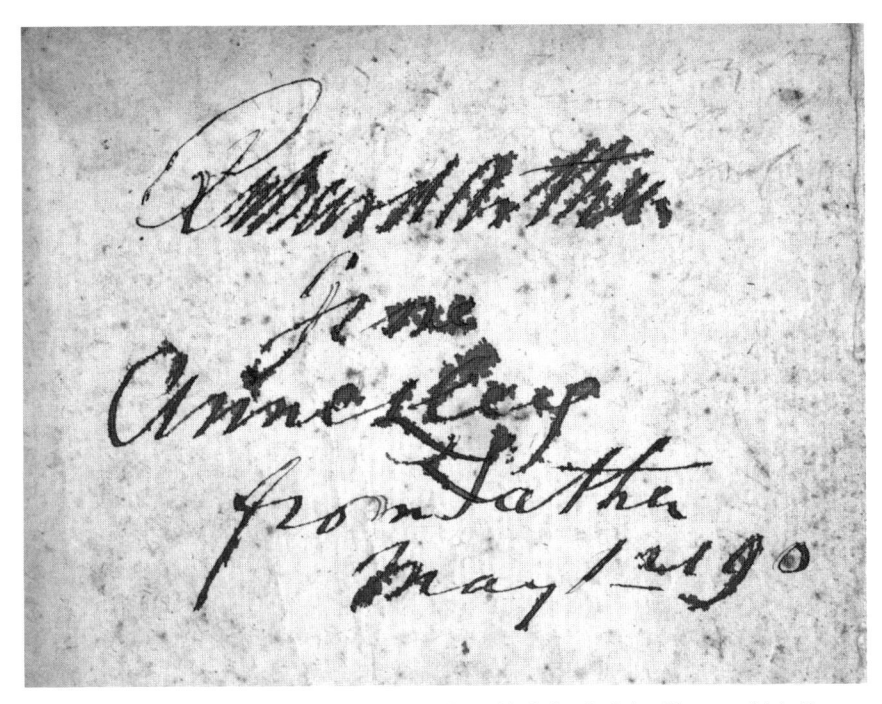

15.3 Inscription to Richard Grove Annesley from his father in John Abercrombie's *Every man his own gardener* (1793). Annes Groves Archive.

prolific gardening writers of the eighteenth century. It is most likely that this book originally belonged to John Mahon of Bessborough, Co. Tipperary, who was Richard's great grandfather, and was handed down through the generations. The inscription on the title page indicates that it was given to Richard by his father on 2 May 1890, when Richard was almost twelve years old.

This general gardening book covered everything from kitchen and fruit gardens to pleasure grounds, from flower gardens to green houses. It provided practical, no-nonsense gardening advice on a month-by-month basis. This was not a book for the dreamer or visionary, and was seen as a good starter book for a very young man. We know that Richard senior had introduced new types of conifers from America to Annes Grove and would have been a major influence on the young Richard. Whatever the extent of his encouragement to his son, this ended with the death of Richard senior in 1892. Before gaining full control of the estate, Richard struggled to obtain enough money to run the Annes Grove farm and there were very limited funds available for the gardens. Although it would take Richard a few years more to begin his own garden projects, it seems that his ideas had been formed from an early age. The book is annotated throughout by different hands, with special attention being shown to glasshouses and the growing of flowers and vegetables, along with many notes in the margins of types of soil.

From these small beginnings, a lifelong passion developed. The most influential gardening books of the period were often consulted, including those by the most famous gardening authors of the nineteenth and twentieth centuries, such as Gertrude Jekyll, William Robinson, Reginald Farrer, E.T. Cook, Walter P. Wright and Lewis B. Meredith. Titles by these authors can be found on the shelves in Annes Grove. Harry Higgot Thomas, who had worked with Jekyll and who was the first regular gardening columnist for the *Daily Telegraph*, is also among these books. While many of these titles were aimed at the dedicated amateur gardener, the library also contains specialist reference books such as by the Swiss botanist Gustave Hegi, editor of some of the most comprehensive reference works of floras of the world, including *Alpine flowers*, which was translated into English in 1930, as well as writings by the New Zealand botanist Leonard Cockayne, and the four-volume work *A general system of gardening and botany* (1831) by George Don, the Scottish botanist and plant collector. These are the books that provided Richard with the tools to understand his soil, to learn of new plants, trees and flowers and to equip him with the most up-to-date thinking of his time. From his readings, he chose what was best suited to his environs and according to his taste.

Upon entering the walled garden today, the influence of Gertrude Jekyll can still be seen. Colour was a fundamental part of the garden for Jekyll and an important, if not essential, component of garden design. Her books on colour and planting are prominent in the Annes Grove library.[4] In the gardens, dahlias, delphiniums and other herbaceous plants are still arranged in blocks of colours, moving from warm to vibrant on the colour spectrum. The use of a single colour, particularly red (a favourite of Jekyll), remains an important part of the garden design in Annes Grove and reflects the continuation of Richard's garden to the present time. Photographs from as early as the late 1920s show how relatively unchanged many of the borders have remained.

Annes Grove Gardens are often described as Richard Grove Annesley's interpretation of a Robinsonian garden. As expected, books by his fellow Irishman, William Robinson, are to be found in his library. One of Robinson's most significant concepts was the idea of naturalistic gardening, which was introduced in *The wild garden* and further developed in *The English flower garden*.[5] Robinson admired nature's diversity and brought what he called 'the untidy edges', where a garden blended into the larger landscape. His ideas were well suited to the Annes Grove landscape. The development of the river garden and island reflect Robinson's influence, albeit with Richard's own stamp. These were important books in Richard's library that nourished his imagination and the photo albums in particular document the development of these Robinsonian elements of the garden landscape.

4 G. Jekyll: *Wall and water gardens* (London, 1902); eadem, *Some English gardens* (London, 1904); eadem, *Colour schemes for the flower garden* (London, 1919).   5 W. Robinson, *The wild garden* (London, 1870); idem, *The English flower garden* (London, 1883).

In addition to the collection of horticultural and botanical books, Richard subscribed to many journals and yearbooks. The journals are a mix of the general and the academic. In the January 1939 issue of *New Flora and Silva*, one can read about Davidias by W.J. Bean or Berberis by Camillo Schneider. The Davidias are to this day an important part of the garden in Annes Grove. In the August 1950 issue of the *Journal of the Royal Horticultural Society*, there were articles about the Wisley trials for experimental planting of new varieties of plants, and even a piece about an expedition to Nepal. In this issue Richard annotated information on the growing of rudbeckias, heleniums and salvias wondering if they would be suitable for Annes Grove. He was interested also in the Wisley trials for narcissus between 1948 and 1950, and commented on the varieties used for garden decoration. The presence of the *Journal* and the rhododendron and daffodil yearbooks show his continued interest in the latest horticultural developments.

Annes Grove often featured in the RHS journals. In 1950, the English horticulturalist G.S. Thomas visited and described a *cornus controversa variegata* as 'just at its best and showing the light beauty of its white variegated foliage, tier upon tier up to some 25 feet ... Mr. Annesley's specimen was the most stately I saw.'[6] In 1959, R.C. Jenkinson described the same tree, except it had by then grown to 33 feet. Jenkinson thoroughly enjoyed his May visit to Annes Grove, remarking on the diversity of plants and trees. Of particular interest to him were the rhododendrons that 'Mr Annesley grows so surprisingly well.'[7] The Annes Grove library contains an important collection of books written by plant hunters, particularly George Forrest and by Frank Kingdon Ward. From the photographs and letters that have been found within the pages of these books, it is clear how crucial they were in understanding Richard Grove Annesley's gardens. There are photographs of Forrest and Annan Bryce, of Ilnacullin, with Richard in Annes Grove with a large Hessian bag of seeds and cuttings.[8] A letter from Lionel de Rothschild in June 1931 to Richard mentions that Forrest had 'gone out on another expedition to China and some seeds from his native collectors have come back'.[9] He enclosed, in the letter, a packet of seed of *r. croceremo* and wrote that he was expecting more interesting seeds the following year, wondering if Richard would like a little. George Forrest never did return to Europe, as he died of a heart attack in January 1932 while plant hunting in China.

The largest collection of books by a single author in the Annes Grove horticultural library were written by Frank Kingdon Ward. There is no doubt that Richard Grove Annesley held him in very high regard, referencing him throughout his notes, particularly when considering rhododendrons. The letters that were found within the pages of the books highlight their close and amiable

6 G.S. Thomas, 'Some famous Irish gardens', *Journal of the Royal Horticultural Society*, 74 (1950), pp 315–23. 7 R.C. Jenkinson, 'Irish gardens and gardeners', *Journal of the Royal Horticultural Society*, 84 (1959), pp 460–7. 8 Annes Grove Archive (AGGA). These papers are only partially catalogued as of November 2023. 9 AGGA.

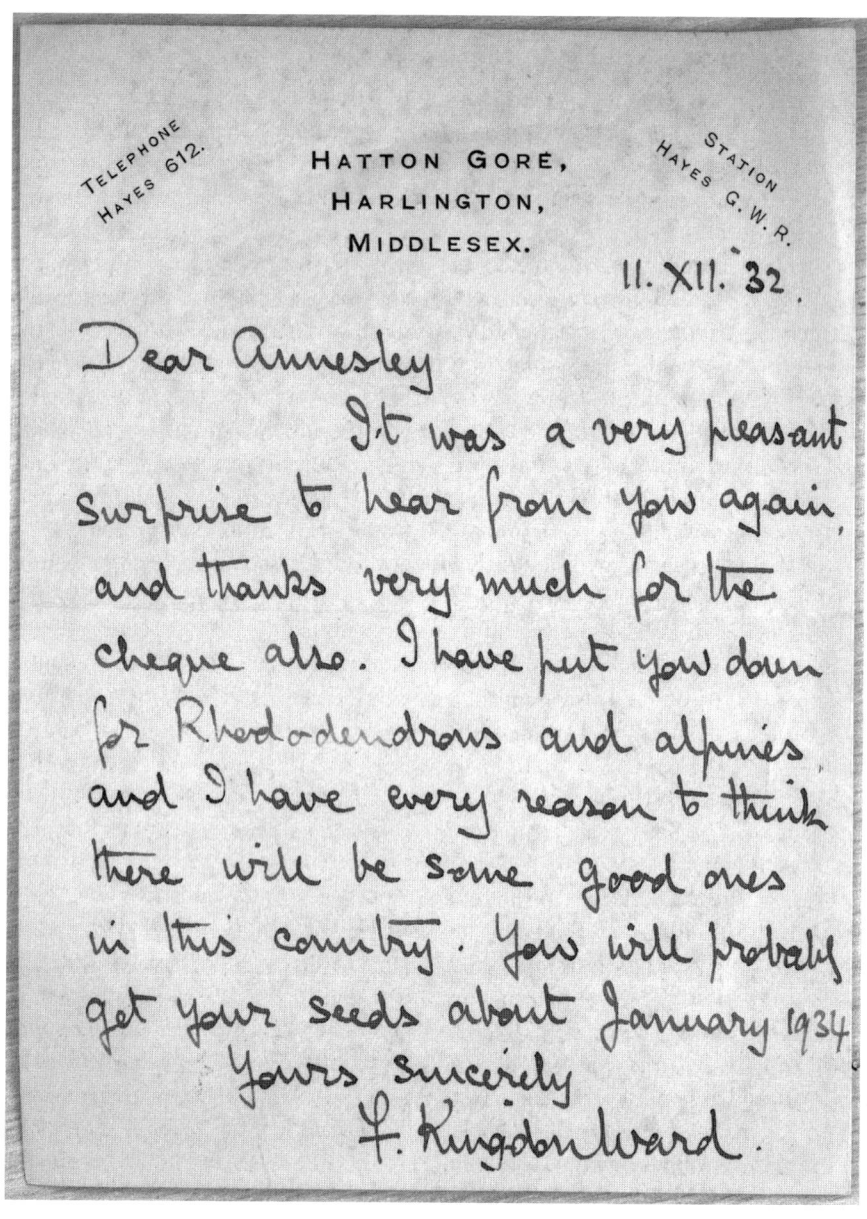

> HATTON GORE,
> HARLINGTON,
> MIDDLESEX.
>
> TELEPHONE HAYES 612.
> STATION HAYES G.W.R.
>
> 11. XII. 32
>
> Dear Annesley
>
> It was a very pleasant surprise to hear from you again, and thanks very much for the cheque also. I have put you down for Rhododendrons and alpines, and I have every reason to think there will be some good ones in this country. You will probably get your seeds about January 1934
>
> Yours Sincerely
> F. Kingdon Ward.

15.4 Frank Kingdon Ward letter to Richard Grove Annesley of 11 Dec. 1932. Annes Grove Archive.

working relationship. Just eight letters, dating from 1932 to 1957, remain of what was most likely a more extensive correspondence. These letters, written from Tibet, Calcutta, Ceylon and Birkenhead, described his journeys, the problems with transportation and food, the climate and topography, as well as the seeds he was collecting.[10] Kingdon Ward's expeditions were primarily financed by subscription and Richard not only subscribed but arranged for others to contribute also. In 1932, Ward wrote that he had put Richard down for rhododendrons and alpines. A year later, he mentioned that the murder of his mail runner in Tibet had 'rather jammed things'. As late as September 1955, Kingdon Ward was pleased to hear that Richard was interested in lilies, 'having become a fan himself'.

Letters from R.M.K. Buchanan, the representative for Kingdon Ward's plant hunting expedition in 1934, informed Richard that the final batch of seeds would soon be distributed and that Kingdon Ward was preparing his field notes on the expedition for publication, which would be in the subscribers' hands later in the year.[11] This publication forms part of the library, and is well annotated with Richard's own handwriting and was used as part of his day-to-day work. Richard used these field notes to recreate how the rhododendrons were planted in the wild, paying particular attention as to what plants were grown nearby, commenting on the soil and overall physical nature of the landscape from which they came.

The final letter from Kingdon Ward was from Ceylon, in which he noted he had 'had a sticky time in the Chin Hills but got some good plants in the end'. The letter outlined the growing difficulties he was experiencing in getting plants and seeds out of the country. However, he informed Richard that he should receive 'the primulas, rhododendrons and alpine saxifraga as well as hypericum and alliums which should prove both hardy and acceptable'. This letter went on to describe the tea estate where he was staying, that he was going to an orchid show and mentioned the places he intended to visit once the weather improved. He finished by letting Richard know he was very anxious to see the Ceylonese pitcher plant.[12]

The correspondence from the seed and plant suppliers indicate that Richard was buying from the best and constantly enquiring as to whether they had seeds or bulbs in which he was interested. He dealt with suppliers from Ireland, UK and throughout the world to source what he needed. He used his subscription to published journals in particular, to keep up to date and his correspondence with the suppliers shows that he was keen to buy what was new but also what he considered to be relevant to his collection. In 1932, he was buying *acer rufinerve* and *circinatum*, *viburnum oculus*, *euonymus planipes* and *latifolius* from W.J. Marchant in Wimborne in Dorset, while in 1938 he purchased from the Japanese supplier, K.Wanda, camellias and also new types of lillies, in particular *lilium auratum*, which the suppliers asked him to see if it would grow in Ireland. The replies from the suppliers often contained advice and suggestions as to what might grow in Ireland, as well as enquiring whether he had considered growing other varieties. At times, Richard was asked if he could spare any seeds because

10 AGGA.   11 AGGA.   12 AGGA.

of the reputation of his displays; for example, in January 1966, the Dutch seed merchant Van Tubergens in Haarlem asked him for spare seeds of *primula vialii*. Considering this occurred not long before Richard Grove Annesley died, the letters provide insight into just how active he was in creating his gardens right up until his death aged eighty-five.

The contents of the Annes Grove library – the combination of books, journals, letters, and photographs – provide the evidence that Richard Grove Annesley was a committed gardener with a clear idea of what he wanted to do. He researched and read widely, he met and/or corresponded with the plant hunters and suppliers, he sponsored their expeditions, and then he planted the seeds, paying close attention to the field notes, particularly of Kingdon Ward, in order to achieve the best results. A quick look at Richard's annotations and notes written upon Kingdon Ward's published field notes or books show how important they were to him.

One book in the library deserves a final mention. *My shrubs*, written by Richard Grove Annesley, was bound in 1928.[13] It is primarily a list of shrubs planted in Annes Grove, but to a large extent, it is a record of his early work in the garden. Some of the plants and trees that survive today in the garden are recorded in this book. It serves as a fitting testament to his research and his collaboration with the best of his age. The books, letters and photographs give a glimpse of a well-connected world in which a small rural corner of Ireland was able to remain at the forefront of the gardening world. While we may know some of the influences that shaped work at Annes Grove, we may never know everything: for example, why he desired to include exotics in his garden paradise? It is hoped that further examination of the archive will shed extra light on Richard's plans and projects. What began with a fascination for the new developed into so much more. As well as having the resources, Richard had time, knowledge and an abundance of energy. Like all gardeners, his optimism was apparent in every corner of the garden and in his library.

In the front page of a book written by Frank Kingdon Ward and given to Richard by his wife Hilda in 1930 were a few lines from a poem by an anonymous poet:

> Here's a book above the level,
> As is Himalaya's self;
> Let me tell – but why the devil?
> Just you take it off your shelf
> And let flowers and high adventure
> Fill a humdrum Autumn night
> While they equally content your
> Taste for 'Someone who can write'.

13 AGGA.

Contributors

BEN COWELL is director general of Historic Houses. He is the author of *The heritage obsession: the battle for England's past* (Stroud, 2008) and most recently, *The British country house revival* (Martlesham, Suffolk, 2024).

DEIRDRE CULLEN is a PhD candidate at University College Dublin. Her research is focused on the eighteenth-century painted decorations in the Long Gallery of Castletown House, Co. Kildare, and is funded by the Irish Research Council and the Office of Public Works. She was joint awardee of the Irish Georgian Society's Desmond Guinness Scholarship in 2021.

IAN D'ALTON is the author of *Protestant society and politics in Cork, 1812–1844* (Cork, 1980) and was co-editor of *Protestant and Irish: the minority's search for place in independent Ireland* (Cork, 2019). A former visiting fellow at Sidney Sussex College, Cambridge, he is currently a visiting research fellow in the Centre for Contemporary Irish History, Trinity College Dublin.

KRISTINA DECKER is a doctoral candidate in history at University College Cork. She was awarded a Government of Ireland Postgraduate Scholarship from the Irish Research Council for her research project, 'Women and improvement in eighteenth-century Ireland: the case of Mary Delany (1700–1788)' and previously received a Desmond Guinness Scholarship from the Irish Georgian Society for her work on Mary Delany.

TERENCE DOOLEY is head of department, professor of history, and director of the Centre for the Study of Historic Irish Houses and Estates at the Department of History, Maynooth University. His most recent monograph is *Burning the big house: the story of the Irish country house in war and revolution* (London, 2022).

CATHAL DOWD SMITH is curator and collections manager of Newbridge House and Malahide Castle for Fingal County Council. He is a graduate of Trinity College Dublin where he studied the history of art and architecture and history; his current research interests are in the Irish country house, and architectural and landscape history of the eighteenth and nineteenth centuries.

R.F. (ROY) FOSTER is emeritus professor of Irish history at the University of Oxford. His many books include *Modern Ireland 1600–1972*, the two-volume authorized biography of W.B. Yeats, *The apprentice mage* (Oxford, 1998) and *The arch-poet* (Oxford, 2003), *The Irish story: telling tales and making it up in Ireland* (London, 2021), *Vivid faces: the revolutionary generation in Ireland* (London, 2014) and most recently, *On Seamus Heaney* (Princeton, 2020). The holder of several honorary degrees, he is a Fellow of the British Academy and an honorary member of the Royal Irish Academy. In 2021 he received the President's Distinguished Service Award.

JAMES FRAZER completed a PhD at Queen's University Belfast in 2023. His research interests include the political and religious history of nineteenth-century Ireland. He is currently employed as research officer at the Irish Linen Centre & Lisburn Museum.

RAYMOND GILLESPIE was emeritus professor of history, Maynooth University, until his untimely death in February 2024. He published widely on social change in early modern Ireland, most recently *Reforming Galway: civic society, religious change and St Nicholas's collegiate church, 1550–1750* (Dublin, 2024).

ELIZABETH GRUBGELD is regents professor of English at Oklahoma State University and author of three books on Irish autobiography, each of which was awarded the American Conference for Irish Studies Rhodes Prize for Literature in its respective year: *George Moore and the autogenous self* (Syracuse, 1994); *Anglo-Irish autobiography: class, gender, and the forms of narrative* (Syracuse, 2004); and *Disability life writing in post-independence Ireland* (Cham, 2020).

ANNA-MARIA HAJBA is a senior archivist at University of Limerick's Glucksman Library. She holds postgraduate degrees in English philology, cultural history, and archive administration, and is currently a PhD candidate in history at UL. She is the author of a wide range of works on architectural history, including most recently, *The building of Adare Manor: a family chronicle* (Dublin, 2023).

JEREMY HILL, sometime airline pilot, farmer and gallery owner, now promotes heritage and manages the Monksgrange Archive – a vast resource of family papers, letters, diaries, personal artwork and photographs facilitating post-graduate research.

ELIZABETH JAMIESON is an independent researcher, lecturer and art historian. She is director of the Attingham Study Programmes for the study of the British country house and curatorial advisor to the National Trust on horse-drawn carriages and historic stables.

KATE RETFORD is professor of history of art and head of the School of Historical Studies at Birkbeck, University of London. She has published widely on eighteenth-century British art, particularly on gender, portraiture, and the country house. Her recent publications include *The conversation piece: making modern art in eighteenth-century Britain* (New Haven, 2017) and *The Georgian London town house: building, collecting and display*, co-edited with Susanna Avery-Quash (London, 2019). She is currently working on a book about print rooms in

Contributors

eighteenth-century country houses, which was funded by a Leverhulme Research Fellowship in 2021–2.

CHRISTOPHER RIDGWAY is curator at Castle Howard and adjunct professor at Maynooth University.

AILEEN SPITERE is a qualified archivist and has a masters in history. She was previously the head of the London Office of the National Archives of Canada. At present she is sorting and cataloguing the Annes Grove archive in Castletownroche in north Cork.

Index

The index adopts the standard academic practice of referring to the city and diocese of Derry, but the county of Londonderry.

Abbey School, Tipperary, 122
Abbeyleix House, Co. Laois, 75
Adam, Robert, 140, 155
Adare Manor, Co. Limerick, 108–21
Adminton House, Gloucestershire, 138
Althorp House, Northamptonshire, 142
America, *see* United States of America
Annes Grove, Co. Cork, 74, 184–94
Antrim, earls of, *see* McDonnell family of Co. Antrim (earls of Antrim)
Armagh county, 61
Atget, Eugène, 124–35

Ballisk, Co. Dublin, 63–4
Ballyfin, Co. Laois, 74, 75
Ballynatray House, Co. Cork, 39, 74
Bandon, Lord and Lady, 38
Banville, John, 29
  Birchwood, 29, 74
Barber, Mary, 42
Beaufort, Lady Margaret, 138
Belfast, 91, 93, 94
Belfast Castle, 93
Bence-Jones, Gillian, 31
'bible gentry' *see* evangelical Protestantism
Binney, Marcus, 7, 11, 67
Birr Castle, Co. Offaly, 172
Birr workhouse, Co. Offaly, 76
Blythe, Ernest, 68, 69
Boland Kevin, 69
bookselling and book buying, 89–98, 101, 103–7, 108–9, 112–21, 179–81, *see also* libraries
Bord Fáilte, 77
botany, 41–51, 181–3, 184–94
Bowen, Elizabeth, 29–40, 71, 74
  Bowen's Court, 40
  Eva Trout, 31

The last September, 31, 32, 33, 34, 37, 39, 74
A world of love, 39
Bowen's Court, Co. Cork, 30, 31, 32, 33, 34, 40, 75
Bowood, Wiltshire, 10
Brehon Law Commission, 117
Brennan, Maeve, 74
  Springs of affection, 74
Brighton, 58
British Archaeological Association, 142
British Museum, 59, 142
British Tourist Authority, 4, 5
British Travel Association, 4, 11
Browne, Elizabeth, 140–1
Browne, George, 8th Lord Montague, 140
Brownlow, Arthur, 96
Brugha, Cathal, 73
Brussels, 18
Buckminster Park, Leicestershire, 148
Bulstrode Park, Buckinghamshire, 43, 44, 45
Bunbury, Sarah, 19
Bunratty Castle, Co. Clare, 91
Bunyan, John, 80
  Pilgrim's progress, 58, 80
Burton Constable, East Yorkshire, 172
Burton Hall, Co. Cork, 92
Butler, Col. [Francis?], 90, 92

Cambrian Archaeological Association, Wales, 117
Campbell, Patrick, 90
Carter-Brown, J., 11
Carton House, Co. Kildare, 18
Cassiobury Park, Hertfordshire, 171
Castle Bernard, Co. Cork, 38
Castle Brown, Co. Kildare (Clongowes Wood College), 152

Castle Howard, North Yorkshire, 176, 178–80
Castle Hyde, Co. Cork, 39, 74
Castle Ward, Co. Down, 94
Castleisland, Co. Kerry, 91
Castlemaine, Lady, 38
Castletown Cox, Co. Kilkenny, 74
Castletown House, Co. Kildare, 13–28, 74
Castlewellan, Co. Down, 187
Cavendish Bentwick, Margaret, duchess of Portland, 42–51
Cavendish, Georgina, countess of Carlisle, 176–9
Cavendish, Georgina, 5th duchess of Devonshire, 176
Celtic Society, 117
Chancery Lane Safe Deposit, London, 146–7
Charlotte, Queen, 42
Chastleton House, Oxfordshire, 139
Chatsworth House, Derbyshire, 138, 176
Chichesters *see* Donegall family of Antrim
Clandeboye, viscounts, *see* Hamilton family of Co. Down (viscounts Clandeboye)
Clongowes Wood College, *see* Castle Brown, Co. Kildare (Clongowes Wood College)
Cobbe, Charles, 60–1
Cobbe, Frances Power, 52–66
    Duties of women, 57
    'The Fenians of Ballybogmucky', 63
Cobham Hall, Kent, 175
Cole family of Co. Fermanagh, 95, 97
Coleman, David, 5
Collins Barracks, 76
Conolly, Louisa, 13–28, 151
Conolly, Thomas, 13–28
Conservative Party, 5, 12
Constable, William, 172–3
Conway, Edward, 94
Cooke, Henry, 87
Coole, Co. Galway, 30
Cornforth, John, 5–7, 11
Cork county, 91, 92, 184–94
Cosgrave, William T., 68
Cowdray House, West Sussex, 136–49
Cowdray, Viscount, 140
Coyningham family of Co. Londonderry, 95
Crossfield, Co. Leitrim, 95
Curraghmore, Co. Waterford, 35, 76

Darwin, Charles, 53, 181
Darwin, Erasmus, 181–2
decorative arts, 41–51
Delany (née Pendarves), Mary, 41–51, 93, 151
Delany, Patrick, 41–3, 46, 49–50
Delville, Co. Dublin, 41–51, 151
de' Rossi, Domenico, 154–6
destruction of country houses, 37–9, 71–4, 75, 140
de Vere White, Terence, 69
Derrylahan Park, Co. Tipperary, 74
Development of Tourism Act (1969) (UK), 4, *see also* legislation
d'Hervart, Sabine, 140
Dockrell, Maurice, 69
Dolan, Turlough, 97
Dolly's Brae, 79
domestic servants, 54–5, 70, 81–2
Donegal county, 62
Donegall family of Antrim, 93, 94
    Chichester, Arthur, 4th earl of Donegall, 93
Doneraile Court, Co. Cork, 74
Dorchester Hotel, 4
Drishane, Co. Cork, 30, 31
Dublin Castle, 91
Dublin city, 69, 74, 79, 89–91, 93, 95, 106
Dublin county, 41–51, 52–66
Dublin Philosophical Society, 96
Dundalk House, Co. Louth, 79, 83, 88
Dundas, Sir David, 168
Dundas, Thomas, 161
Dunluce Castle, Co. Antrim, 91
Dunraven, earls of, *see* Wyndham Quin family of Co. Limerick (earls of Dunraven)
Dunsany, Lord, 70
    The curse of the wise woman, 70
Dunton, John, 89, 92, 93

Echlin, Henry, 90
Echlinville, Co. Down, 90
Edgeworth family of Longford, 90, 101, 106, 188
    Edgeworth, Maria, 101, 106, 188
education, 15, 18, 28, 53–4, 57–60, 85–7, 122, 126
Elizabeth, Charlotte, 81–2, 87, 88
Elstob, Elizabeth, 44–5

Index

Emo Court, Co. Laois, 74
England, 44, 46, 53–4, 58, 74, 94, 136–49
evangelical Protestantism, 61, 64, 78–88
exhibitions
> *The destruction of the country house*, Victoria and Albert Museum (1974), 7–8, 11, 67–8
> *Treasure houses*, National Gallery of Art, Washington DC (USA) (1985), 11

Eyrecourt, Co. Galway, 75

Farley, Maurice, 35
> 'Stately home', 35

Farnham family of Cavan, 78, 80
> Farnham, 5th baron, 80, 86

Farrell, J.G., 38, 70
> *Troubles*, 38

Farrell, Michael, 71
> *Thy tears might cease*, 71

Fenianism, 63–4
Finance Act (1975) (UK), 10, *see also* legislation
Finance Act (1976) (UK), 10, *see also* legislation
fires, *see* destruction of country houses
First World War, 8
FitzGerald, Emily, duchess of Leinster, 19, 153, 166, 167–8, 169–70, 178
FitzGerald, James, duke of Leinster, 169–70
FitzGerald, William Robert, marquis of Kildare (later, 2nd duke of Leinster), 153
Fitzwilliam Street, Dublin, 69
Florence, 18, 18 n., 15, 127
Florence Court, Co. Fermanagh, 95, 97
Fraigneau, William, 18

Gaelic League, 126
gardens, *see* landscape design and management
Garth, Samuel, 23
Gascoigne Cecil, Robert, 3rd marquess of Salisbury, 172
Geashill Castle, Co. Offaly, 91
Geddes, Ross, 4
Geneva, 15, 18
Geneva Academy, 15, 18
George III, 42
Gibbs, James, 136
Goodwood, Sussex, 18

Gosford family of Armagh, 78
Gowers, Sir Ernest, 2–3
> Gowers Report (1950), 2–3, 5

Glenavy, Lady (Beatrice Moss Campbell), 38
Grand Tour, 15, 16, 18, 26, 28, 152, 179, *see also* travel, foreign
Gray, Sir James, 18
Granville Dewes, Mary, 44, 46
Green, Henry, 72
> *Loving*, 72

Gregory (Isabella) Augusta, Lady Gregory, 30
Grierson, Constantia, 42
Grove Annesley family of Co. Cork, 184–94
> Annesley, Francis Charles, 1st earl Annesley (1740–1802), 184
> Grove, Mary (d. 1791), 184
> Grove Annesley, Arthur (1774–1849), 184
> Grove Annesley, Richard (1815–92), 184
> Grove Annesley, Richard Arthur (1879–1966), 184, 187–94

Haldane, Robert, 87
Ham House, London, 146–9
Hamilton family of Co. Down (viscounts Clandeboye), 94, 96
> Hamilton, Anne, 94
> Hamilton, James, 94

Hamilton, Sir William, 153, 154
Hardwick, P.C., 114
Hardwick Hall, Derbyshire, 138
Harris, John, 7, 8
Hartnett, Michael, 34
> 'A visit to Castletown House', 34

Hatfield House, Hertfordshire, 172
Healey, Denis, 10
Heard family (of Pallastown), 39
Heath, Edward, 5
Heritage Council, 77
Hibernian Bible Society, 79, 85
Hillsborough Castle, Co. Down, 95
Hippisley-Cox, Richard, 157–9, 162–3
Historic Houses Association (UK), 2, 5, 9, 10, 11, 12
Hope, Thomas, 161
Hopetoun House, South Queensferry, 138
Horsely, Samuel, 60–1

Howard family of Castle Howard
    Howard, George, 11
    Howard, Frederick, 5th earl of Carlisle, 179–82
    Howard, George, 6th earl of Carlisle, 176, 182
    Howard, George, 9th earl of Carlisle, 168
    Howard, Mary, Lady Andover, 44
    Howard, Rosalind, 9th countess of Carlisle, 176
Hughes, John, 37
    'The Big House on the hill', 37
Hume Street, Dublin, 69
Humewood Castle, Co. Wicklow, 74
Huntingdon Library, California, 140

Irish Archaeological Society, 117
Irish Architectural Archive, 74–5
Irish Georgian Society, 75
Irish Museum of Modern Art, *see* Royal Hospital Kilmainham
Irish Society, the, 85

Jay, William, 60
Jekyll, Gertrude, 190
Jenkin, Hugh, 9
Jocelyn, Robert, 3rd earl of Roden, 78–88
    Lord Roden and the servant girl, 80
Johnston, Jennifer, 36
    The gates, 36
Jones, Martha, 54

Keane, Molly, 31, 32, 34, 38, 71–2
    Loving and giving, 34
    Two days in Aragon, 31, 32, 38, 72
Kildare, earl of, 91
Kildare Place, Dublin, 69
Kimmage, Co. Dublin, 38
Kingdon Ward, Frank, 191–3
Knockninny, Co. Fermanagh, 95
Knole, Kent, 143–6, 148–9

La Demeure Historique (France), 2
Labour Party (UK), 5, 7, 10
Lancashire County Record Office, 148–9
Lancaster, Osbert, 7–8
Land Commission, 68
landscape design and management, 33, 41–51, 184–94

languages, 18, 102, 108
Le Fanu, Sheridan, 70
legislation
    Development of Tourism Act (1969) [UK], 4
    Finance Act (1975) [UK], 10
    Finance Act (1976) [UK], 10
    Planning and Development Act, 2000 [RI]
libraries, 23–5, 58–60, 78, 80, 89–98, 99–107, 108–21, 136–49, 150–63, 164–83, 184–94
Lickorish, Len, 4–5
London, 15, 23, 59, 62, 93, 94, 99, 100, 106, 126, 151
Lorton family of Co. Roscommon, 78
Lucan House, Co. Dublin, 151
Lunar Society, 181
Luton Hoo, 4
Lutton, Anne, 87
Lyell, Sir Charles, 53
Lyons, Co. Kildare, 74

MacBeth, George, 37
    'A conversation with grandfather', 37
Madden, John, 95, 97
Maguire family of Co. Fermanagh, 97
    Maguire, Brian, 95–6, 97, 98
Mahon, John, 189
Major, Thomas, 151
Makinney, Tom (Thomas McKenny), 69
Malan, César, 87
Malone, Mary, 54
Manchester family of Armagh, 78, 80, 84
    Manchester, 6th duke of (Lord Mandeville), 80
Mandeville, Lord, *see* Manchester family of Armagh
Manor Waterhouse, Co. Fermanagh, 95
Marsh's Library, Dublin, 95
Martin, Violet Florence ('Martin Ross'), 70
    see also Somerville and Ross; Somerville, Edith
Martineau, Harriet, 53
Maturin, Charles, 70
Mayo, Lord, 39
Mazell, Peter, 160
McBride, John, 93
McDonnell family of Co. Antrim (earls of Antrim), 97
    4th earl of Antrim, 97

Index 203

Méjanel, Pierre, 87
Mentmore House, Buckinghamshire, 10 n., 2
Mill, John Stuart, 53, 175, 176
Moira, earl of, 93
Molyneux, William, 91
Monksgrange, Co. Wexford, 122, 127
Montagu (née Robinson), Elizabeth, 42, 43, 44
Montagu, Lord, of Beaulieu, 1, 4, 7, 10, 11
Montgomery family of Co. Down, 96–7
    Montgomery, William, 96–7
Moore family of Co. Mayo, 99–107
    Moore, Augustus, 106
    Moore, George (1729–99), 100
    Moore (II), George Henry (1810–70), 102, 104
    Moore, George Augustus (1852–1933), 99–107
    Moore, Julian, 106
    Moore, John, 100
    Moore, Louisa, 100
    Moore, Maurice, 99–107
Moore Hall, Co. Mayo, 99–107
Mountcashell family of Cork, 78
Moydrum Castle, Co. Westmeath, 38
Murdoch, Irish, 32
    The red and the green, 32
    The unicorn, 32, 34

Naples, 15, 18, 153–4
National Gallery of Art, Washington DC, 11
National Gallery of Ireland, 48
National Heritage Memorial Fund, 10
National Museum of Ireland, 75, 76
National Portrait Gallery, 7–8, 145
National Register of Archives, 148–9
National Trust, 68, 94, 146
natural history, 45, 48–50, 59
Newbridge House, Co. Dublin, 52–66
Noel, Wriothesley, 87
Norman, William, 92
Nostell Priory, West Yorkshire, 139–41

O'Brien, Kate, 71
    The ante-room, 71
O'Connell, Daniel, 88
O'Donnell family of Donegal, 91
Office of Public Works, 75, 77

O'Malley, Ernie, 35
Orange Order, 79
Ormond, duke of, 91, 92
Ó Rodaigh, Tadhg, 95, 97, 98
Orpen, Adela, 122–35
Orpen, Goddard, 122–35
Orpen, John, 122
Orpen, Sir William, 127
Orrery, earl of, 92
Oscott, West Midlands, 101
Ovid, *Metamorphoses*, 20–8
Owenson, Sydney, 70
Oxford Movement, 116
Oxford Society for Promoting the Study of Gothic Architecture, 112

Pain, James, 112
Pallastown, Co. Cork, 39
Palmerstown, Co. Kildare, 39
Paris, 105, 122–35, 152
Parker, Theodore, 53
Parsons, William, 3rd earl of Rosse, 172
Perceval, Sir John, 92
Percy, Hugh, 1st duke of Northumberland, 155
Petrie, George, 117
Pilkington, Letitia, 42
Piper, John, 6
Pellegrini, Giovanni Antonio, 22
petitions, 10
Petworth, Sussex, 155–7
Planning and Development Act, 2000 [RI], *see also* legislation
politics, 8, 12, 68, *see also* petitions; taxation
Portmore, Co. Antrim, 94
Powerscourt family of Wicklow, 78, 80, 88
    Powerscourt, Viscountess, 88
Pugin, Augustus Welby Northmore, 114, 115–16
Puttenden Manor, 4

Rathrobin, Co. Laois, 74
Religious Tract and Book Society, 85
Reni, Guido, 27
Reuben Ryley, Charles, 19
Ricci, Sebastiano, 22
Richards, Ellen, 132
Richmond House, London, 18
Roberts, Miss, 58
Robin Wade Associates, 8

Robinson, Lennox, 30, 34, 36, 39
  The Big House, 30, 34, 36
  Killycregs in twilight, 39
Robinson, William, 190
Roden, 3rd earl of, *see* Jocelyn, Robert, 3rd earl of Roden
Roden family of Louth and Down, 78–88
Rome, 18, 152, 154, 156, 159, 161
Rousham, Oxfordshire, 5
Royal Horticultural Society of Ireland, 188
Royal Hospital Kilmainham, 76
Royal Irish Academy, 116
Royal Society, 172
Rubens, Peter Paul, 22
Runciman, Miss, 58
Rundle, Thomas, bishop of Derry, 93
Russborough House, Co. Wicklow, 68–9, 74, 75

Sackville family of Kent, 143–9
  Sackville, Arabella Diana, 145
  Sackville, John Frederick, 3rd duke of Dorset, 143–5
  Sackville West, Eddie, 143
Sackville-West, Vita, 143, 145
Savage family of Co. Down, 97
Scharf, George, 145
Second World War, 8, 146, 148
servants, *see* domestic servants
Shavington Hall, Shropshire, 139
Sheridan, William, 97
Sican, Elizabeth, 42
Smith, Sydney, 178
Solander, Daniel, 44
Somerville, Edith, 30, 70
Somerville and Ross, 70
Springhill, Co. Londonderry, 95
Stanley, Edward Henry, 15th earl of Derby, 175
St Mary's Church, Bruton, 138–40
Stearne, John, bishop of Clogher, 95
Stoker, Bram, 70
Stokes, Margaret, 117
Ston Easton Park, Somerset, 157
Stowe Archive, 140
Strong, Roy, 7–8, 67–8
Strozzi family of Rome, 159
Summerhill House, Co. Meath, 75
Sunday School Society for Ireland, 85

Surrey Record Office (Surry History Centre), 148
Sussex Archaeological Society, 142
Swift, Jonathan, 42
Syon House, Middlesex, 155

Tandragee Castle, Co. Armagh, 84
taxation, 5–12
Taylor, Mentia, 53
tenantry, 61, 86–8
Tennison, Margaret, 42
Thackeray, Elias, 83, 84
Thames & Hudson, 8
Theaker, George, 94
Thomond, earl of, 91
Thompson, Brian, 4
Thurston, Katharine Cecil, 70
  The fly on the wheel, 70–1
Tischbein, Wilhelm, 154
Toibín, Colm, 71–2
  The heather blazing, 71, 72–3
  The south, 71
Tollymore Park, Co. Down, 79–88
Tonson, Jacob, 23
Townley Hall, Co. Louth, 75
travel, foreign, 18, 62, 102, 113, 119, 122–35, 152, 159–61, 179, 192–3
Trevor, William, 36, 70
  The story of Lucy Gault, 36
Trimbleston, Lord, 63
Trinity College Dublin, 93, 95, 116, 122
tourism, 1–4, 10–11
Turvey House, Co. Dublin, 63
Tynetesfield, Somerset, 174–5

United States of America, 120, 179

Vesey family of Co. Dublin, 151
Victoria and Albert Museum (V&A), 7–8, 11, 67–8
  The destruction of the country house exhibition, 7–8, 11, 67–8
Vierpyl, Simon, 26
Vivares, François, 151, 160

Ward family of Co. Down, 94
  Ward, Michael, 94
Waterford county, 30
Waterford, Lord, 35

Index

Waugh, Evelyn, 1
  Brideshead revisited, 1
Wedgwood, Josiah, 152
Wentworth, William, 2nd earl of Strafford, 18
Wernher, Sir Harold, 4
West Sussex Record Office, 140, 142
Westminster School, London, 15
Wexford county, 72
Wilberforce, William, 80
  A practical view, 80
Wilson, Harold, 5
Wilson, Richard, 25
Winn, Sir Roland, 140
Wogan Browne, Thomas, 154
Wolff, Joseph, 87
women, 52–66
Wontner, Hugh, 4
Woodlawn, Co. Galway, 39

Worlidge, Thomas, 160–1
Wraxall, Sir Nathaniel, 143–6
Wyndham, Charles, 2nd earl of Egremont, 155
Wyndham Quin family of Co. Limerick (earls of Dunraven), 108–21
  Edwin, 3rd earl of Dunraven, 109, 115–18
  Windham Henry, 2nd earl of Dunraven, 109, 110–14
  Windham Thomas, 4th earl of Dunraven, 109, 118–21

Yeats family of Co. Sligo, 74, 77, 126
  Yeats, Elizabeth (Lolly), 126
  Yeats, W.B., 74, 77
    The tower, 74

Zincke, Christian Friedrich, 44